B 738.893

HIGHWAY
TRAFFIC
CON-
DITIONS
AND
PROPOSED
RELIEF
MEASURE
FOR
N. Y.

Transp.
HE
372
.N5
D28

TRANSPORTATION LIBRARY
HE
372
.N5
D28

REPORT

TO THE

Honorable James J. Walker, *Mayor*

ON

HIGHWAY TRAFFIC CONDITIONS

AND

PROPOSED TRAFFIC RELIEF MEASURES

FOR THE

CITY OF NEW YORK

Prepared by

DAY & ZIMMERMANN, Inc.
ENGINEERS

NEW YORK   PHILADELPHIA   CHICAGO

REPORT

TO THE

Honorable James J. Walker, *Mayor*

ON

HIGHWAY TRAFFIC CONDITIONS

AND

PROPOSED TRAFFIC RELIEF MEASURES

FOR THE

CITY OF NEW YORK

Prepared by

DAY & ZIMMERMANN, Inc.
ENGINEERS

NEW YORK   PHILADELPHIA   CHICAGO

Presented to the Board of Estimate and Apportionment by his Honor, the Mayor, on October 24, 1929 (Cal. No. 197).

Transportation
Library

HE
372
.N5
D28

LETTER OF TRANSMITTAL

DAY & ZIMMERMANN, INC.,
  Engineers
New York, Philadelphia, Chicago.

Report 2739
New York, October 22, 1929.

To the Honorable JAMES J. WALKER,
  Mayor of the City of New York,
  New York, N. Y.

Sir—Complying with your request and pursuant to action taken by the Board of Estimate and Apportionment on November 27, 1928, we have made a comprehensive survey and analysis of the vehicular traffic conditions in the City of New York and of the various relief measures proposed by the administrative departments, civic organizations of the five boroughs and others for the purpose of developing the measures of relief which would be afforded by the more important projects to serve as a basis for a rational program of procedure which would yield the best results from the standpoint of present conditions and probable future growth in population and centres of congestion.

The ground work of our investigation was laid on the voluminous information and statistical data contained in the records of the various City departments, the Public Service Commission, Port Authority, Board of Transportation, Regional Plan, Holland Tunnel Commission, civic and business organizations, public service and other corporations, and in the report of the City Committee on Plan and Survey, all of which were freely placed at our disposal. Everywhere we found entire accord for the impartial development of facts to the end that sound conclusions could be reached. The subsequent collection of supplemental data necessary to complete our studies was greatly facilitated by the splendid co-operation of the City departments of Police and Plant and Structures.

The results of our investigation are set forth in detail in the following report which is briefly summarized as follows:

PRESENT CONDITIONS.

Highway traffic problems in some form are always present in urban centres and are continually assuming new aspects because of changing conditions. In New York City they are aggravated by the tremendous volume of financial, commercial and industrial activities; the physical characteristics of the City; and the long delayed construction of major facilities required for the free movement of traffic through and between the five boroughs constituting the City. The activities of the entire metropolitan area, having a population in excess of 10,000,000, are centred in a relatively small area in the lower end of the Borough of Manhattan, which is entirely surrounded by navigable waters.

Although roughly 50 per cent. of the vehicular movements into and out of Manhattan to and from the other boroughs originate in or are destined to points across the East River in the Boroughs of Brooklyn and Queens, no additional crossings have been provided in the last 20 years. During this period the number of vehicles crossing the river has increased from about 15,000 to nearly 200,000 per day. The tremendous volume of traffic concentrating on and dispersing from the four existing bridges through inadequate bridge heads to mingle with or cross substantially like volumes of traffic moving in other directions, create conditions in Manhattan which are rapidly reaching unmanageable proportions from the standpoint of regulation and which are intolerable to the public in general.

Scattered throughout the five boroughs are many areas of varying sizes in which business has centred and in which traffic problems have developed to a greater or lesser degree. In most instances, these conditions are aggravated by through traffic which might well use other and more direct routes if they were available.

The delays and difficulties experienced in their daily journeys by trucks, passenger cars, street cars and other means of conveyance of goods and people, as well as by pedestrians, result not only in inconvenience, but also in tremendous money losses which have been stated by the City Committee on Plan and Survey to approximate $500,000,000 per annum. In addition, the permanence of existing business and industry and of the investments incident thereto, as well as the favorable development and use of the many areas available in the City for purposes of industry, business and housing, are of necessity imperiled or hindered by conditions preventing freedom of vehicular access and communication.

The formulation of a rational program for relief involves consideration of measures falling in four major groups as follows:

    1. The initiation and fostering of general measures regulating, directing or encouraging the development of the City and its activities, such as building, transit and transportation, along lines that will tend to reduce street traffic of all kinds and particularly its concentration in specific areas.

    2. Modifications and extensions of regulatory and control measures looking towards an improved utilization of the existing streets, bridges and similar facilities.

    3. Improvements and extensions to existing facilities.

    4. Creation of new facilities.

CITY PLANNING.

The matters referred to in paragraph one are developed to considerable length in the report of the City Committee on Plan and Survey, and have to do with the decentralization of industrial and commercial activities, urban and suburban transit operations, zoning and the regulation of building construction, co-ordinated planning of the highway system, port development, belt line railways, housing and other miscellaneous matters, all of which obviously were beyond the scope of our investigation.

TRAFFIC REGULATION.

The problem of regulation becomes exceedingly difficult where the facilities are being utilized far in excess of their efficient capacity, as is the case in many sections of New York City. Considering the conditions to be met, the traffic department is amazingly efficient. The provision of additional facilities as hereinafter set forth will undoubtedly change to a substantial degree the present characteristics of traffic in the more congested areas.

Theoretically the further regulation of traffic affords substantial possibilities of relief through the abolition of parking in congested areas, more rigid control of pedestrian traffic and other restrictions in the use of the highways, but practically the many diverse interests to be reconciled make progress extremely slow. The fundamental issues in this connection have been clearly defined and are recognized by the City Administration and the general public.

IMPROVEMENTS TO EXISTING FACILITIES.

Improvements to existing facilities in the nature of roadway widening, removal of obstructions, minor extensions, paving, etc., offer a very practical means of facilitating the free flow and circulation of traffic, the cumulative effect of which is often quite substantial. In illustration, there are 14 avenues across Manhattan on the line of 34th street, with curb to curb widths ranging from 45 to 72 feet, mostly 60 feet. In four of these the effectiveness of the useful street widths is much reduced by the combination of double track street railways and elevated columns, and five others are similarly affected by the presence of double track railways. Material increase in vehicular capacity would accompany the elimination of these facilities. However, it will probably take many years before the transit situation will permit the removal of the elevated lines, and relief from this source will be very gradual.

Improvements to existing facilities and affecting the main arterial highway systems of the five boroughs have been considered in detail by us and are set forth in the attached report. Those having only local aspects have not been considered by us.

CREATION OF NEW FACILITIES.

Under present conditions it is apparent that the creation of any new facility would be helpful, but the character of construction and the order of procedure to yield the maximum advantage from a City-wide standpoint is not so obvious. When it is considered that the total estimated cost of the projects which we believe from a traffic standpoint to be desirable improvements and extensions to the existing arterial highway system of the City would probably approach the staggering sum of one billion dollars, it is apparent that some projects must be deferred and that the judgments exercised with respect thereto will be affected by financing problems, City-wide versus local interests, and other considerations more or less intangible in their nature.

In its broader aspects the street plan of Manhattan has been given a fixed status by the intensive building development, particularly in the areas where additional street capacity would be most hedpful in relieving congestion. Under existing circumstances the suggested opening of new north and south through avenues and new east and west highways through the midtown section would involve costs of such magnitude as to demand that other relief measures be first sought for and tried out. Similarly with respect to extensive grade separations at congested intersections of important highways.

The principal we believe should be followed is to provide facilities the use of which would reduce the number of vehicles and the distances vehicles travel in congested areas. This can be accomplished by providing facilities elsewhere that will divert traffic now passing through congested areas on its way from outside origins to outside destinations, and by providing facilities that will give traffic originating in or destined for points in congested areas the most direct routes of entrance and exit.

Improvements that would contribute to such a result are of the following nature:

(a) Additional interborough connections which, together with a distributing and collecting highway system crossing the main approaches to the bridge and tunnel heads, would enable the most direct entry and exit from origin to destination.

(b) Marginal and other through highways, together with by-pass highways, of large capacity and maximum freedom from cross traffic by reason of their diversion effect.

The improvements of this nature which we believe merit consideration constitute a large number of individual projects, all of which are set forth in the attached report. The resulting effect on the arterial highway system of the City is indicated on the map (page IX). Those offering the greatest advantages from a City-wide standpoint although construction in some instances is not immediately urgent, are discussed briefly as follows:

INTERBOROUGH CONNECTIONS.

There can be no question but that additional interborough connections across the East River are urgently needed, particularly between Manhattan and Brooklyn and Queens. In our judgment those offering the maximum measure of relief singly and collectively are the Triborough Bridge, 38th Street Tunnel and Battery Tunnel. A substantial part of the congestion in Manhattan is undoubtedly caused by north and south weaving of vehicles seeking the existing river crossings, and by the large amount of traffic to and from points in Brooklyn, Queens and The Bronx, moving long distances over Manhattan highways. These facilities will provide more direct routes for this traffic and should afford very substantial relief.

Under present conditions a connection between Brooklyn and Manhattan in the vicinity of 10th street appears desirable from a traffic standpoint. We are of the opinion that if the other facilities enumerated above are created, the urgency of the 10th street crossing will be greatly reduced and for this reason suggest that the matter be deferred until the resulting effect is determined by actual experience.

The Narrows Tunnel connecting Brooklyn and Richmond is not a measure to relieve existing congestion, but rather one to provide convenient access to Staten Island with its large areas suitable for housing, industry and shipping, and thereby stimulate the development of these valuable assets. Although the present volume of traffic is not sufficient to make the project self-supporting, a rapid rate of growth can assuredly be expected.

OTHER IMPROVEMENTS.

Other arterial highway improvements of outstanding City-wide importance from a traffic standpoint are briefly discussed as follows:

North-South Vehicular Tunnel, Manhattan.

This project has been proposed to afford a through highway extending the length of Manhattan, in which vehicles could move long distances at high speeds and with a minimum of interruptions.

The most desirable location from the standpoint of convenience and minimum of conflict with existing subsurface structures is in 5th avenue. The cost would approximate, $200,000,000, and the annual cost would amount to about $30,000,000. Although a large volume of traffic would be afforded freer movement, we doubt very much whether the use would be sufficient to make the project self-supporting on a reasonable toll basis. There would necesarily be a long construction period with much interference with traffic and business. We are of the opinion that the money required could be more advantageously expended at this time for other projects.

Marginal Highways, Manhattan.

Marginal highways of large capacity are proposed to extend the full length of Manhattan on both east and west sides. We believe these are meritorious projects which will prove to be important factors in affording traffic relief. At the present time the section of the west side project extending from Canal to 72d street and the east side project extending from 23d to 54th street, are urgently needed to improve conditions in the mid-town area. The section of the east side project extending along the Harlem River from 2d avenue to the Harlem River driveway, is necessary to provide a direct connection between the Hudson River and Triborough Bridges and is desirable to afford relief in the Harlem River sections of Manhattan and The Bronx.

North-South Highway in Brooklyn and Queens.

The proposed north-south highway to extend from the Narrows Tunnel, through Brooklyn and Queens is essential to the full development of the traffic relief possibilities of the East River bridges and tunnels. In addition it will provide an urgently needed route for the free movement of traffic in and between the river front sections of Brooklyn and Queens. The adopted route should utilize existing highways to the fullest possible extent and to this end we have suggested a tentative location which we believe meets that requirement. We believe that this project will in effect add capacity to the street system of Manhattan.

Astoria Avenue and Northern Boulevard, Queens.

The Astoria avenue and Northern boulevard projects considered together will provide a desirable outlet from the Triborough Bridge through Flushing to points on the north shore of Long Island. At present there is no urgency for these projects except the section of the Northern boulevard in the Flushing district, where roadway widening and other improvements are badly needed.

Borden Avenue, Queens.

The Borden avenue improvement will be necessary in order to provide an adequate outlet from the 38th Street East River Vehicular Tunnel and connect with the arterial highway systems of Brooklyn and Queens. The project may be considered as a necessary part of the tunnel improvement.

Atlantic Avenue, Brooklyn and Queens.

Atlantic avenue is one of the principal highways leading from the bridge head area in Brooklyn, eastwardly through Brooklyn to the Jamaica section in Queens. The highway is occupied in part for a considerable length by the tracks of the Long Island Railroad, which seriously reduce the space available for vehicular traffic and in addition create barriers to cross traffic. The project includes the removal of the tracks from the surface, the widening of the roadway and other general improvements, and constitutes a traffic relief measure urgently needed. Other related improvements in the Jamaica district not enumerated here are essentially a part of this project.

Grand Boulevard and Concourse, Bronx.

It is proposed to extend the Grand Boulevard and Concourse by widening Mott avenue in The Bronx to about East 153d street and to provide a high level bridge across the Harlem River connecting with 7th and Lenox avenues in Manhattan. The improvement is urgently needed to provide a more adequate connection between the boulevard and the street system of Manhattan.

East 172d Street, Bronx.

One of the outstanding features of The Bronx street system is the limited number of adequate crosstown arteries. The East 172d street project will tend to improve this condition and in addition will provide very desirable direct crosstown connection with the Hudson River Bridge.

Arterial Highway Across Staten Island.

At the present time the highway traffic in the Borough of Richmond is largely local in character. Upon the completion of the Narrows Tunnel it will be necessary to provide adequate facilities at the tunnel head and a cross island highway to connect with the Goethals and Kill Van Kull Bridges.

The foregoing are projects involving the construction of major vehicular connections between the Boroughs and of certain arterial highways which appear for the most part to be of more City-wide interest and directly related to the relief of the congested areas of Manhattan. In addition there is a large number of projects involving the improvement of or extension to the arterial highway systems throughout the five Boroughs, the execution of which we believe to be very desirable from a traffic standpoint as set forth in our report. In view of their nature and location and the local aspects involved, it is impractical for us to develop a definite schedule of procedure, but in this connection we have endeavored to set forth the particular advantages which would be afforded by the individual projects.

Additional crossings of the Hudson River will undoubtedly be constructed from time to time, and while they will create tunnel or bridge head problems in Manhattan, the resulting City-wide effect will be an improvement in traffic conditions. The completion of the 178th Street Bridge now under construction will not afford major relief in lower and mid-Manhattan, but will provide a much needed facility in the northern part of the City.

In our judgment the major projects now under way or authorized have been wisely considered and will undoubtedly afford a very substantial measure of relief. The whole problem has many aspects, some of which can not be developed in an investigation of this character, and our report is submitted with the hope that the impartial presentation of the various projects will prove helpful in the important decisions which must be made.

Respectfully submitted,

DAY & ZIMMERMAN, Inc.
H. E. Ehlers, Vice-President
H. R. Martz, Vice-President

Oversized Foldout

INDEX

	INTRODUCTION	1–3
	Photograph showing Downtown Manhattan	4
I	PHYSICAL CHARACTERISTICS OF THE CITY OF NEW YORK FROM THE STANDPOINT OF TRAFFIC MOVEMENT	5–20
	Magnitude of Traffic Flows	5
	Photograph showing Manhattan	6
	Photograph showing Harlem River Bridges	7
	Photograph showing Three Lower East River Bridges	8
	Population and Development	9
	Manhattan	9
	Photograph showing The Brooklyn Water Front	10
	Photograph showing The Downtown Section of Brooklyn	11
	Photograph showing General View in Queens	12
	Brooklyn and Queens	13
	Photograph showing The River Front Section of Queens	14
	Photograph showing The Concourse in The Bronx	15
	Photograph showing Staten Island	16
	The Bronx	17
	Richmond (Staten Island)	17
	Photograph showing St. George, Staten Island	18
	Photograph showing Manhattan, south from Times Square	20
II	CHARACTERISTICS OF HIGHWAY TRAFFIC	21–48
	Classification of Traffic	21
	Pedestrian Traffic	21
	Vehicular Traffic	21
	Horse Drawn Vehicles	21
	Motor Vehicles	21
	Photograph showing Crosstown View in Mid-Manhattan	22
	Street Railway	23
	Traffic Flows	25
	Traffic Flows Entering and Leaving Manhattan	25
	Diagram showing Distribution of Weekday Vehicular Traffic Flows	24
	Traffic Flows in Mid-Manhattan	27
	Diagram showing Traffic at Principal Intersections	26
	Traffic Flows in Lower and in Upper Manhattan	28
	Traffic Flows in Other Boroughs	29
	Traffic Congestion	29
	Traffic Speeds	29
	Speeds in 1924	30
	Speeds in 1926	30
	Speeds in 1929	30
	Manhattan Avenues	31
	Crosstown Streets	31
	South of Canal Street	32
	East River Bridges	33
	Summary	35
	Congestion	35
	Pedestrian Traffic	35
	Photograph showing Noon-day Crowd in the New Garment Center	34
	Vehicular Traffic	35
	Downtown Manhattan	35
	Photograph showing views of Shopping Crowds in Manhattan	36
	Photograph showiwng Views of Pedestrian and Vehicular Traffic at 42d Street and Madison Avenue	37

XI

			PAGE
II	CHARACTERISTICS OF HIGHWAY TRAFFIC		
	Traffic Congestion		
	Congestion		
	Vehicular Traffic—*Continued*		
	Midtown Manhattan		39
	Photograph showing Characteristics of Crosstown Traffic in Mid-Manhattan		38
	Photograph showing views of Traffic Conditions on 5th Avenue in the Midtown Section of Manhattan		40
	Photograph showing views of Mid-day Traffic Conditions on Cross Streets in the Central Section of Manhattan		41
	Photograph showing Traffic Congestion in Madison Avenue at 59th Street		42
	Bridge Heads		39
	Miscellaneous		43
	Other Boroughs		43
	The Cost of Congestion		43
	Photograph showing Rush Hour Traffic Flows on 5th Avenue at 58th Street		44
	Photograph showing Traffic Conditions During Non-Rush Hours at 42nd Street and 5th Avenue		45
	Photograph showing Viaduct in Park Avenue Connecting with High Level Roadways Around Grand Central Station and Through the New York Central Building		46
	Traffic Regulation		47
III	IMPROVEMENTS TO EXISTING FACILITIES		49–55
	Highways		49
	Bridges		49
	Queensboro Bridge		49
	Photograph showing Queensboro Bridge		48
	The Williamsburg Bridge		51
	Photograph showing Traffic Conditions at the Manhattan Terminals of the Willis Avenue and the Williamsburg Bridges		50
	The Manhattan Bridge		53
	Photograph showing Manhattan Terminal of the Manhattan Bridge		52
	The Brooklyn Bridge		55
	Photograph showing views of Manhattan Terminals of the Brooklyn and the Queensboro Bridges		54
	Photograph showing General View in Mid-Manhattan		56
IV	PROPOSED NEW FACILITIES		57–144
	The Proposed Triborough Bridge		57
	The Present Situation		57
	The Relief Afforded		59
	Diagram showing the Nature and Extent of the Traffic Relief Afforded		58
	Proposed Triborough Tunnel		60
	Proposed Utilization of Hell Gate Bridge		60
	Proposed Triborough Bridge		61
	Location and General Features		61
	The Bronx Terminal		61
	Map showing General Location of the Triborough Bridge		62
	The Manhattan Terminal		63
	The Queens Terminal		63
	The Bridge Roadways		64
	The Cost of the Project		64
	Tolls and Traffic		65
	Conclusion		65
	Proposed 38th Street-East River Vehicular Tunnel		65
	The Present Situation		65
	General Traffic Flows and Distribution		66
	Traffic Flows Subject to Inferior Routing		66

IV PROPOSED NEW FACILITIES
   Proposed 38th Street-East River Vehicular Tunnel—*Continued*   PAGE
      The Relief Afforded.. 67
         Superior Routing 67
         Diversion of Traffic.. 69
            Diagram showing Nature and Extent of Relief Afforded.... 68
      Description of the Project... 69
         Original Proposal 69
            Diagram showing General Location of the Proposed Tunnel 70
         Alternate Proposals 71
         The Queens-Brooklyn Terminals................................ 71
         The Manhattan Terminals..................................... 72
      The Cost of the Project... 73
      Tolls and Traffic... 73
      Conclusion 73
   The Proposed Narrows Vehicular Tunnel Connecting Richmond and Brooklyn 73
      The General Situation... 75
      Present Connections and Traffic................................... 75
      The Need for Improved Connections................................ 75
            Diagram showing the Relative Location of Major Existing and Proposed Vehicular Bridges and Tunnels............. 74
            Photograph showing Staten Island and The Narrows........ 76
      The Development of the Project.................................... 77
      Description of the Project... 77
         General Features 77
            Plan showing General Location of the Proposed Narrows Vehicular Tunnel 78
         The Staten Island Terminals................................... 79
         The Brooklyn Terminal....................................... 79
      The Cost of the Project... 79
      Potential Traffic 80
         Present Flows 80
         Future Conditions 80
      Summary and Conclusions... 81
   The Proposed Manhattan-Brooklyn Vehicular Tunnel from West Street, Manhattan, to Hamilton Avenue, Brooklyn (Battery Tunnel)......... 81
      Description of Project.. 81
            Plan showing General Location of the Proposed Manhattan-Brooklyn Vehicular Tunnel............................ 82
         Manhattan Terminal 83
         Brooklyn Terminal 83
      Present Situation 83
      Relief Afforded 85
            Diagram showing Nature and Extent of Traffic Relief Afforded 84
      Cost of the Project... 87
      Tolls and Traffic... 87
      Conclusion 87
   The Proposed Brooklyn-Manhattan Bridge Connecting 1st Avenue and 9th Street, Manhattan, with Metropolitan and Union Avenues, Brooklyn (10th Street Bridge).. 87
            Plan showing General Location of the Proposed Manhattan-Brooklyn Bridge 86
      Description of the Project... 87
      The Present Situation... 88
      Relief Afforded 89
         Superior Routing 90
         Relief Afforded to Streets and Bridges.......................... 91
            Diagram showing Nature and Extent of Relief Afforded.... 92
      Effect of Other Proposed Relief Measures.......................... 93
      Capacity and Type of Structure.................................... 94
      The Cost of the Project... 95
      Conclusions 95

	PAGE
IV PROPOSED NEW FACILITIES—*Continued*	
The Proposed North-South Highway Through Brooklyn and Queens....	95
Photograph showing General View of Navy Yard Section in Brooklyn	96
Effect of Street Plans upon Traffic Flows	97
Interborough Traffic Flows and Effects	97
Nature of Relief Needed and Afforded	97
Photograph showing General View in Queens Showing Newtown Creek and East River	98
General Requirements of the Project	99
Description of the Project	100
South Brooklyn Section	100
Map showing A Suggested Location for The Proposed North-South Highway	101–102
Mid-Brooklyn Section	103
North Brooklyn Section	104
Queens Section	104
Grade Separations	104
Type and Width of Roadway	105
The Cost of the Project	105
Conclusion	106
West Side Marginal Highway, Manhattan	106
Proposed Route	106
Development of Project	106
Description of Facilities	106
Map showing Major Existing and Proposed Arterial Highways, Bridges and Tunnels	107–108
Relief Afforded	109
Conclusions	109
East Side Marginal Highway, Manhattan	109
Photograph showing General View in Manhattan Along East River	110
Proposed Route	111
Development of Project	111
Relief Afforded	111
Conclusion	111
The North-South Vehicular Tunnel in Manhattan	111
Development of the Project	112
Cost of the Project	113
Relief Afforded	113
Conclusions	114
Extension of Park Avenue from 96th Street to Grand Boulevard	114
Lower Manhattan Highway Extensions	114
Sixth Avenue, Carmine Street to Fulton Street	115
Canal Street, Mulberry Street to the Bowery	115
Essex Street, Houston to East Broadway	115
Chrystie Street, Houston Street to Canal Street	115
Madison Avenue Extension, 23d Street to Franklin Street	116
Allen Street, Delancey to East Broadway	116
Lexington Avenue Extension	116
5th Avenue, 120th to 124th Street	116
Miscellaneous Arterial Highway Projects in Manhattan, Bronx, Brooklyn, Queens and Richmond	117
Manhattan	117
Riverside Drive, 115th Street to The Bronx	117
West Side Improvement Plan	117
Manhattan Approach to Hudson River Bridge	118
Broadway Bridge	118
Extension of Harlem River Speedway	118
Connection Between West and South Streets at the Battery	118
The Bronx	118
Extension of Grand Boulevard and Concourse	118
Map showing Major Existing and Proposed Arterial Highways, Bridges and Tunnels	119–120

IV PROPOSED NEW FACILITIES
    The Bronx—*Continued*

	PAGE
Extension of Bronx River Parkway at 233d Street	121
Photograph showing The Bronx from Washington Heights	122
Extension of Bronx River Parkway Southerly to Bronx and Pelham Parkway	123
Improvement of Routes between Washington Bridge and the Proposed Triborough Bridge	123
Route No. 1	123
Route No. 2	123
New Cross-Bronx Artery, Washington Bridge to Clason's Point	123
Widening of Southern-Eastern Boulevard Route, Cypress Avenue to City Line	124
Improvement and Extension of University Avenue	124
Widening of Boston Post Road, Van Cortlandt Avenue with Roads Around Reservoir, and Gun Hill Road	125
Improvement of Webster Avenue, Gun Hill Road to 233d Street	125
Connection from Gun Hill Road to Bronx River Parkway	125
Extension of Riverside Drive and Improvement to 261st Street	125
Widening and Improvement of Existing Streets across the Northern Section of The Bronx	126
Widening of 233d Street and Baychester Avenue	126
Widening of Sedgwick Avenue	126
Improvement of Cross-Bronx Route	126
Improvement of Park Avenue	127
Tremont Avenue Bridge	127
Brooklyn-Queens	128
Atlantic Avenue Improvement	128
Atlantic Avenue Extension and Connections East of Morris Park Station	128
Construction of a Diagonal Street from Morris Park Station to 101st Avenue	128
Construction of a Diagonal Street between Chichester and Liberty Avenues	128
Map showing Major Existing and Proposed Arterial Highways, Bridges and Tunnels	129–130
Construction and Improvement of Liberty Avenue, 109th Street, Hollis Avenue and Hempstead Turnpike	131
Improvement of Westchester and Foch Boulevards	131
Improvements to Northern Boulevard	131
Ditmars Avenue to Flushing River	131
Construction of New High Level Bridge over Flushing River	131
Photograph showing General View of Queens	132
Widening Between Flushing River and Main Street	133
Widening at Douglaston	133
Improvements to Nassau Boulevard	133
Widening Harmon Street from Myrtle Avenue to Metropolitan Avenue	134
Construction of Elliot Avenue from Metropolitan Avenue to Queens Boulevard	134
Construction from Queens Boulevard to Strongs Causeway	134
Construction of Viaduct Over Alley Pond Creek	134
Improvement of Stewart Railroad Right-of-Way	134
Nassau Boulevard to Hillside Avenue, Queens	135
Main Street to Nassau Boulevard	135
Widening of Woodhaven Boulevard	135
Improvement and Extension of 137th Street, Queens	135
Widening of Van Wyck Avenue	135
Construction of Plaza at Van Wyck Avenue and 101st Avenue	136
Widening of 101st Avenue	136
Paving Liberty Avenue between Sutphin and Merrick Boulevards	136
Merrick Road Widening	136
Construction of New High Level Bridge over English Kills at Grand and Metropolitan Avenues	136

		PAGE
IV	PROPOSED NEW FACILITIES	
	Brooklyn-Queens—*Continued*	
	Construction of Circumferential Highway Through Brooklyn and Queens	137
	Widening of Astoria and Ditmars Avenue	137
	Proposed Route from Astoria Avenue to Nassau Boulevard	137
	Construction of Express Highway from Proposed Upper Deck of Queensboro Bridge	138
	Borden and Caldwell Avenue Improvements	138
	Replacement of Present Retractile Drawbridge at Borden Avenue Over the Dutch Kills	138
	Widening of 9th Street from Hamilton Avenue to Smith Street	138
	Construction of Two New Bridges Over the Gowanus Canal at Hamilton Avenue and 9th Street	138
	Miscellaneous Projects for Ultimate Development	139
	Richmond	141
	Map showing Major Existing and Proposed Arterial Highways, Bridges and Tunnels	143
	Miscellaneous Bridge Projects	144
	Ferry Point-Whitestone Connection	144
	86th Street Bridge	144
V	DETAILS OF STREET TRAFFIC IN MANHATTAN	145–150
	Available Data	145
	Traffic Flows	145
	Mid-Manhattan	145
	Avenue Traffic, Mid-Manhattan	145
	Diagram showing The Distribution of the Combined Northbound and Southbound Vehicular Traffic on Individual Avenues	146
	Effective Traffic Lanes	147
	Crosstown Traffic, Mid-Manhattan	147
	Diagram showing the Distribution of the Eastbound and Westbound Vehicular Traffic	148
	Canal Street Traffic Flows	149
	Fluctuations in Traffic Flows	149
	Commercial Vehicles	149
VI	DETAILS OF BRIDGE, TUNNEL AND FERRY TRAFFIC	151–169
	Available Data	151
	East River Bridges	151
	Harlem River Bridges	151
	Municipal Ferries	151
	East River Private Ferry	151
	Holland Tunnel	151
	Hudson River Ferries	152
	Staten Island-New Jersey Bridges and Ferries	152
	Traffic Volumes in 1928	152
	East River Bridges	152
	Harlem River Bridges	152
	East River Municipal Ferries	153
	Clason's Point Ferry	153
	East River Private Ferry	153
	Staten Island Municipal Ferries	153
	Hudson River Ferries	153
	Holland Tunnel	153
	Staten Island-New Jersey Bridges and Ferries	155
	Motor Vehicle Registration	155
	Registration in 1928	155
	Growth in Registration	155
	Diagram showing Growth and Distribution by Boroughs of Motor Vehicle Registration	154
	Diagram showing Growth and Distribution by Classes Motor Vehicle Registration	154
	Diagram showing Growth of East River Bridge Traffic and Motor Vehicle Registration	156

VI DETAILS OF BRIDGE, TUNNEL AND FERRY TRAFFIC
    Motor Vehicle Registration
        Growth in Registration—*Continued*

	PAGE
Semi Log Diagram showing Comparison in Rates of Growth East River Bridge Traffic and Motor Vehicle Registration	156
Diagram showing Growth and Distribution by Classes East River Bridge Traffic	156
Estimates of Future Registration	157
Growth in Traffic	157
East River Bridges	157
Harlem River Bridges	157
Municipal Ferries	157
Hudson River Ferries and Tunnel	158
Comparison of Rates of Growth	159
Semi Log Diagram showing Comparison of Rates of Growth in Vehicular Traffic on New York Bridges and Ferries	158
Analysis of East River Bridge Traffic	159
Day and Night Traffic	159
Passenger and Commercial Car Traffic	161
Hourly Flow of Week-day Traffic	161
Diagram showing Variations in Combined Vehicular Traffic Flow over the Four East River Bridges for Eastbound, Westbound and Total Traffic	160
Diagram showing Variations in Passenger Car and Commercial Car Traffic Flow over the Queensboro Bridge, Both Directions Combined	162
Accumulation of Vehicles in Manhattan	161
Relative Utilization of Bridges	161
Maximum Traffic Flows	163
Analysis of Holland Tunnel Traffic	163
Traffic in 1928	163
Relation of Daily to Annual Traffic	165
Passenger and Commercial Car Traffic	165
Hourly Flow of Traffic	165
Diagram showing Variations in Hourly Traffic Flow for the Holland Vehicular Tunnel Eastbound, Westbound and Total Traffic	164
Diagram showing Variations in Hourly Traffic Flow for the Holland Vehicular Tunnel Eastbound, Westbound and Total Traffic	166
Analysis of Daily Traffic	165
Analysis of Municipal Ferry Traffic	167
Monthly Flow of Traffic	167
Diagram showing Variation by Months of Typical Daily Vehicular Traffic for all Municipal Ferries	168
Passenger Cars and Commercial Car Traffic	167
Relation of Daily to Annual Traffic	167

VII DETAILS OF ORIGIN AND DESTINATION STUDIES 171–201

Purpose and Scope	171
Representativeness of Samples	171
Holland Tunnel Traffic	173
Analysis of Sample	173
Results of Count	173
Diagrams showing Vehicular Traffic Through the Holland Tunnel	170–172
East River Bridge Traffic	173
Collection and Analysis of Data	173
Comparison of Traffic Flows	174
Presentation of Results	174
Tabulation showing the Sample of East River Bridge Traffic	175–176
Queensboro Bridge Traffic	179
Diagram showing Vehicular Traffic on the Queensboro Bridge	178
Williamsburg Bridge Traffic	181
Diagram showing Vehicular Traffic on Williamsburg Bridge	180

VII DETAILS OF ORIGIN AND DESTINATION STUDIES
    East River Bridge Traffic—*Continued*

	PAGE
Manhattan Bridge Traffic..	183
Diagram showing Vehicular Traffic on the Manhattan Bridge	182
Brooklyn Bridge Traffic...	185
Diagram showing Vehicular Traffic on the Brooklyn Bridge	184
Williamsburg, Manhattan and Brooklyn Bridges, Combined..........	187
Diagram showing Combined Vehicular Traffic on the Brooklyn, Manhattan and Williamsburg Bridges................	186
Queensboro, Williamsburg, Manhattan and Brooklyn Bridges, Combined	189
Diagram showing the Combined Vehicular Traffic on the Brooklyn, Manhattan, Williamsburg and Queensboro Bridges	188
Ferry Traffic	191
Staten Island-Battery Ferry...	191
Diagram showing Vehicular Traffic on the Staten Island-Battery Ferry	190
Staten Island-Brooklyn Ferry.......................................	191
Diagram showing Vehicular Traffic on the Staten Island-39th Street, Brooklyn Ferry...........................	192
Clason's Point-College Point Ferry................................	193
East River Municipal Ferries.......................................	193
Astoria Ferry	193
Greenpoint and Grand Street Ferries..............................	193
Atlantic, Hamilton and 39th Street Ferries.......................	193
Traffic on Manhattan Avenues at 51st Street...........................	193
The Traffic Sample...	195
Volume of Traffic..	195
Distribution on Basis of Districts.................................	195
Diagram showing the Northbound and Southbound Vehicular Traffic Crossing 51st Street on Eastside and Westside Avenues	194
Distribution on Basis of Distance Traveled......................	195
Diagram showing the Northbound and Southbound Vehicular Traffic Crossing 51st Street on Eastside and Westside Avenues	196
Extent of Long Haul Traffic.......................................	197
Traffic South of 51st Street..	198
Eastbound and Westbound Traffic in Mid-Manhattan..................	198
The Traffic Sample...	198
The Volume of Traffic...	198
Distribution on Basis of Districts.................................	199
Distribution on Basis of Distance traveled......................	199
Extent of Long Haul Traffic.......................................	199
Diagrams showing the Eastbound and Westbound Vehicular Traffic Crossing 5th Avenue Between 30th and 59th Streets, Inclusive	200–201

REPORT 2739

on

HIGHWAY TRAFFIC CONDITIONS

and

PROPOSED TRAFFIC RELIEF MEASURES

for

THE CITY OF NEW YORK

to

THE HONORABLE JAMES J. WALKER, MAYOR OF THE CITY OF NEW YORK

INTRODUCTION

Pursuant to a resolution adopted by the Board of Estimate and Apportionment on November 27, 1928, we have made a comprehensive survey and analysis of the vehicular traffic conditions in the City of New York and of the various relief measures proposed by the administrative departments and civic organizations of the five boroughs for the purpose of developing the relative merits of the more important projects and of providing a basis for a rational program of procedure which would yield the best results from the standpoint of present conditions and probable future growth in population and centres of congestion.

Traffic relief problems ever present in urban centres are aggravated in New York City by reason of the diversity and tremendous volume of business transacted and the physical characteristics of the limited area in which it is centred. On the lower portion of the island of Manhattan within an area about two miles in width by about five miles long are centred the financial and commercial activities of the country. The streets are narrow and the office buildings large in area and many stories in height and in many instances house more people than are found in our smaller cities.

The volume of vehicular traffic at the present time in the principal highways of Manhattan and those leading to the surrounding metropolitan areas has grown so far beyond the efficient capacity of the facilities afforded as to interfere with the orderly conduct of business and to tax the efforts of the traffic department of the City to the point where traffic regulation becomes at times more a matter of accident prevention than that of expediting vehicular movement.

For many years the problem of affording relief from existing conditions and adequately providing for the continual increase in volume of traffic has continually engaged the attention of the City Administration and the various civic organizations within the five boroughs. Construction projects and drastic traffic regulations are constantly being suggested, any of which would be helpful to a greater or lesser degree. Unfortunately, construction projects of sufficient magnitude to afford a substantial measure of relief involve not only large expenditures but also, in varying degrees, complicated financial, legal and engineering problems, and consideration of more specific advantages to certain sections and interests than to others, or to the City at large, with the result that there is usually a conflict of opinion as to their relative merits and inevitably an extended period of negotiation and consideration prior to final authorization and construction.

The various departments of the City and Borough governments are well organized and number among their personnel many able and experienced men who have not only shown extraordinary ability in coping with past and present traffic conditions but have also given much time and thought to the best program of procedure for the future. As a result much has been accomplished by the City in its efforts to keep pace with the extremely rapid growth in vehicular traffic experienced in recent years, as is evidenced by construction completed and under way and also by many projects under active consideration and in various stages of development ranging from recommendations through consideration, authorization, preparation of plans, etc., to construction.

The recent consummation, after many years of study, strife and negotiation, of the agreement between The City of New York and the New York Central Railroad Company covering removal of railroad track and yards from west side streets to private property, the development of new terminals with overhead tracks, express highways and other improvements along the Hudson River between Canal street and Spuyten Duyvil is an outstanding accomplishment toward traffic relief.

The need of additional interborough connections has been generally recognized for a number of years and has resulted from time to time in recommendations for construction of bridges and tunnels in various locations. Preliminary plans for a bridge across East River from a point in the vicinity of 10th street in Manhattan to a point in the Greenpoint section in Brooklyn were under active consideration by the Board of Estimate and Apportionment in 1923, but the project failed of approval.

In 1916 a recommendation was made for a Triborough Bridge connecting The Bronx, Manhattan and Queens, and in 1923 an appropriation was made for a preliminary study. In 1926 a recommendation was made to the Board of Estimate and Apportionment for a vehicular tunnel under the East River at 38th street, Manhattan. Early in 1927 the Board appropriated funds for the preparation of preliminary plans for both the Triborough Bridge and the 38th Street Tunnel.

All of the foregoing projects and many others not enumerated have been the subject of much study and consideration by City officials and interested civic organizations and individuals throughout the five boroughs. The magnitude of the expenditures involved not only present serious problems of financing but also add to the desirability of developing the relative merits of the various projects.

As already stated, under date of November 27, 1928, the Board of Estimate and Apportionment authorized the employment of Day & Zimmerman, Inc., engineers, for the purpose of making a survey and study of traffic conditions in the various boroughs to be followed by the submission of a report presenting their views with respect to the most logical procedure to be followed by the City in its efforts to afford relief from present conditions and to adequately provide for future growth. The investigation was begun in December, 1928, and included among other things the following principal matters:

1. The determination of the characteristics of vehicular traffic moving on the streets of the City and over, through and on the various bridges, ferries and tunnels with respect to class of traffic, volume, time of flow, points of origin and destination and general routes followed.

2. A study of the characteristics of the various major highway, bridge and tunnel projects proposed for traffic relief, including the purposes intended to be accomplished and the means of accomplishment, the general feasibility of the projects and their relations to existing and other proposed facilities and measures.

3. The determination insofar as was practical of the measures of relief which would be afforded by the various projects considered, and estimates of their potential use and the cost of construction and operation where tolls would be charged.

4. The preparation of a report containing the results of our investigation including recommendations based upon a consideration of the general City-wide situation as it appears to us in the light of the information, suggestions and opinions gathered from officials and others directly concerned and the results of our analysis of traffic data developed and our general observations and studies.

Transit and transportation by railroads were specifically not included in the matters to be covered by our study and are therefore only referred to in general terms in connection with their influence upon the development of the City and hence its traffic problems. No consideration has been given by us to improvements to existing highways designed to give local relief throughout the various Boroughs.

Theoretically the further regulation of traffic affords substantial possibilities of relief through the abolition of parking in congested areas and other restrictions in the use of the highways, but practically the many diverse interests to be reconciled make progress extremely slow. The fundamental issues in this connection have been clearly defined and are understood by the City administration and the general public. The matter of traffic regulation generally is in the hands of the Police Department, which is efficiently organized, keenly alive to the situation, and continually endeavoring to improve conditions. We have considered these matters beyond the scope of our investigation, and have treated them only in the most general way in our report.

The exhaustive report of the "City Committee on Plan and Survey" submitted to the Mayor in June, 1928, presents many recommendations for improvements as a basis for future study and analysis. This report established a valuable and helpful starting point for our study. Additional recommendations and suggestions were developed in response to an appeal to the public by the Mayor and through conference with Borough and City officials and with representatives of other public and semi-public agencies, civic associations, corporations and interested individuals to the end that in carrying on our work and reaching our conclusions with respect to the various relief measures proposed, we would have the benefit of the widest possible viewpoint.

In the development of data submitted the maximum possible use was made of the material presented in the report of the City Committee on Plan and Survey and that readily available in the various City departments as well as data placed at our disposal by the courtesy of agencies such as the Public Service Commission, the Port Authority, the Board of Transportation, Regional Plan, Holland Tunnel Commission, civic and business organizations, public service and other corporations. The data thus obtained included much helpful information particularly with respect to the traffic flow at specific street intersections and over the various bridges, ferries and tunnels, but there was a lack of specific information as to where the traffic came from, where it was going to and by what route or routes it moved. Informataion of the latter type has its direct application in and is essential to a well-rounded consideration of the various express highways, tunnels, bridges and other measures proposed for traffic relief. With the help and co-operation of the Police Department, the Department of Plant and Structures and others interested, origin and destination data were collected covering the traffic flow across the Hudson and East Rivers by means of bridges, tunnels and ferries and in the principal avenues and cross-town streets of Manhattan.

The data and general information thus assembled were supplemented by a knowledge of conditions obtained through appropriate observations in the field. These included a general survey of the various sections of the City with particular reference to topography, street plan, nature of territory, traffic conditions, etc., in the vicinity of or affected by the various highway, bridge and tunnel projects. They also included observations in the areas where the congestion of traffic was most evident, as well as in other locations, covering the general and any special characteristics of the traffic movements at such points, the extent of the congestion and the contributory causes where apparent or local. Special consideration was given to conditions in the various bridge and tunnel head areas and on the existing structures in view of their bearing on future design.

Special studies were made to develop by observation and by contact with representatives of the industry and those conversant with or affected by the characteristics of trucking movements, taxicab operation and practice and bus operation and practice, street car traffic and similar matters having a bearing on traffic problems.

For convenience of presentation, we have divided our report into the following principal sections:

I. *Physical Characteristics of the City of New York from the Standpoint of Traffic Movement.*

II. *Characteristics of Highway Traffic—*
   (a) Classification of traffic.
   (b) Traffic flows.
   (c) Traffic congestion.
   (d) Traffic regulation.

III. *Improvements to Existing Facilities—*
   (a) Highways.
   (b) Bridges.

IV. *Proposed New Facilities—*
   (a) Triborough Bridge.
   (b) 38th Street Tunnel.
   (c) Narrows Tunnel.
   (d) Battery Tunnel.
   (e) 10th Street Bridge.
   (f) North-South Highway, Brooklyn-Queens.
   (g) West Side Marginal Highway, Manhattan.
   (h) East Side Marginal Highway, Manhattan.
   (i) North-South Vehicular Tunnel, Manhattan.
   (j) Park Avenue Elevated Highway, Manhattan.
   (k) Lower Manhattan Highway Extensions.
   (l) Miscellaneous Arterial Highway Projects in Manhattan, The Bronx, Brooklyn, Queens and Richmond.
   (m) Miscellaneous Bridge Projects.

V. *Details of Street Traffic in Manhattan.*

VI. *Details of Bridge, Tunnel and Ferry Traffic.*

VII. *Details of Origin and Destination Studies.*

DOWNTOWN MANHATTAN

SECTION I

PHYSICAL CHARACTERISTICS OF THE CITY OF NEW YORK
from
THE STANDPOINT OF TRAFFIC MOVEMENT

THE CITY OF NEW YORK

The City of New York is generally recognized as the financial, business and shipping centre of the country and one of the great cities of the world. It has a present population in excess of 6,000,000 people and its area is some 316 square miles. It extends almost 40 miles from the upper end of The Bronx to the lower tip of Staten Island and about 18 miles from the Hudson River shore of Manhattan to the easternmost limit of the City along the Rockaway Beach section of Queens.

The adjoining and surrounding portions of New York and New Jersey, particularly adjacent to the harbor waters, while separated in a political sense, are in fact an integral part of the life and activities of this great City, and together with it constitute a vast metropolitan area with a population in excess of 10,000,000 people, a dense concentration of railroad and shipping terminals, warehouses, factories, etc., and an intense activity in industry and trade. Into and out of this area, and between the various portions of it, there flows daily a great tide of people and of foodstuffs, merchandise and materials of all kinds, most of which involves trucking movements to or from the rail heads or waterfronts to storehouses and other points of delivery.

Politically the City is divided into five boroughs: Manhattan, Brooklyn, Queens, The Bronx and Richmond. The separation of these boroughs from each other or from the adjoining mainland, by the East River, the Harlem River, the Hudson River, or the waters of New York Bay, has imposed restrictions and limitations on the means of vehicular communication of all kinds far reaching in their effect upon the development of the City and upon its problems of transit, transportation and traffic.

Magnitude of Traffic Flows.

During the year ended June 30, 1928, the rapid transit lines in New York City carried 2,000,000,000 passengers and the surface railways and buses over 1,000,000,000 passengers. About 485,000,000 passengers were carried by taxicabs. The report of the City Committee states that over 400,000 carloads of perishable products pass through the port each year merely to supply the needs of New York City, as well as building materials for a yearly construction program in excess of $1,000,000,000, and materials and products incident to manufacturing activities having an annual payroll in excess of $844,000,000.

The magnitude of the vehicular traffic flows taking place within the City is evidenced by the following statements, based on 1928 week day conditions as developed more fully later in this report:

The registration of motor vehicles in New York City in 1928 totaled over 681,000, of which number about 75 per cent. were passenger cars, 17 per cent. were commercial vehicles and 6 per cent. taxicabs and buses.

Approximately 21,000 taxicabs are operating on the streets of the City, chiefly in the areas of greatest vehicular activity.

The daily vehicular flow into and out of Manhattan totals substantially 450,000 vehicles per day. About 58,000 of these move across the Hudson River by tunnel or ferry, about 195,000 move across the East River over the four bridges, and about 190,000 move over the eight Harlem River Bridges.

The combined northbound and southbound flow on all the avenues in the midtown section of Manhattan is in the order of 200,000 vehicles in the hours from 7 a. m. to 7 p. m., and of these approximately 17 per cent. find their way over the East River bridges and approximately 20 per cent. over the Harlem River Bridges.

The combined eastbound and westbound flow at 5th avenue on all crosstown streets from 30th to 59th streets, inclusive, is about 160,000 during the day time 12 hours, and of these approximately 11 per cent. move over the East River bridges.

Commercial car traffic, largely trucking, accounts for from 20 per cent. to 30 per cent, of the total traffic figures just given for the various tunnels, bridges and combinations of streets.

MANHATTAN

HARLEM RIVER BRIDGES CONNECTING MANHATTAN AND THE BRONX

Photo by Curtiss Flying Service—Photo Division

THE BROOKLYN, MANHATTAN AND WILLIAMSBURG BRIDGES

Population and Development.

The population of the City as a whole is steadily increasing, but at a less rapid rate than surrounding suburban areas. The population of all of the Boroughs except Manhattan has shown a steady increase since the 1910 census, the greatest growth occurring in Queens and The Bronx. The present distribution and density of the population, according to the official directory of the City of New York, is shown in the following tabulation:

Borough.	1929 Population.	Per Cent. of Total.	Population per Square Mile.
Manhattan	1,689,419	28	86,800
Brooklyn	2,342,781	38	28,900
Queens	899,791	15	7,660
Bronx	977,819	16	23,600
Richmond	154,674	3	2,710
Total	6,064,484	100	19,200

The tendency towards the development of the outlying sections, particularly for residential and industrial purposes, has undoubtedly been accentuated by and accompanied the development of transit facilities and improved highways and has been somewhat checked in recent years by the failure to provide additional interborough bridges, highways, etc., and to otherwise keep pace with the growing requirements for vehicular traffic. Although at the present time the greatest undeveloped areas are in Queens and in Richmond (Staten Island), there is also opportunity for favorable development both in industry and housing in all of the other Boroughs, not excepting Manhattan.

Manhattan.

The focal point of the metropolitan area is the Borough of Manhattan, occupying an island about two miles in width and 13 miles in length, on which is to be found probably the greatest concentration of business and industry, and certainly the greatest development of sky-scrapers as to number and size in the world.

The concentration of buildings in the downtown and midtown sections, along the upper west side, and along the east side of Central Park is strikingly shown in the photograph on page 6. Practically all of it is along streets laid out many years prior to the advent of the skyscraper, the automobile and the motor truck.

The street plan of Manhattan, with the exception of sections south of 14th street and in the vicinity of Dyckman street, is laid out on a checkerboard system with the north and south avenues much further apart and in most instances almost twice as wide as the crosstown streets. There are 14 avenues across Manhattan on the line of 34th street, about 1,000 feet apart, with curb to curb widths mostly 60 feet and ranging from 45 to 72 feet. In four of these avenues the effectiveness of the street width is much reduced by the combination of double track street railway and elevated columns, and five others are similarly affected by the presence of double-track railways.

The crosstown streets are spaced about 200 feet apart and are mostly 30 feet between curbs, with wider streets about every ten blocks, about 60 feet between the curbs. Most of the wider crosstown streets have double track railways along them.

The general continuity of the checkerboard system is broken by the long diagonal of Broadway and by Central Park, through which, however, several cross thoroughfares and longitudinal drives are provided. Marginal streets of generous width extend along the waterfront on the Hudson and lower East River, where extensive docks and wharf developments have been provided for accomodation of large passenger liners, freight steamers, river and sound steamers, car floats and ferries.

The railroad facilities connecting the Grand Central Station with the Bronx are all below or above the street grade and those connecting the Pennsylvania Station with New Jersey and Long Island are all in tunnel. Tracks and yards of the New York Central extend along the Hudson River front in Manhattan, mostly at street grade below about 72d street, as are the freight yards and rail connections to car float wharves belonging to a number of the railroads having their main terminals on the New Jersey side of the Hudson River.

In addition to these railroad connections between Manhattan and points in New Jersey, Long Island and The Bronx, there are a number of other connections for rapid transit lines and vehicular and pedestrian traffic, including ferries, bridges and tunnels. There are at present 25 ferry routes operated for the public use between Manhattan and points in New Jersey, Brooklyn, Queens and Staten Island. Of these, 14 operate across the Hudson River and 11 across the upper bay or the East River.

THE BROOKLYN WATER FRONT

Photo by Fairchild Aerial Surveys Inc., N. Y. C.

THE DOWNTOWN SECTION OF BROOKLYN

Photo by Curtiss Flying Service—Photo Division

GENERAL VIEW IN QUEENS

Communication between Manhattan and The Bronx across the Harlem River is afforded by 11 bridges, 8 of which serve pedestrian, vehicular and street railway traffic and three railroad or rapid transit lines exclusively. The bridges, with one exception, are relatively low level draw bridges subject to opening for navigation and in general spaced more closely toward the eastern side of Manhattan.

Four high level bridges span the East River, three connecting with Brooklyn and one with Queens. The Manhattan terminals of the three lower bridges are quite closely spaced and in an area where the street plan is rather irregular. It is about 3 miles between the Queensboro Bridge, connecting mid-Manhattan with Queens, and the Williamsburg Bridge, the nearest of the three lower bridges. All of these bridges carry rapid transit and street railway, as well as pedestrian and vehicular traffic.

Brooklyn and Queens.

Occupying the western end of Long Island, the Boroughs of Brooklyn and Queens are separated from the other boroughs and the mainland by the harbor waters and the East River. The area occupied extends about 20 miles north to south and 15 miles from east to west and has a present population in excess of 3,000,000. In addition to its outstanding development as a place of residence for people having their daily occupation in Manhattan, it includes within its limits shipping, industrial and other activities commensurate with its size, location and population, with ample waterfront and other areas available for further development for residential, industrial and recreational purposes.

Brooklyn, with an area of about 81 square miles, ranks first among the boroughs for population, and second in density of population. The section extending eastwardly from the Manhattan and Brooklyn Bridge plazas, roughly along Flatbush avenue, to its intersection with 4th avenue and Atlantic avenue, includes a high building area and most of the principal office buildings, department stores, theatres, hotels, etc. The extensive development of piers, yards, terminal buildings and other activities connected with shipping, extend along the harbor and the East River waterfronts as well as along the various kills and creeks extending inland from the main waterfront. Industrial development has in general been most pronounced along the riverfront sections of the City. Noteworthy residential and recreational development is found in the extreme southern section of the borough, facing the Narrows and the Lower Bay and Ocean.

The Borough of Queens, with an area of about 117 square miles, has a present population of about 900,000, giving it a density of population less than one-tenth of that of Manhattan. It has no high building areas, its development has been essentially residential in character, and its large open areas offer ample opportunity for favorable extension and continuance of growth in this direction. Industrial development is found chiefly along the sections bordering the East River and along Newtown Creek and Flushing Creek, as well as in scattered inland locations. Recreational and summer resort development is found largely in the extreme southern end of the Borough along the Rockaway Peninsula and to some extent along the northern shore.

The separation of these Boroughs from Manhattan by the East River with the limited number of crossings in the nine miles of waterfront and the natural growth of these Boroughs towards the east and south has been reflected in the street arrangement. One noticeable characteristic is the natural tendency of the main highways leading from the outlying section to converge upon rather narrow areas lying back of the four East River bridge crossings. Another is the large number of different checkerboard street arrangements which have developed along these main highways and are particularly noticeable in the sections near the East River, where, for example, seven different checkerboard arrangements of streets are found in Brooklyn between Newtown Creek and Atlantic avenue. In the more outlying sections of the Boroughs there are fewer variations in the street plan and larger areas of uniformity.

There is a marked absence of direct or continuous highways traversing the Boroughs in a north and south direction, and particularly is this true in the sections immediately adjoining the East River. In addition, traffic moving through and between the industrial sections along the East River, as well as interborough traffic, is restricted in its freedom of movement by the limited crossings available over natural barriers such as the Newtown Creek and over artificial barriers such as the extensive Sunnyside Yards of the Long Island Railroad.

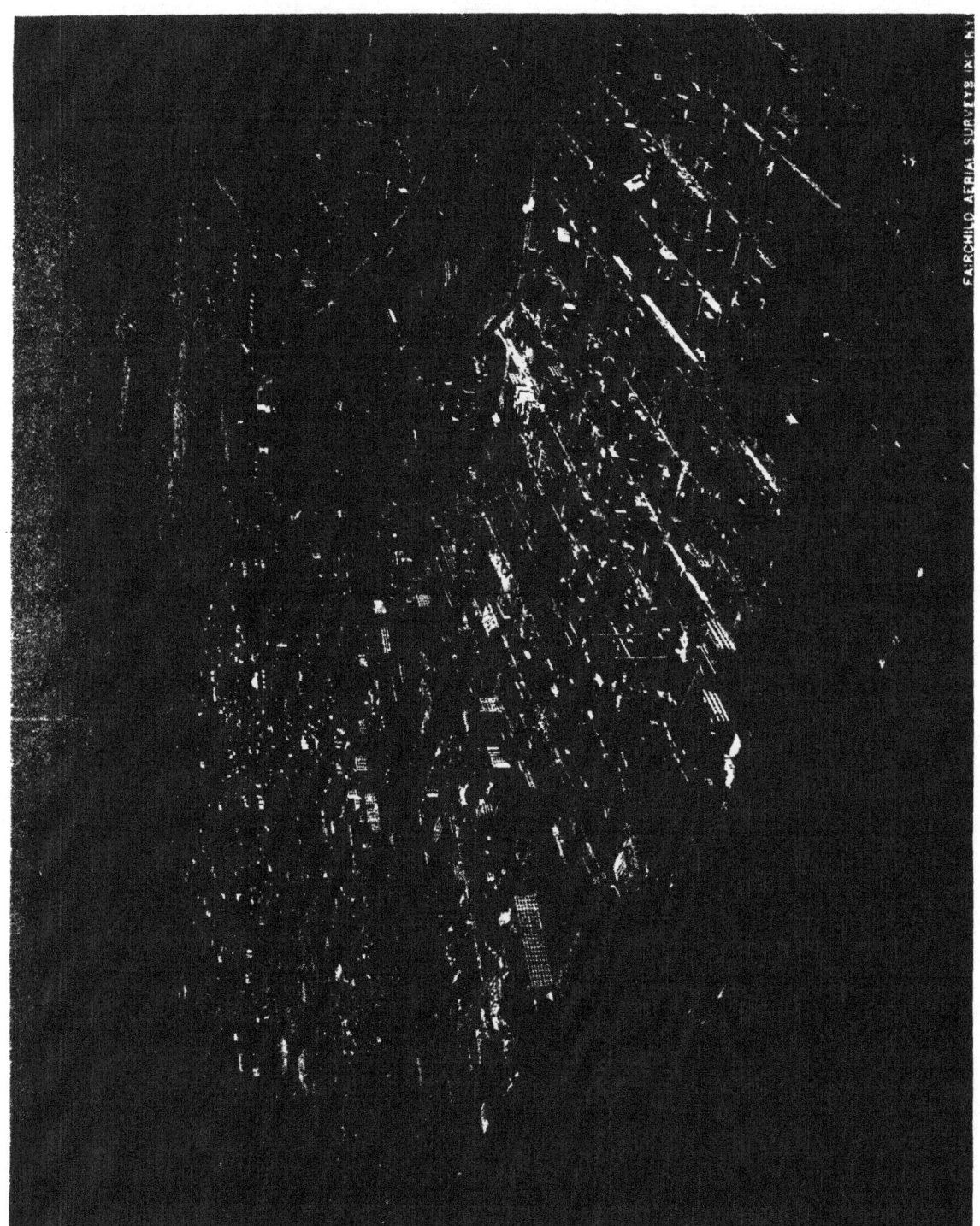

THE RIVER FRONT SECTION OF QUEENS

THE CONCOURSE IN THE BRONX

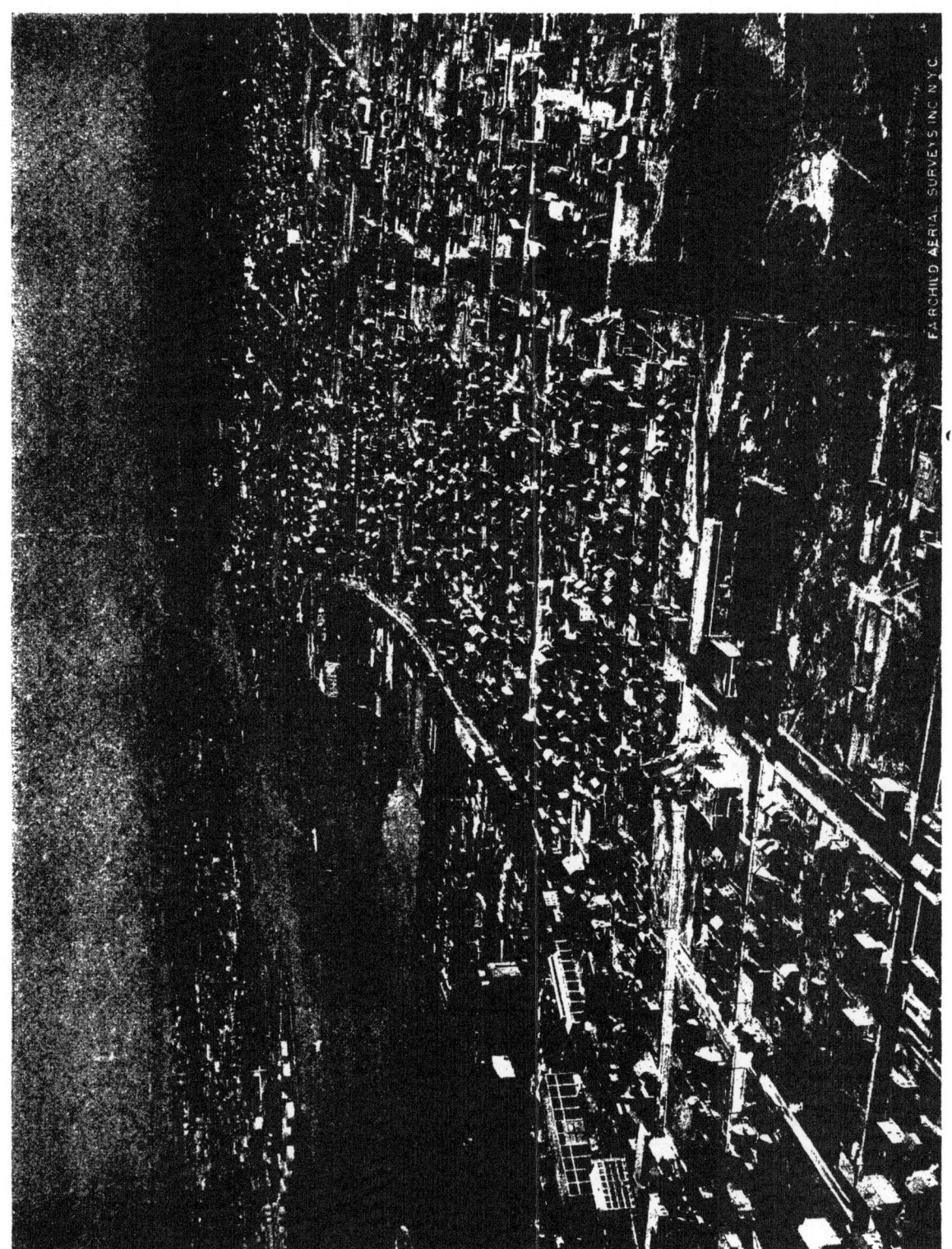

STATEN ISLAND

In general the main highways referred to above and the larger streets in the Boroughs are of liberal widths, ranging up to 80 feet between curbs. In Brooklyn, a large proportion of the streets are 80 feet wide, with roadways 44 feet from curb to curb, whereas in Queens most of the streets making up the regular street plan are 60 feet wide with 30-foot roadways. A number of highways and boulevards intersecting the main east and west highways, or leading to the beaches and resorts beyond the City limits, form an important element in the highway system of these two Boroughs, particularly in view of the tremendous traffic flows to be accommodated on week-ends and holidays.

The Bronx.

To the north of Manhattan and separated from it by the Harlem River is the Borough of The Bronx, ranking third among the Boroughs in number and density of population, and primarily residential in character. It has a present population of 978,000 and its population density closely approaches that of Brooklyn. It occupies an area of about 41 square miles, extending approximately nine miles east and west and eight miles in a north and south direction.

The eastern section of the Borough is the least developed, the greatest development being found between the Bronx and Harlem Rivers and south of about Fordham road. Its residential character is reflected in the preponderance of buildings of moderate height, mostly six stories or less, used for dwelling, retail business, and the miscellaneous purposes of such a community. Industrial development is largely confined to the waterfront areas.

Several railroad lines traverse the Borough or skirt its outer edges with a notable absence of crossings at grade. The various terminal and freight yards of these Boroughs are in general either below the street grade or else so located as not to conflict with the street system.

Reference has already been made to the bridges across the Harlem River connecting Manhattan and The Bronx and to the large volume of vehicular traffic they accommodate. Vehicular communication with Queens and Brooklyn at the present time is largely via Manhattan, the only direct connection being Classon Point Ferry. More direct and incidentally much needed access will be furnished by the recently authorized Triborough Bridge.

The street plan in general reflects its more recent development, the limitations imposed by topography and the traffic demands. The series of ridges and valleys running in a north and south direction through the Borough has favored building and street development in the same direction and made difficult the establishment of continuous and direct through highways from east to west. The necessity of handling not only strictly local traffic and traffic to and from Manhattan, but also the considerable volumes of traffic passing through The Bronx on its way to or from points in New England or in Westchester County has also favored the development of north and south highway facilities and Harlem River crossings.

The main highways and streets in general have curb to curb widths ranging from 50 to 60 feet. Special highways, such as the Grand Boulevard and Concourse, have a roadway width totaling up to 123 feet, with grade separations at important intersections. The section as a whole is in need of a fuller development of through highways with adequate connections to the avenues of Manhattan and to the main highways and boulevards of Westchester County as well as additional cross highways and provisions for meeting traffic requirements expectable upon the completion of the 178th Street Hudson River Bridge and the Triborough Bridge across these rivers.

Richmond (Staten Island).

The Borough of Richmond completely occupies Staten Island, which has an area of about 57 square miles, and is approximately 7½ miles wide and 12½ miles long. It has a present population of some 154,000, ranking last among the Boroughs in population and in population density, and third in area.

Staten Island is separated from the rest of the City by the Upper Bay and the Narrows and from New Jersey by the Kill von Kull, Newark Bay and Arthur Kill. A railroad bridge a Elizabethport, vehicular toll bridges at Elizabeth and Perth Amboy, and ferry lines at Perth Amboy, Carteret, Elizabethport and Bergen Point connect the island with New Jersey, An additional vehicular connection with Bayonne, the Kill von Kull Bridge, is under construction.

It is approximately five miles across the Upper Bay from the northern end of Staten Island to the southern tip of Manhattan, but only about a mile across the Narrows to the lower end of Brooklyn. Municipally operated ferries furnish the only means of direct communication for either vehicles or pedestrians with Manhattan and Brooklyn. Additional and more direct communication with Brooklyn will be afforded by the recently authorized vehicular tunnel across the Narrows.

ST. GEORGE, STATEN ISLAND

Population and development have, without doubt, been retarded by the comparative isolation of Staten Island with respect to the rest of New York City, and until recently with respect to New Jersey. Development has in large measure been confined to the area extending southward from the ferry terminals at St. George, including the immediately adjacent retail business and more remote residential sections and to the areas extending southward along either shore of the Island. Shipbuilding and allied industries are located along the west shore, down to about opposite Elizabeth, with residential development extending inland from the shore line. Extensive docks and warehouses occupy the waterfront along the Narrows, and further along the eastern shore are a number of recreational and residential centres. The south end of the Island and the more central portions include scattered residential sections and a single large industry. The utilization of the large areas still available for residential and industrial purposes will undoubtedly be quickened by the improved means of communication recently completed, under construction or authorized.

Railroad facilities extend along the north shore, connecting with the wharves, the terminal yards at Arlington and St. George and with the railroad bridge at Elizabethport. An electrical railroad extends along the entire eastern side of the island and together with a number of bus lines and local street railway lines furnishes local transportation. Gradual replacement of street railway operations by buses is stated to be under consideration.

The highway system reflects the demand for connection of the various points of crossing and also the traffic demands created by the recreational opportunities found along the eastern shore of the island. The existing main highways in general lead from the vicinity of the ferry terminals at the northern end of the island towards the various bridge and ferry terminals along the western shore and towards the beaches and settlements along the eastern shore. The main streets are mostly 70 feet wide, with 40 feet width between the curbs. The Hylan boulevard, extending along the eastern shore to the southern end of the island, is 100 feet wide with 60 feet roadway widths. The more urgent needs of the street system include the provision of additional highway connections to and between the recently completed or authorized bridges and tunnel, suitably by-passing the more densely built-up sections, as well as the provision of more direct connection between areas along the eastern and the western shores.

20

Photo by Fairchild Aerial Surveys Inc., N. Y. C.   MANHATTAN LOOKING SOUTH FROM TIMES SQUARE

SECTION II

CHARACTERISTICS OF HIGHWAY TRAFFIC

CLASSIFICATION OF TRAFFIC

The term highway traffic as here considered includes movement of pedestrians and of vehicles of all kinds upon the public streets. A presentation of the nature and extent of the elements contributing to such movements is given prior to the consideration of traffic flows, congestion and proposed relief measures as follows:

Pedestrian Traffic.

Pedestrian traffic is much more local in its nature than vehicular traffic. It is made up of relatively short movements, as for example between a subway station or railroad terminal and a place of employment, or between office buildings or stores in the same general neighborhood. Its extent reflects the concentration of activities, and hence of persons, in a particular district. It reaches its greatest proportions in areas immediately surrounding the various railroad, railway, ferry and transit terminals, in the theatrical and shopping districts and in the high building areas of down-town and mid-town Manhattan.

The pedestrian traffic on the streets of New York is occasioned by the movements from place to place of a resident population of 6,000,000 people, augmented by a large commuting population from the surrounding portion of the metropolitan area and a transient population variously estimated at from 50,000 to 100,000 persons. In its report on "Highway Traffic," the Regional Plan estimates the day-time population of the section of Manhattan to the south of 59th street, for a typical business day in 1924, to have been some 2,900,000, of which number about two-thirds moved into and out of the district each day.

The City Committee on Plan and Survey estimated the number of pedestrians using the streets of New York as approximately 6,000,000. The rapid transit, surface railway and bus lines in New York carried some 3,000,000,000 passengers in 1928, or about 9,500,000 passengers for an average business day. Practically all of these contribute to the pedestrian traffic at one or at both ends of their journeys. The passengers carried by taxicabs, approximating 1,500,000 per day, and those carried into and out of Manhattan by the 340,000 passenger car movements per day over bridges, ferries and tunnels, also contribute in varying degrees to the pedestrian traffic.

Vehicular Traffic.

The elements contributing to vehicular highway traffic are horse-drawn vehicles, passenger automobiles, taxicabs, buses, trucks and street cars. An indication of their relative importance in the traffic problem is afforded by a consideration of the number in use or authorized, and of the nature of their use of the highways.

Horse Drawn Vehicles.

There are no official records from which the number of horse drawn vehicles can be ascertained. Estimates based on data furnished by the industries and trade associations indicate that the number in use in 1928 approximated 29,000, which is approximately 54 per cent. of the number in use in 1919. They are extensively used for the delivery of milk and bread during the early morning hours, and for heavy trucking along the waterfront where long periods of waiting are involved. Wherever they mingle with general vehicular traffic, they cause delays to an extent far greater than indicated by the ratio of their number to the total number of vehicles on the streets.

Motor Vehicles.

The motor vehicle registration in New York City in 1928 was some 681,000, of which 75 per cent. were passenger cars, 17 per cent. commercial cars and 6 per cent. busses and taxicabs. Registration has grown rapidly, the total in 1928 being more than three times that in 1919. Detailed analysis indicates clearly a lessening rate of growth during recent years, and that passenger car registration is increasing much more rapidly than that of commercial vehicles. Registration of all classes in Brooklyn and in Queens is increasing considerably faster than in Manhattan.

Comparison of the growth in registration and the growth in traffic on special highways, such as the East River bridges, shows that for the larger areas they connect, there is a fairly definite relationship between total registration and total traffic. In smaller areas, as for example in mid-Manhattan, the traffic on individual streets has not increased as fast as the total registration, due in part to the greater spreading of the traffic and in part to the large proportion of the traffic more local in its nature.

Photo by Fairchild Aerial Surveys, N. Y. C.

CROSSTOWN VIEW IN MID MANHATTAN

Dealing with main traffic streams only and not with individual streets or intersections, commercial cars constitute from 20 to 30 per cent. of the total flow. The burden of this traffic upon the streets, due to the size of the trucks, their slower movement and more general cumbersomeness is far greater than the above percentages or those of total registration would indicate.

In the early months of 1928, there were about 21,000 taxicabs on the streets of the City, over two-thirds of which number operated in two shifts from about 6 a. m. to 2 a. m. Records of mileage are rather meagre but indicate about 150 miles per day as fairly representative. Random observations at five points in the midtown area covered 1,071 taxicabs, 27 per cent. of which were empty, and general observations indicate that a more complete and extensive count would show a considerably greater proportion of empty cabs. The relation between taxicabs and total vehicles varies widely with both time and location, reaching its greatest proportions in the principal streets of the midtown and downtown sections during the late afternoon rush hours.

Based on a survey made early in 1929, motor busses are operated in local transportation service by the Fifth Avenue Coach Company, and by the City, and in less local service by the interurban lines and railroads. The latter group operate in general from terminals over definite routes to the city portals, and account for about 1,700 traffic movements per day. The Emergency Bus System of the City includes seven crosstown lines in Manhattan, 11 in The Bronx and 18 in Queens. The Manhattan lines traverse streets and sections where their bearing on traffic problems is relatively minor.

The bus operations on 5th avenue reach their greatest density in the section between 34th and 57th streets. Scheduled headways at 42d street call for about 144 busses per hour during the afternoon north bound peak, indicating bus movements at this point approximately 10 per cent. of the total vehicular flow. The size of the busses, the stopping for passengers, and close headways create traffic burdens on the streets far greater in effect than the numbers above would indicate.

Street Railway.

There are street railway operations on most of the principal highways of the five boroughs. The number of revenue passengers carried during the year 1928, by boroughs was as follows:

Borough.	Number of Revenue Passengers Carried.
Manhattan	308,600,000
Bronx	153,100,000
Brooklyn-Queens	530,700,000
Richmond	10,300,000
Total	1,002,700,000

The maximum scheduled cars per hour in one direction at certain points in Manhattan, based on minimum headways during rush hours are as follows:

Location.	Maximum Cars per Hour.
North and South Bound—	
Essex and Clinton from 2d street to Delancey street	168
Park Row-Post Office Loop to Brooklyn Bridge	108
Bowery, Grand street to 8th street	78
2d avenue, 8th street to 59th street	48
4th avenue and Madison avenue	54
7th avenue, 42d street to 59th street	88
Crosstown—	
14th Street Line	103
23d street, Lexington avenue to Broadway	83
34th Street Line	61
42d street, Park avenue to Madison avenue	124
125th street, 3d avenue to Amsterdam avenue	49

Although the street car movements are small compared to other vehicular movements their occupancy of the middle of the highway and the necessity for passengers to cross the general traffic lanes greatly reduce the capacity of the roadways for general vehicular traffic.

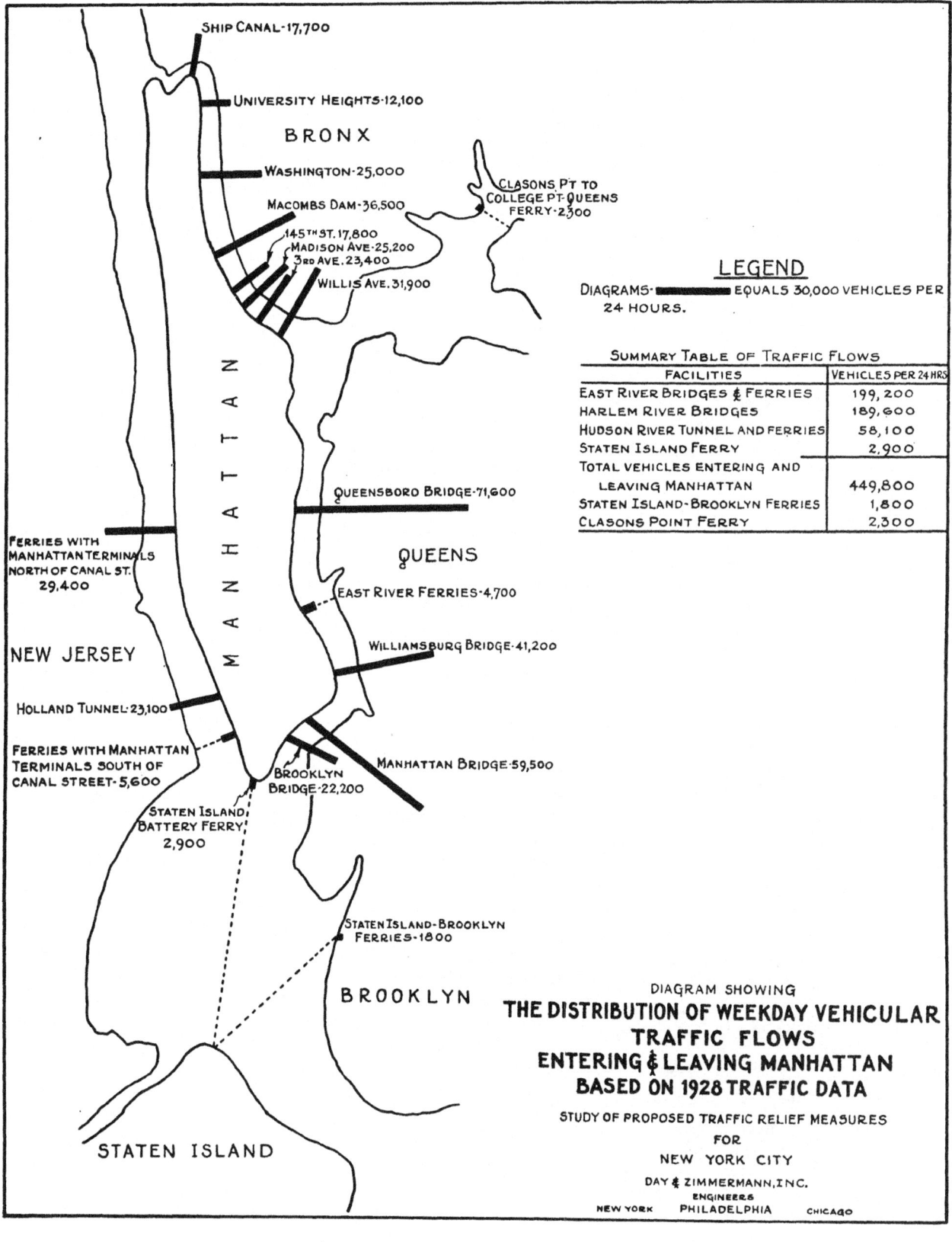

TRAFFIC FLOWS

A detailed presentation of the proportions and general characteristics of vehicular traffic on the streets, bridges, ferries and tunnels, the points between which it is moving and the general routes followed will be found in later sections of this report and forms the basis for the following more general presentation:

The greatest traffic flows are encountered in Manhattan and represent a combination of a heavy traffic local to the island and a large volume of traffic moving across the surrounding rivers to or from points in the other boroughs and in New Jersey. An indication of the relative magnitude of these flows is afforded by the following result of counts made in January, 1929:

Dealing with the combined traffic on all the avenues at 51st street, about one out of every five vehicles moved across the Harlem River, about one out of every six across the East River, and about one out of 40 across the Hudson River.

Traffic Flows Entering and Leaving Manhattan.

The typical week day vehicular traffic flow into and out of Manhattan totals substantially 450,000 vehicles per day, distributed as shown diagrammatically on page 24. The movements across the Harlem and East Rivers are nearly equal and together account for 86 per cent. of the total. About two-thirds of the East River bridge traffic is concentrated on the three bridges connecting Lower Manhattan with Brooklyn, and the remainder on the Queensboro Bridge. The latter is located about midway between the Williamsburg Bridge and the mouth of the Harlem River, and is the only major crossing in a distance of over six miles.

The ferry and tunnel traffic across the Hudson totals some 58,000 vehicles per day, 40 per cent. of which move through the Holland Tunnel portals at Canal street.

Over two-thirds of the East River bridge traffic moves between the hours of 7 a. m. and 7 p. m., with heavy directional peaks, westbound in the morning and eastbound in the evening hours, caused almost entirely by passenger car traffic which is commuting in its nature. The commercial car traffic, amounting to about one-quarter of the total, is characterized by relative uniformity of flow during working hours. An indication of the volume of night trucking is afforded by the fact that almost one-fifth of the interborough commercial car traffic over the bridges moves between the hours 7 p. m. and 7 a. m.

Based on a count of week day traffic in October, 1928, the maximum hourly flow over the bridges in both directions is approximately one and one-half times the maximum flow in one direction and about two times the average flow during the 24 hours. The maximum hourly flow in both directions totalled, for the four bridges, some 15,200 and for the Queensboro Bridge alone about 5,700 vehicles per hour.

Traffic over the Harlem River bridges is considered to be of the same general nature as over the East River bridges and to possess generally similar characteristics. Except for a slightly greater proportion of commercial car traffic and less pronounced peak flows. Analysis of the week day traffic through the Holland Tunnel shows general characteristics similar to those of East River bridge traffic.

As previously stated, about 21 per cent. of the traffic on all Manhattan avenues near 51st street moves across the Harlem River, and constitutes about one-third of the traffic over these bridges. The remainder is in most part traffic local to the northern sections of Manhattan.

Only a small portion of the Queensboro Bridge traffic moves to or from Brooklyn, the most of its being attributable to the sections near the bridge head and Flushing. The greater portion is destined for points in mid-Manhattan, with about 21 per cent. of the total moving to points north of 110th street, and about 10 per cent. moving through the congested midtown section on its way to points below 14th street. About one-third of the total is destined for West Side districts. East Side avenues and crosstown streets between 30th and 59th streets carry the greater portion of the traffic to and from the bridge.

The traffic over the Williamsburg Bridge in most part moves to or from Brooklyn sections south of Newtown Creek and to the east of the bridge. About 57 per cent. of the total is destined for points in Manhattan south of 14th street and about 34 per cent. to points between 14th and 72d streets. About one-half of the traffic uses east side avenues, chiefly 1st avenue and Lafayette street, for movements to the north of the bridge.

The Manhattan Bridge derives about 90 per cent. of its traffic from districts in Brooklyn to the east and south of the bridge. On the Manhattan side about 85 per cent. of the traffic is quite evenly distributed between the east side and west side districts south of 47th street. About two-thirds of the traffic uses east side avenues, chiefly Lafayette street and 4th avenue, and substantially all of the remaining traffic moves

DIAGRAM SHOWING
FOR
**THE PRINCIPAL INTERSECTIONS IN MID-MANHATTAN
THE DISTRIBUTION OF THE TOTAL TRAFFIC**
ON THE BASIS OF
THE FLOW IN EACH DIRECTION
BASED ON 1928 AVENUE & STREET TRAFFIC COUNTS
7 A.M. TO 7 P.M.
STUDY OF PROPOSED TRAFFIC RELIEF MEASURES
FOR
NEW YORK CITY
DAY & ZIMMERMANN, INC.
ENGINEERS
NEW YORK   PHILADELPHIA   CHICAGO

LEGEND
1- LENGTHS OF BANDS ARE PROPORTIONAL TO THE AVERAGE HOURLY TRAFFIC FLOWS IN EACH DIRECTION.
   SCALE ▬▬▬ EQUALS 1000 VEHICLES PER HOUR.
2- ■ DENOTES COMMERCIAL CAR TRAFFIC.
3- ☐ DENOTES PASSENGER CAR TRAFFIC.
4- * NO DATA AVAILABLE, AND IN CASE OF 8TH AVENUE COMPARABLE TRAFFIC FLOW NEGLIGIBLE
   DUE TO SUBWAY CONSTRUCTION.
5- ** INCLUDED WITH 6TH AVENUE.   6- *** INCLUDED WITH 5TH AVENUE.

directly across town, mostly on Canal street, using 7th avenue or West street for north and south movements.

Regulations restrict the vehicular use of the Brooklyn Bridge almost exclusively to passenger cars, about 83 per cent. of which moves to or from Brooklyn points to the south and east of the bridge. There is an even greater concentration of traffic on the Manhattan side, where about two-thirds of the traffic moves to points south of Canal street over diverse routes. Traffic toward the north in large part moves via Centre and Lafayette streets.

Dealing with the three lower bridges collectively, with a combined traffic of 123,000 vehicles per day, about 95 per cent. of the total is attributable to the area lying south of Newtown Creek on the Brooklyn side and about 81 per cent. to Manhattan districts lying south of 47th street. About 6 per cent. of this traffic moves to and from points north of 110th street and about 5 per cent. to New Jersey.

Approximately two-thirds of the Holland Tunnel week-day traffic, which totals about 23,000 vehicles, moves to or from points in Manhattan, chiefly in west side districts below 47th street and mostly using Varick street and 7th avenue. About one-fourth of the total traffic moves across lower Manhattan streets on its way to points in Brooklyn and Queens, by far the larger portion using Canal street and the Manhattan Bridge. On the west side of the Hudson about one-half of the traffic is attributable to Jersey City, Newark and their immediate environs.

The major vehicular traffic streams across the East River may be summarized as flowing between:

(1) Points in Queens and points in upper Manhattan and The Bronx, using the Queensboro Bridge and its approaches and traveling long distances on Manhattan streets due to the indirectness of the route.

(2) Points in Queens and points in mid-Manhattan, using the Queensboro Bridge and approaches on its way into and through the most congested sections of the City.

(3) Points in southern Brooklyn and along its waterfront and points in lower Manhattan, using chiefly the Manhattan and the Brooklyn Bridges and passing through the congested approach areas on both sides of the river.

(4) Points in the northern section of Brooklyn and points in lower Manhattan, using chiefly the Williamsburg Bridge, and more local in its nature than the other streams.

There are in addition two appreciable flows involving counter movements, passage through congested sections and long distances traveled on Manhattan avenues. These are between Queens and lower Manhattan via the Queensboro Bridge and between Brooklyn and upper Manhattan or The Bronx via the three lower bridges.

Traffic Flows in Mid-Manhattan.

The available data as to vehicular traffic on the streets of the City in general covers week-day flows between the hours of 7 a. m. and 7 p. m. at principal intersections in areas where traffic conditions are in greatest need of relief, and for such areas reasonably satisfactory determinations of the main flows can be developed.

A consideration of the shape of Manhattan and its street plan, the distribution of business and housing and the location of bridge, tunnel and ferry terminals indicates and the traffic data establishes that with but few exceptions the north and south movements exceed in volume and in distance traversed those in an east and west direction.

The average hourly traffic flows in each direction for a number of principal intersections in mid-Manhattan are showwn diagramatically on page 26. In all cases the volumes are greater on the avenues than on the crosstown streets, the ratio of north and south to east and west traffic averaging about 2.5 to 1 for the intersections shown, and being least along 57th street. The greater flows on preferred highways such as 5th avenue and Park avenue, and on the avenues offering superior facilities for through traffic such as 1st, 7th, 10th and 11th avenues, is quite marked. Traffic, particularly commercial car traffic has a tendency to follow the more marginal streets, such as 1st avenue and 10th avenue, in an effort to avoid the midtown congestion.

The average hourly traffic on Park avenue at 42d street is about 2,800 and on 5th avenue about 2,000 vehicles per hour. The combined north and south movements on all the avenues at 42d street is about 18,400 and at 23d street about 12,800 vehicles per hour, of which about 22 per cent. and 30 per cent respectively, are commercial cars.

Crosstown traffic on 42d street at 5th avenue is about 700, and on the one-way streets ranges from 300 to 450 vehicles per hour. On all the crosstown streets from 30th to 59th, inclusive, a distance of about 1½ miles, the combined average flow at 5th avenue is about 13,300 vehicles per hour, commercial car traffic averaging about 20 per cent. of the total and being somewhat greater in the streets south of 39th street. On the basis of allowing two lanes in each street for standing vehicles, the average flow per effective lane on the crosstown streets is in the order of 200 and on the avenues about 300 vehicles per hour, with rather wide variations on the individual streets. The cycle of traffic control lights at most intersections is practically three minutes, during two of which traffic flows on the avenues, thereby restricting crosstown movements at intersections to one minute out of every three.

Traffic on most of the avenues shows a south bound peak during the morning hours and a north bound peak in the afternoon, with the greatest total flows occurring in the afternoon hours. With the exception of 1st avenue and of 57th street, the hourly variations in traffic between 8 a. m. and 6 p. m. are in general much less pronounced on the avenues than on the bridges, and still less so on the crosstown streets. The ratio of the maximum to the average hourly flow varies rather widely and on the avenues is in the order of 1.5 to 1.0.

Analysis of the traffic crossing 5th avenue on streets between 30th and 59th streets, inclusive, develops that in general from 50 per cent. to 60 per cent. of the traffic moves between points in areas directly east or west of the crossing. Considerable portions move to or from points well to the north or the south, and about 11 per cent. moves across the East River, chiefly via. the Queensboro Bridge. It is evident from the data collected and from observations in the streets, that there is a large number of Z and L movements in this section of Manhattan. About 8.5 per cent. of the traffic crossing 5th avenue on the streets enumerated above moves on these streets from at least 9th avenue to at least 3d avenue, and in addition about 11.7 per cent. from at least 7th avenue to at least 3d avenue. These figures give a measure of the extent of "longhaul" crosstown traffic in this area.

The combined north bound and south bound flow on all the avenues at 51st street averages about 18,000 vehicles per hour between 7 a. m. and 7 p. m., about two-thirds of the movement taking place on avenues from 1st to 6th, inclusive. About one-fourth of the traffic moves across Manhattan on its way to or from the point at which it crosses 51st street, and consequently makes an L shaped journey. The very considerable portion of the total traffic moving to or from points far to the north or to the south of 51st street is evidenced by the following distribution:

    35 per cent. moved to or from points north of 110th street.
    24 per cent. moved to or from points between 72d and 110th streets.
    17 per cent. moved to or from points between 33d and 14th streets.
    26 per cent. moved to or from points south of 14th street.

A more concrete measure of the distances traveled in a north and south direction by this traffic is afforded by the following:

    About 39 per cent. of the total avenue traffic crossing 51st street traveled between points involving north and south movements in Manhattan ranging from 5 to 8 miles and averaging about 6 miles.

    About 31 per cent. of the total involved north and south movements in Manhattan ranging from 2.5 to 3.5 miles and averaging practically 3 miles.

    The remaining 30 per cent. moved north and south distances ranging from 2 miles downwards and may be considered to represent avenue traffic local to mid-Manhattan.

There is a very general similarity between commercial car traffic and total traffic as to distribution and distances traveled in Manhattan.

Traffic Flows in Lower and in Upper Manhattan.

In lower Manhattan, with its irregular street plan, traffic flows are not so definite or susceptible of summarization as in the midtown section. The most pronounced north and south flows are found on Centre street, Lafayette street and the Bowery on the east side, and on West street and Varick street on the west side. The heaviest crosstown movements are found on Canal street to the east of Broadway, where the average hourly flows approximate 1,500 vehicles per hour, about two-thirds of which is through traffic using the East River Bridge or the Holland Tunnel. Commercial vehicles constitute over one-half of the Canal street traffic, and the percentage of the total varying widely and reaching a maximum of 72 per cent. at Washington street. With the exception of the Lafayette street intersection, where the flows are approximately equal, the east and west movements in Canal street exceed the north and south movements. At practically all other intersections of major streets in the downtown section the north and south flows are the greater.

In upper Manhattan there is a similar preponderance of north and south traffic, the flows in general being less than in the midtown area and including a considerable volume of traffic local to upper Manhattan and to The Bronx. Average flows on upper Broadway are of the order of 2,000 and on 5th and 7th avenues about 1,500 vehicles per hour.

Traffic Flows in Other Boroughs.

As in Manhattan, the traffic flows on the streets of The Bronx, Brooklyn and Queens are a combination of the local traffic and the heavy volume of interborough traffic moving over the various bridges and ferries. The available data as to volumes and directions of flow is more scattered and in general confined to intersections along the main highways leading to and from the bridge heads. No data of this nature is available for the Borough of Richmond.

In The Bronx, where the larger flows follow the north and south highways, the week day volumes are considerably less than on Manhattan avenues, in general averaging less than 1,000, with Fordham road showing about 1,250 vehicles per hour at its intersection with the Boston Post road.

In Queens, the greatest flows are in an east and west direction and are found on the highways converging upon the Queensboro Bridge, particularly in the vicinity of the bridge, and in locations further east where existing routes tend to converge, as in the Jamaica region. Typical week day flows along the Queens boulevard average about 2,000 and along the Northern boulevard about 1,600 vehicles per hour. Crossing traffic is in general relatively small.

In Brooklyn, the convergence of streets and of traffic upon the area back of the Manhattan and Brooklyn Bridges is most marked, creating heavy flows along main streets such as Flatbush, Fulton and Atlantic and 4th avenues in this section, and an effective barrier against easy movement in a north and south direction. Hourly flows on these streets are quite comparable with those found in Manhattan, a week day count on Flatbush avenue at Myrtle avenue, averaging 2,200 vehicles per hour. The heavy holiday and week-end traffic to the beaches and to the more outlying sections of both Brooklyn and Queens in large measure moves across the East River bridges and follows the same general routes as the week day traffic, but encountering somewhat greater cross flows and conflicts.

TRAFFIC CONGESTION

Traffic congestion is encountered in varying degrees in every section of the City and is by no means confined to certain hours of the day or periods of the year. It is due primarily to the great numbers of people and of vehicles of all kinds using the highways and to the intense concentration of this use in restricted areas on a highway system established long before the days of the skyscraper, the rapid transit subway, the automobile and the motor truck.

The greatest traffic congestion, and the most serious consequences, are found in the following districts:

(1) The midtown and downtown sections of Manhattan.

(2) In the vicinity of, and along the streets leading to the various bridge and tunnel heads in Manhattan, Brooklyn, Queens and The Bronx.

(3) Along the main highways leading from the bridge heads to the outlaying sections of Brooklyn, Queens and The Bronx.

Traffic Speeds.

One measure of traffic congestion is afforded by the over-all speeds at which automobiles can travel when moving with the traffic and under the existing system of traffic control. The continual changes in traffic conditions from hour to hour and from day to day account for considerable variations in observed speeds on a specific route, particularly shorter routes.

In considering the results of observations of traffic speeds on Manhattan avenues and streets, it is of interest that under the control system in effect, avenue traffic in general flows for two minutes and is then entirely stopped for one minute to allow cross town traffic to move. Avenue traffic then moves again, traveling at maximum permissible speeds until again stopped by the traffic light. It moves two-thirds of the time and is stopped one-third of the time. East and west traffic can move across the avenues only one-third of the time. These conditions have a controlling effect upon the over-all or average speeds with which traffic can move from origin to destination.

Speeds in 1924.

In its report on highway traffic, the Regional Plan gives the results of an extensive series of observations on the volume and speed of traffic on typical Manhattan streets, made during business hours in October and November, 1924. The results given are average findings for street sections ranging in length from 0.4 to 1 mile. The weighted average speed for all the observations was 11.3 miles per hour. On 5th avenue south of 59th street the average speed maintained between points eight or nine blocks apart ranged from 5.4 to 10.5 miles per hour. The average speeds maintained throughout the individual routes ranged from a maximum of 15.3 to a minimum of 7.8 miles per hour.

Speeds in 1926.

Observations made by the Regional Plan in 1926 indicated a falling off in speeds on the busier streets. On 5th avenue speeds as low as 2.5 to 3 miles per hour were found not unusual during peak hours in the busiest sections.

Observations made by the Police Department during either the morning or afternoon rush hours in May, 1926, cover longer trips and indicate somewhat higher speeds. On 5th avenue between 14th and 110th streets, a distance of about five miles, the over-all speed reported was 12 miles per hour, the speeds over one mile sections of the route ranging from 8½ to 20 miles per hour. On crosstown streets, the trips extended practically from river to river and showed over-all speeds in the midtown section ranging from 5.4 to 7.1 miles per hour. The streets involved and the range in over-all speeds observed are shown in the following tabulation:

Table Showing Speeds of Passenger Car Traffic as Observed by the Police Department in May, 1926.

Street.	Approximate Distance in Miles.	Over-All Speeds, Miles Per Hour.
3d avenue	7.0	12.7
4th and Park avenues	6.0	10.5
Lexington avenue	5.5	10.0
Madison avenue	6.0	10.5
5th avenue	5.0	12.0
6th avenue	2.4	6.7
Broadway	8.0	8.7
7th avenue	3.8	9.3
10th and Amsterdam avenues	7.8	11.3
14th street	2.0	8.3
23d street	2.0	6.9
34th street	1.8	7.4
37th street	2.0	5.4
38th street	1.9	5.4
42d street	2.0	6.6
59th street	2.0	7.1
125th street	2.0	10.0

Speeds in 1929.

The results of some observations made by outside interests on a typical week day afternoon early in January 1929, have been placed at our disposal. They cover single observations in each direction on Park, 5th, 6th and 7th avenues from 14th to 59th streets, a distance of about 2¼ miles, and on 42d street from 1st avenue to 11th avenue, a distance of about two miles.

The eastbound trip on 42d street showed an over-all speed of 5.5 and the westbound trip of 4.5 miles per hour. On the avenues, the over-all speeds ranged from 6.7 to 11.3, with crest speeds in excess of 25 miles per hour, and southbound speeds slower than northbound in nearly every instance. The variations in speeds over quarter-mile sections ranged from a low of 2.1 to a high of 22.5 miles per hour. Over-all speeds on Park avenue were about two miles per hour faster than those observed on 5th, 6th and 7th avenues.

Miscellaneous observations made at various times during the first five months of 1929 indicate that under ordinary rush-hour conditions a passenger car would make about eleven blocks between successive "go" signals on Park avenue and about eight on 5th avenue, the latter figure dropping to between five and six blocks during periods of heavy congestion. Under the present timing of signals, the number of blocks traveled between successive signals is approximately equal to the over-all speed in miles per hour.

More specific observations on a number of routes were made under our direction by the Police Department during the latter part of May, 1929. Unmarked passenger cars, with observers in civilian attire, were driven over the various routes selected at the same rate as the general traffic. All of the observations were made on week days, with weather conditions varying but for the most part clear. Five round trips were made over each route, two during the morning rush hours, one in the middle of the day and two during the late afternoon rush.

Manhattan Avenues.

The tabulation below shows for traffic on the avenues the over-all speeds by routes between the limits stated and also the speeds observed in the midtown sections extending from 23d to 59th streets.

Table Showing Speeds of Week Day Vehicular Traffic on North and South Avenues in Manhattan as Observed in May, 1929.

Avenue and Limits of Trip.	Distance in Miles.	Direction, Northbound or Southbound.	Over-all Speed in Miles Per Hour.			
			Slowest Trip.	Fastest Trip.	Average of Five Trips.	Average Speed Between 23d Street and 59th Street, Distance 1.8 Miles.
1st—Schiff parkway and 125th street	6.5	N. B.	10.6	12.0	11.1	10.5
		S. B.	9.3	12.9	11.1	10.5
3d — Canal street and 125th street	6.8	N. B.	10.4	13.5	11.9	11.4
		S. B.	10.3	11.5	11.0	9.9
Lexington—23d street and 125th street	5.0	N. B.	8.3	10.2	9.1	9.7
		S. B.	8.3	9.7	8.8	9.1
Park—Canal street and 125th street	6.8	N. B.	11.4	13.1	12.2	11.8
		S. B.	8.8	12.5	10.7	8.3
5th — Canal street and 125th street	6.8	N. B.	8.3	11.8	10.0	6.8
		S. B.	9.0	11.0	10.2	7.8
7th — Canal street and 59th street	3.4	N. B.	7.5	15.6	10.2	8.3
		S. B.	8.7	12.0	10.6	7.7
9th — Canal street and 125th street	6.9	N. B.	12.1	14.1	13.3	12.1
		S. B.	13.1	16.3	14.1	12.6
10th—Canal street and 125th street	6.7	N. B.	11.5	13.2	12.4	12.6
		S. B.	11.2	14.0	12.6	12.9

It may be further summarized as follows:

Range in Speed; Entire Route—
Slowest trips, 7.5 to 13.1 miles per hour.
Fastest trips, 9.7 to 16.3 miles per hour.
Average of five trips, 8.8 to 14.1 miles per hour.
Range in Speed; Midtown Section—
Average of five trips, 6.8 to 12.9 miles per hour.

The time required for an entire trip at the above speeds ranges from a maximum of 54 minutes to a minimum of 25 minutes. The time required to travel between 23d street and 59th street at 6.8 miles per hour would be about 16 minutes, and at 12.9 miles per hour about 8.4 minutes.

Dealing with the average of both northbound and southbound observations, over-all traffic speeds were highest in 9th avenue and lowest in Lexington avenue, with 10th, Park, 3d, 1st, 7th, 5th avenues falling between in the order named.

Vehicles moving over the two north and south drives in Central Park are not stopped by traffic signals and are subject to less delay due to intersecting traffic streams than on the avenues. Tests made during the same period showed average speeds of 20 miles per hour.

Crosstown Streets.

The speeds of crosstown traffic were observed on eleven routes, using eight streets with two-way traffic and six streets on which traffic is restricted to movement in one direction. With one exception, the trips covered the width of the island, a distance of practically two miles. The tabulation below shows by routes the over-all speeds observed between the limits stated:

Table Showing Speeds of Week Day Vehicular Traffic on Crosstown Streets in Manhattan as Observed in May, 1929.

Route or Street and Limits of Trip.	Distance in Miles.	Direction, Eastbound or Westbound.	Speed in Miles Per Hour.		
			Slowest Trip.	Fastest Trip.	Average of Five Trips.
Canal—Bowery and West street......	1.0	W. B.	6.6	13.1	9.3
		E. B.	7.8	13.2	9.6
14th—Avenue D and 11th avenue....	2.2	W. B.	7.4	8.5	7.9
		E. B.	6.4	7.2	6.9
23d—Marginal street and 13th avenue	2.0	W. B.	6.3	8.8	7.1
		E. B.	6.8	10.4	8.3
27th—1st avenue and 12th avenue....	1.9	W. B.	5.6	8.1	6.5
28th—1st avenue and 12th avenue....	1.9	E. B.	6.0	8.1	7.2
34th—1st avenue and 12th avenue....	1.9	W. B.	6.1	7.7	7.0
		E. B.	6.1	7.7	7.0
37th—East River and 12th avenue....	2.0	W. B.	4.7	6.9	6.0
38th—East River and 12th avenue....	2.0	E. B.	5.1	7.8	6.0
42d—East River and 12th avenue.....	2.0	W. B.	6.0	7.2	6.4
		E. B.	5.9	8.1	6.9
49th—Beekman place and 12th avenue	2.0	W. B.	7.5	9.8	8.3
50th—Beekman place and 12th avenue	2.0	E. B.	7.5	9.8	8.6
57th—Sutton Place South and Riverside drive	2.0	W. B.	6.8	8.7	7.5
		E. B.	6.4	7.6	7.2
110th—Pleasant avenue and Riverside drive	1.9	W. B.	9.8	11.2	10.2
		E. B.	8.5	11.8	10.0
125th—Pleasant avenue and 12th avenue	1.9	W. B.	7.9	9.6	8.9
		E. B.	8.5	9.6	8.9

It may be further summarized as follows:
    Range in Speed—
        Slowest trips, 4.7 to 9.8 miles per hour.
        Fastest trips, 6.9 to 13.2 miles per hour.
        Average of five trips, 6.0 to 10.2 miles per hour.

For a two-mile trip, the corresponding time required for the trip ranges from 26 minutes as a maximum to nine minutes as a minimum. Dealing with the averages of the eastbound and westbound traffic speeds, the 37th-38th Street Route shows the lowest and the 110th Street Route the highest speeds, with the 42d Street, 27th-28th Street, 34th Street, 57th Street, 14th Street, 23d Street, 49th-50th Street, 125th Street and Canal Street Routes falling between in the order named. The showing of the lower speeds in the midtown section is quite definite and significant.

South of Canal Street.

South of Canal street, traffic speeds were observed on five routes, four of which lead to or through the financial district. They are as follows:

    Lafayette Street Route: Between Canal street and the intersection of Broadway and Park Row via Lafayette street, Centre street, Park Row, Mail street and Broadway, southbound; and Park Row, Centre street, Peach street and Lafayette street, northbound. Distance, 0.7 miles.

    Broadway Route: Between Canal street and Battery place on Broadway. Distance, 1.2 miles.

    Varick Street Route: Between Canal street and Battery place via Varick street, West Broadway, Greenwich street, Day street and Washington street, southbound; and Greenwich street, West Broadway and Varick street, northbound. Distance, 1.3 miles.

    West Street Route: Between Canal street and Battery place on West street. Distance, 1.5 miles.

    South Street Route: Between Whitehall street and Montgomery street on South street. Distance, 1.6 miles.

The Lafayette Street Route is a continuation of the north and south Park Avenue Route, which carries the heaviest traffic of all the avenues. Along Park row the traffic filters into various streets leading farther south towards the financial district, with much of it using Broadway.

A study of the tests made on both the Lafayette Street and the Broadway Routes showed ranges in speed in one direction as follows:

Range in Speed—
  Slowest trips, 3.5 to 6.4 miles per hour.
  Fastest trips, 8.3 to 13.8 miles per hour.
  Average of 5 trips, 6.7 to 8.3 miles per hour.

Comparing the above with observed speeds on the avenues above Canal street, it will be noted that they are much lower, and hence that traffic conditions south of Canal street were even more restrictive of free movement than in the midtown sections.

The Varick and the West Street Routes are also continuations of main north and south avenue routes such as 7th, 9th, 10th and 11th avenues. Results of tests on these two routes combined are as follows:

Range in Speed:
  Slowest trips, 7.0 to 12.3 miles per hour.
  Fastest trips, 16.2 to 19.5 miles per hour.
  Average of 5 trips, 11.5 to 13.5 miles per hour.

The streets used for these two routes do not have traffic lights, and also are subject to less interference by cross traffic than either Lafayette street or Broadway.

South street was selected for tests to ascertain normal speeds on a marginal thoroughfare that has no traffic congestion. Of the ten one-way trips made the fastest was at 19 miles per hour, with seven trips at 16 miles per hour, which was also the slowest speed. The average of all ten trips was 16.6 miles per hour.

East River Bridges.

An indication of traffic conditions encountered in crossing the East River bridges is afforded by the observed speeds set forth in the following tabulation:

Table Showing Speeds of Weekday Vehicular Traffic on East River Bridges and Approach Streets as Observed in May, 1929.

Bridge and Route.	Number of One Way Trips.	Average Speed in Miles per Hour.		
		On Bridge.	On Approach Streets.	Entire Trip.
Brooklyn	10	18.8	10.9	14.1
Manhattan, Lower Level	7	21.5	11.5	14.0
Manhattan, Upper Level	3	18.3	8.6	10.8
Williamsburg	10	14.5	10.3	12.1
Queensboro (a)	4	14.2	11.3	14.0
Queensboro (b)	6	13.7	13.0	13.3

Routes and Distances.

Bridge and Limits of Trips.	Distance in Miles.		
	Bridge.	Approach Streets.	Total.
Brooklyn—Spruce street and Park row, Willoughby and Flatbush avenues	1.13	.98	2.11
Manhattan, Lower Level—Mulberry and Canal streets, Flatbush avenue and Plaza	1.32	2.03	3.35
Manhattan, Upper Level—Bowery and Hester street, Flatbush avenue and Plaza	1.32	2.09	3.41
Williamsburg—Bowery and Delancey street, Broadway and Flushing avenue	1.50	1.52	3.02
Queensboro (a)—3d avenue and 59th street, eastbound, 3d avenue and 60th street, westbound, Northern boulevard and Broadway	1.40	2.10	3.50
Queensboro (b)—3d avenue and 59th street, eastbound, 3d avenue and 60th street, westbound, Queens and Roosevelt boulevards	1.40	1.61	3.01

VIEW SHOWING A RESULT OF CONCENTRATION OF INDUSTRY AS ILLUSTRATED BY NOON-DAY CROWD IN THE NEW GARMENT CENTER

Photo by Ewing Galloway, N. Y.

View on 36th Street Between 8th Avenue and Broadway. Street Completely Closed to Vehicular Traffic by Police Regulations

The routes extended from points in the immediate vicinity of the respective Manhattan terminals over the bridges and along the main highways on the Long Island side for distances ranging from one to two miles. The variations in observed speeds on individual trips were of the same order as set forth for the Manhattan streets and avenues, and are in large part responsible for some apparent inconsistencies in the resulting averages. Average speeds over the various bridges ranging from 14 to 22 miles per hour and average speeds on the approach streets ranging from 9 to 13 miles per hour show clearly that the greater hindrances to free movement across the East River are found in the approach areas rather than on the bridge roadways.

Summary.

The results of the observations made in May, 1929, using rounded averages, may be summarized as follows:

Traffic speeds on Manhattan avenues ranged from 9 to 14 miles per hour for entire trips and from 7 to 13 miles per hour through the midtown section.

Crosstown traffic moved at speeds ranging from 6 to 10 miles per hour, the lower speeds occurring in the midtown area.

Traffic between the Battery and Canal street moved at speeds ranging from 7 to 8 miles per hour via Broadway and Lafayette street, and from 12 to 14 miles per hour via West street or Varick street.

East River bridge traffic moved over the bridges and along the approach streets at speeds ranging from 11 to 14 miles per hour.

In considering the above speeds in relation to traffic conditions, it must be kept in mind that the tests were limited in number and made during a period of the year in which traffic volume and congestion are not at their peak. It is believed that tests made during the winter months would in many instances show lower speeds.

Congestion.

A brief description of characteristic examples of congestion in several sections of the City is given as follows:

Pedestrian Traffic.

The most striking examples of congestion resulting from pedestrian traffic are found in the high building areas of downtown and midtown Manhattan and in the vicinity of the various ferry, rapid transit and railroad terminals. One result of piling acre upon top of acre of floor space is a volume of pedestrian traffic so great that it has become necessary to bar vehicular traffic from streets, such as Nassau street, during certain hours of the day. A similar situation has developed in the new centre of the garment industry. The photograph (page 34) shows a noon-day crowd on 36th street between 8th avenue and Broadway and is illustrative of this extreme of congestion.

In addition to causing congestion on the sidewalks, where pedestrian traffic is heavy, it tends to disregard traffic signals and to encroach upon the roadway space at intersections, thereby greatly retarding the flow of vehicular traffic. The two views of conditions at 42d street and Madison avenue, shown on page 37, indicate typical examples of this conflict between pedestrians and vehicular traffic.

In the upper view, pedestrian traffic in 42d street has the right-of-way, but is being interfered with by the taxicabs making left turns into Madison avenue. In the lower view, vehicular traffic in Madison avenue has the right-of-way, but is being retarded by the pedestrians who have crowded into the roadway and by those who have gotten into the midst of the vehicular traffic.

Conflicts of this nature are so general and widespread as to constitute an outstanding cause of traffic congestion, and particularly because of the slowing up of vehicles. Control of pedestrian traffic in such situations is one of the most difficult problems in traffic regulation, but also offers great possibilities of relief. It was an essential element in the general plan developed early in 1929 for the general regulation of traffic in the theatrical district.

Vehicular Traffic, Downtown Manhattan

The narrow streets and the irregular street plan of lower Manhattan, together with the constant flow of vehicular traffic in all directions on these streets, result in much congestion. Broadway traffic, large in volume and varied in make-up, is continually held up by cross traffic at frequent intervals. Trucks, taxicabs, passenger cars and street cars move in close order and at low speeds, and midday conditions are almost as bad as those in the morning and late afternoon. The proposed extension of several of the avenue routes farther south and the improvement of the marginal highways should result in spreading traffic which now tends to concentrate.

VIEWS SHOWING SHOPPING CROWDS IN MANHATTAN

Photo by Underwood & Underwood, N. Y.
Looking North on Broadway at 34th Street

Photo by Underwood & Underwood, N. Y.
Looking East on 42nd Street From 6th Avenue

VIEWS SHOWING CONFLICT OF PEDESTRIAN AND VEHICULAR TRAFFIC AT 42ND STREET AND MADISON AVENUE

Photo by Ewing Galloway, N. Y.

42nd Street Traffic Has the Right of Way

Photo by Ewing Galloway, N. Y.

Madison Avenue Traffic Has the Right of Way

VIEW SHOWING CHARACTERISTICS OF CROSS TOWN TRAFFIC IN MID MANHATTAN

Photo by Underwood & Underwood, N. Y.

View Looking East on 39th Street From 5th Avenue. Note Horse Drawn Vehicle, Trucks and Restriction of Moving Traffic to 2 Lanes

Park row, connecting via Centre street with the much-used Lafayette Street Route uptown, has liberal roadway width, but the free flow of traffic is hindered by the four lines of street car tracks and by the cross flows of traffic moving over the Brooklyn Bridge. Much crowding and congestion occurs between its intersections with Nassau and Centre streets due to these causes. The view on page 54 shows the general situation, although not during a period when traffic is heavy. The proposal to narrow the sidewalk on the City Hall Park and to widen and straighten out the roadway of Centre street where it passes under the bridge terminal should afford much relief in this vicinity. Further relief would be afforded if the street car operation could be restricted to two tracks or better yet removed entirely.

Canal street is the main thoroughfare between the west side waterfront and the Manhattan Bridge. It carries a greater volume of traffic, and a greater proportion of truck traffic, than any of the streets which it intersects. The conflict between this east and west traffic, and that flowing on main north and south routes is most marked at Varick, Broadway and Lafayette streets, and is the cause of much congestion and delay. Any measure which would tend to reduce appreciably the crosstown traffic in this section of the City by providing by-pass routes, as for example the proposed West Street-Hamilton Avenue Tunnel, would greatly relieve the situation.

Midtown Manhattan.

The crosstown streets of mid-Manhattan offer examples of extreme congestion without particularly heavy traffic flows. In general they are operated as one-way streets, and have a roadway barely wide enough for four lanes of traffic. The development along these streets is so much of a commercial and industrial nature that trucks, either moving or stopped for purposes of loading or unloading, occupy a considerable section of the roadway area, and together with the large amount of passenger car parking, so restrict the general movement of traffic as to create intolerable conditions. Horse-drawn vehicles in considerable numbers also use these streets and are an additional cause of congestion and delay.

The photograph on page 38 and the views on page 41 show conditions quite clearly. The large proportion of trucks, the presence of horse-drawn vehicles, the narrow roadway and the parked cars and trucks are all apparent. The view taken in 38th street is particularly illuminating. The occupancy of curb space by trucks for loading and unloading of materials in itself is a heavy burden on traffic, but if the truck is placed at an angle with the curb, as shown in the photograph, it becomes a positive obstruction. In this particular case, moving traffic has been restricted to one lane. Provision of space within the building line for the receipt and delivery of materials seems to be the only remedy and one that for practical reasons can only be brought about gradually by suitable building regulations.

Much of the crosstown traffic in mid-Manhattan moves long distances under conditions as described above, and its diversion from the surface to an underground roadway, such as will be provided by the 38th Street-East River Tunnel, will afford great relief.

The volume of traffic on 5th avenue in the mid-town section is not as great as that on Park or 1st avenues, but in general congestion is more pronounced and traffic speeds considerably lower. It is a preferred street passing through the great retail district and heavily used by both local and through traffic. In addition, there is a very heavy bus traffic, reaching its greatest density during the rush hours, and adding further to the crowded condition of the roadway. The photograph on page 40 shows conditions existing in May, 1929, in the vicinity of 43d street, at a time when the heavy avenue traffic was stopped to allow crosstown traffic to move. It is characteristic of 5th avenue traffic that frequently conditions are just as bad in the middle of the day as they are during the rush hours. The large amount of 5th avenue traffic which enters or leaves at 57th street, involving left turns, is responsible for the congested conditions so frequently encountered at this intersection and for some distance on either side of it. Further examples, varying only in detail, could be given for Madison, Park, Broadway and other avenues and streets.

Relief of a fundamental nature must be sought by providing new routes which will either shorten the distances traffic now moves on the streets of mid-Manhattan or else enable it to avoid passing through this area at all. The West Side Express Highway, the Triborough Bridge and the 38th Street-East River Tunnel are measures which will each contribute greatly to the desired relief.

Bridge Heads.

Much congestion and delay occurs at and near the terminals of the bridges crossing the East and Harlem Rivers. It is due to a combination of heavy traffic flows and unfavorable street conditions at the terminals. The views on page 52 show condi-

VIEWS SHOWING CHARACTERISTIC TRAFFIC CONDITIONS ON 5TH AVENUE IN THE MID TOWN SECTION OF MANHATTAN

Photo by Ewing Galloway, N. Y.
View Looking North From 43rd Street. Traffic Waiting for the Green Light. Taken During Early Afternoon

Photo by Ewing Galloway, N. Y.
A Noon-Time View Looking South From 47th Street

VIEWS SHOWING MID-DAY TRAFFIC CONDITIONS ON CROSS STREETS IN THE CENTRAL SECTION OF MANHATTAN

Photo by Ewing Galloway, N. Y.
View Looking East on 40th Street Toward Madison Avenue

Photo by Ewing Galloway, N. Y.
View on 38th Street Near 7th Avenue, Moving Traffic Restricted to One Lane

VIEW SHOWING TRAFFIC CONGESTION IN MADISON AVENUE AT 59TH STREET

Photo by Cosmo News Photo Co., N. Y.

Looking South From 60th Street. North-South Movement Held by Traffic Lights

tions at the Manhattan terminal of the Manhattan Bridge. The pathway of bridge traffic towards Canal street is obstructed by the elevated structure, street car line, and crossing traffic in the Bowery, and is further restricted by a narrowing of the roadway, clearly evident on the photograph. Traffic on the bridge is divided between two roadways, the upper level roadway traffic showing on the right. A second upper level roadway is projected, but unless additional and more favorable connections with the street system are provided, will not relieve the terminal congestion.

Similar interferences with the free flow of traffic exist at most of the East River bridge terminals, and result in congestion which frequently extends far beyond the bridges and their plazas. A view of a bad traffic jam at the Williamsburg Bridge is shown on page 50. They are conditions difficult to remedy, and which should be avoided as far as possible in future construction.

Miscellaneous.

In four of the Manhattan avenues, the effectiveness of the roadway widths is much reduced by the combination of double-track street railways and elevated columns, and in five others by the presence of double-track railways. These factors, by reducing the capacity of the streets, create or add to congestion. The substitution of buses for street cars would in some instances afford relief, but not where the street railway traffic is exceptionally heavy. The unfavorable routing of the street car lines, as, for example, the 42d street connection between Madison and Park avenues, is a frequent cause of conflict between street car and other vehicular traffic, resulting in congestion and delay.

The columns supporting the elevated railway structures, where located in the street, are serious obstructions to traffic, and by their location restrict vehicular traffic to two moving lanes in each direction, with no or little opportunity for traffic to adjust itself between them. Improvement in this respect can only come with the gradual replacement of the elevated service by subway service.

Street openings and building construction are unfavorable factors affecting traffic movement. The necessity for these operations cannot be overcome, but much can be done to reduce the consequent obstruction to traffic by proper regulation.

Other Boroughs.

The conditions in the high building area of Brooklyn are substantially similar to those existing in lower Manhattan, with lesser pedestrian traffic problems and in some respects a more difficult situation as far as vehiclar traffic is concerned. The congested area extends from the plaza of the Brooklyn and Manhattan Bridges as a well defined "ridge" to some distance beyond the intersection of 4th, Flatbush and Atlantic avenues. The concentration of East River bridge traffic on highways leading into and through this arca is in most part the cause of congestion, a situation that will only be remedied by the provision of additional East River crossings and suitable highway connections, enabling a wide distribution of this traffic.

Outside of the bridge head areas and the situation set forth above, congestion in other sections of Brooklyn and Queens occurs mostly in districts such as Jamaica, where there is an undue convergence of main highways, and at points where heavy week-end and holiday flows to the resorts and beaches cross each other, as for example at the intersection of Conduit and Rockaway boulevards. Additional cross routes and separation of grades at important intersections are the applicable relief measures of a fundamental nature.

In The Bronx there is a concentration of traffic moving in a north and south direction and crossing the Harlem River bridges. It is on the connections between these bridges and the main north and south highways that considerable congestion exists due to overcrowding, to remedy which additional bridges and improved connecting streets are under consideration. The main highways leading to Westchester County and to New England points carry large volumes of traffic, particularly on holidays, and it is to provide a better distribution of this traffic that additional routes of a marginal nature and crosstown distribution have been proposed.

The Cost of Congestion.

The existence of widespread traffic congestion in New York City is evident to the most casual observer, and conditions are rapidly approaching unmanageable proportions in many sections. The delays and difficulties experienced in their daily journeys by trucks, passenger cars, street cars and other means of conveyance of goods and people, as well as by pedestrians, result not only in inconvenience but also in tremendous money losses, which have been stated to approximate $500,000,000 per year in the report of the City Committee on Plan and Survey.

VIEW SHOWING RUSH HOUR TRAFFIC FLOWS ON 5TH AVENUE AT 58TH STREET

Photo by Cosmo News Photo Co., N. Y.

Looking North. Traffic Held for Cross Town Traffic

VIEWS SHOWING TRAFFIC CONDITIONS DURING NON-RUSH HOURS AT 42ND STREET AND 5TH AVENUE

VIEW SHOWING VIADUCT IN PARK AVENUE CONNECTING WITH HIGH LEVEL
ROADWAYS AROUND GRAND CENTRAL STATION AND THROUGH
THE NEW YORK CENTRAL BUILDING

Looking North in Park Avenue Toward Grand Central Station and 42nd Street During a Period of
Light Traffic Flow
Separation of Grades Extends from 40th Street to 46th Street

The permanence of existing business and industry and of the investments incident thereto are imperiled and the favorable development and use of the many areas avaliable in the City for purposes of industry, business and housing is hindered by traffic conditions preventing freedom of vehicular access and communication.

TRAFFIC REGULATION.

The regulation of highway traffic in the City of New York is a duty of the Police Department, and for all of the Boroughs except Richmond is handled by a Traffic Bureau under the direction of the First Deputy Commissioner. This bureau has a staff totalling about 7,500 and maintains a school for the training of traffic officers. Regulation in Richmond is under the direction of the local police officials. Regulations, both general and specific, governing the control of traffic are issued by the Police Commissioner.

The planning and operation of the traffic control signal systems are a function of the Traffic Bureau. An extensive system of synchronized traffic lights, with a centralized control, regulates the movement of traffic in most of Manhattan. In other sections of Manhattan and in the other Boroughs smaller systems and individual lights have been installed. The newer system of progressive signals has been installed on a section of Riverside drive and on one of the main highways leading to Coney Island, and a wider application of this development is being considered by the Bureau. The lights have the two-color system, red for stop and green for go, with a dark period intervening in which vehicular traffic is supposed to stop.

Traffic officers are stationed at intersections and other critical points and have full authority over the movement of traffic at their stations. When stationed at points with traffic light control the officer is guided by them and is expected to direct the movements of traffic accordingly, but when conditions require he has authority to direct movements other than as indicated by the lights.

Mounted and motorcycle officers patrol main thoroughfares to reduce infractions of regulations and expedite traffic movements. Efforts are made to prevent drivers from unnecessarily obstructing thoroughfares by improper parking or turning or the use of the wrong lane by slow moving vehicles.

One of the most difficult problems of traffic regulation is the one of parking, which presents many aspects of a varied and more or less local nature. In general, parking in excess of one hour is forbidden, and on a number of the more important avenues and streets in Manhattan is entirely prohibited during the morning and evening rush hours. The enforcement of the parking rules, and the determination of modifications to suit changing conditions, is one of the major burdens of the Traffic Bureau.

Most of the crosstown streets in Manhattan have been designated as one-way streets by Police regulations, but on the avenues and on the wider crosstown streets traffic flows in both directions. On 5th avenue and Park avenue commercial vehicles are not allowed to use these highways for more than one block and are entirely barred from the use of the Grand Central Viaduct, Riverside drive and the main drives in Central Park. Empty taxicabs are similarly restricted in their use of portions of 5th avenue during the rush hours. Horse-drawn vehicles are barred from the Manhattan Bridge, and trucks, other than mail and newspaper trucks, from the Brooklyn Bridge.

Examples of regulations governing special situations are afforded by the closure of sections of Nassau street and of 36th street to vehicular traffic during the noonday period, and by the control exercised in the theatrical district. In a rather extensive area, centring about Times square, parking and the making of right or left turns is prohibited and observance of traffic lights by pedestrians enforced during the rush periods prior to and subsequent to the evening performances. The movements of empty taxicabs are supervised and trucks are barred, except under special permit, during the same hours.

In order to have a basis for its regulations and actions the Traffic Bureau carries on special activities as the occasion demands, as for example the collection of data as to traffic flows at critical points, the extent and duration of parking in certain areas, and similar matters.

The Bureau is alive to the important bearing of its activities upon the general traffic problem and active in its efforts to bring about improvement.

THE QUEENSBORO BRIDGE

SECTION III

IMPROVEMENTS TO EXISTING FACILITIES

HIGHWAYS.

The measures proposed for the improvement of the arterial highway system include extensive modifications in existing streets as well as the construction of new highways, and these matters of major importance are presented in a later section of this report. The improvement of the existing streets from a more local viewpoint also offers a very practical means of facilitating the free flow and circulation of traffic. The cumulative effect of such improvements is often quite substantial, and while we have considered their detailed consideration to be beyond the scope of our investigation, a brief reference to them seems desirable.

The condition of the roadway paving is an important consideration from the viewpoint of vehicular traffic, and it is general experience that traffic will avoid as far as possible streets in which the paving is in poor condition and tend to concentrate on the better paved streets. The improvement of the paving in a particular street will usually be quickly followed by an increased utilization. Improvements of this nature make for a better distribution of traffic and offer material possibilities of relief in many situations.

The systematic and extensive clearing of sidewalk areas of obstructions, widening of roadways, and adjustment of curbs at intersections which has been carried on in the midtown section of Manhattan is an example of accomplishment in the gradual improvement of traffic conditions. This has been particularly effective in respect to the crosstown streets. Another illustration is afforded by the widening of the roadway spaces in Park avenue, by reducing the width of the central park strips, thereby adding materially to the capacity and convenience of this important street.

The removal of obstructions such as unused car tracks, subway entrances, and similar obstructions from the roadways is another type of relief measure with considerable potentiality. An example of its effectiveness is afforded by 4th avenue in Brooklyn, where the street area has been widened by the removal of the subway entrances, the conflict between pedestrian and vehicular traffic reduced, and subway passengers relieved of the hazards of moving across a heavy stream of vehicular traffic. The relocation of elevated entrance stairways and columns at critical points, particularly where street widenings are being made, offer relief of the same nature.

Improvements of this character are being made continuously by the various Boroughs and involve much detail work in planning and execution. Each situation requires individual consideration and a detailed knowledge of local conditions which could not be developed in an investigation of this nature.

BRIDGES.

The four East River bridges were all designed and built prior to the development and wide use of motor vehicles. It is about 20 years since the newest of these bridges was opened to traffic. During this period vehicular traffic has increased rapidly and to such proportions that relief of the conditions existing on the bridges and in their approach areas is urgently needed. Changes and additions have been made from time to time, others are now under construction and still others have been proposed as traffic relief measures.

In general, the congestion and delay is mostly due to conditions at the terminals of these bridges, and adding to their roadway capacity will not be an effective relief measure unless at the same time appropriate improvements are made at the terminals.

Queensboro Bridge.

The lower deck of the Queensboro Bridge is occupied by two trolley lines placed outside of a six-lane vehicular roadway. The upper deck at the beginning of 1928 carried two sidewalks and two rapid transit lines and is now being rearranged to provide one sidewalk, two rapid transit lines and a three lane vehicular roadway, which will have its approaches entirely separated from the present bridge approaches.

VIEWS SHOWING TRAFFIC CONDITIONS AT THE MANHATTAN TERMINALS OF THE WILLIS AVENUE AND THE WILLIAMSBURG BRIDGES

The Intersection of 125th Street and First Avenue. Willis Avenue Bridge in Background. Mid-day Traffic

View Looking West from Williamsburg Bridge Esplanade Along Delancey Street Showing Extreme Congestion and Conflict of Traffic Streams

Congestion at the Manhattan terminal arises from the conflicting streams of bridge and normal street traffic, which must move between elevated railroad columns and over street car tracks in 2d avenue. The traffic on the main onbound roadway as observed has usually moved freely, congestion occurring chiefly in the adjoining streets. Offbound traffic tends to congest due to the interruptions of its flow by 2d avenue traffic and to a throat about 27 feet wide on the offbound roadway. The widening of this throat appears practicable and would be very advantageous in facilitating the flow of traffic and in providing greater space for the accumulation of vehicles during periods in which 2d avenue traffic has the right-of-way.

Proposals have been made to extend the plaza to the west of 2d avenue, but do not appear to offer relief commensurate with the probable cost. A more recent proposal is to carry the 2d avenue traffic, street cars and vehicles, past the bridge head in a subway to be built in 2d avenue. Such a facility would undoubtedly help bridge traffic, but 2d avenue traffic would be at a disadvantage. The combination of street car and mixed vehicular traffic in a relatively narrow tunnel is not desirable, and the requirements of surface traffic in the vicinity of the portals would be difficult to meet without extensive street widening.

A proposal to build an additional outlet to the north, consisting of a ramp over 60th street and a new outlet street parallel to 2d avenue and extending to 62d street, was actively under consideration some years ago, but was abandoned due to opposition of local property owners. Its general features were to be similar to those of the outlet now authorized to be built to the south and crossing over 59th street. In our judgment the proposed construction would be a very effective relief measure, particularly because of the resulting wider distribution of bridge traffic, and merits early reconsideration.

Conditions at the Queens plaza of this bridge are very much complicated by the maze of roadways, elevated columns, street car tracks and intersecting streets. The Department of Plant and Structures has proposed plans for improving the roadways in the Queens plaza by widening some, closing others, changing trolley loops, realigning tracks, removing islands and other obstructions. The principal feature of the improvement will be a central roadway leading through the plaza to Jackson avenue. The five intersections in the plaza are to be reduced to three, and the north and south boundary roadways are to be increased from a width of 30 to 45 feet.

The proposed changes seem to strike a practical balance between the conflicting requirements of pedestrian, vehicular and street railway traffic in a most difficult situation and offer prospects of material relief.

Reference has been previously made to construction now in progress to provide an additional roadway on this bridge. The principal traffic feature of this new construction is that it will provide three lanes exclusively for passenger cars on a 22½-foot wide roadway. The cross section will provide three traffic grooves 6 feet 1 inch in width separated by 2-inch high curbs designed to direct traffic in the unusually narrow lanes, to maintain the lateral clearance between vehicles and at the same time permit turnouts in case of necessity. The design constitutes an innovation in highway practice, the working out of which will be followed with great interest by bridge engineers.

The Manhattan approach to this new roadway starts at 57th street a short distance east of 2d avenue, meets 58th street at a revised grade and crosses 59th street by a bridge. The roadway proper will be on the south side of the upper deck and in Queens it will turn south on a ramp which will terminate in two spurs, one leading to Van Alst avenue and Harris street and the other, crossing Jackson avenue above grade, will meet the Thompson Avenue Viaduct over Sunnyside railroad yard near Purves street.

The project will provide needed additional roadway capacity on this bridge and improved distribution of the bridge traffic by the separate and new approaches. Its early completion will afford urgently needed relief of traffic conditions on the Queensboro Bridge.

Repairs to the roadway of the present bridge have caused much traffic delay and congestion. We are advised that a type of bridge floor has been developed by the Department of Plant and Structures which will be much more satisfactory in the particulars of durability and facility for renewal. The placing of this improved type of floor on the main bridge roadway should add to the freedom of movement over the bridge.

The Williamsburg Bridge.

The Williamsburg Bridge, opened to traffic in 1903, was the second bridge built across the East River. Its provisions for vehicular traffic consist of two roadways at the outer sides of the lower deck. These roadways, built in the period of horse-drawn vehicles, provide two traffic lanes each practically ten feet in width and in this respect

VIEW SHOWING MANHATTAN TERMINAL OF THE MANHATTAN BRIDGE

Looking Toward Bridge

Looking Toward Canal Street

provide lanes better adapted to motor traffic on arterial highways than the vehicular lanes on the other East River bridges. Congestion on this bridge appears to be less marked than on the other bridges, although the noticeably larger proportion of horse-drawn vehicles tends to slow up the movement of traffic on the bridge proper. As on the other bridges, terminal conditions are the principal causes of congestion.

At the Manhattan plaza, Clinton street with its single car track crosses the bridge head immediately in front of the portal and is an obstruction to vehicular traffic. The bridge is in alignment with Delancey street, which for a distance of about 500 feet from Clinton street to Norfolk street has a width of 200 feet and then continues at a width of 150 feet for about 1,800 feet to its intersection with the Bowery. Delancey street is occupied in part by grass plots, trolley tracks and passenger stations.

It is not practicable to raise or depress Clinton street at the bridge head, but it appears to be feasible to carry the bridge roadways over Clinton street and at practicable grades reach the surface of Delancey street near Norfolk street. Norfolk street has no car tracks and is a purely local street while Clinton street is part of a continuous route via Avenue B from the river front at 21st street to the river at Clinton and Front streets.

The removal of the conflict between traffic flows at Clinton street and the better distribution of traffic which would result from the extension of the approaches to near Norfolk street offer so much promise of relief that in our judgment this project merits early consideration and detailed study.

The Williamsburg plaza of this bridge contains about 3.6 acres, principally devoted to street car terminals and crossed by an elevated railway structure. The vehicular routes through this plaza are not direct or clearly marked. Some rearrangement of car tracks has been made, but still further adjustment of their points of intersection with vehicular roadways should be made in order to provide a direct vehicular route through the plaza with appropriate and clearly marked junctions to adjacent streets.

Examination was made to ascertain the possibilities for converting the footwalks into vehicular roadways. The critical points for such conversion are found at the intricate bracing of the bridge towers, where the clearance above the footwalks is only about seven feet. The practicability of such rearrangement could only be determined by detailed examination of the plans of the bridge towers. However, the plazas constitute the present restrictions to traffic capacity, and additions to the roadway space should be deferred until adequate terminal facilities are available or provided for as part of such an improvement.

The Manhattan Bridge.

The provision for vehicular traffic on the Manhattan Bridge when opened in 1909 consisted of a 35-foot roadway in the centre of the lower deck. This roadway is now used only by trucks and passenger cars, as horse-drawn vehicles are barred from the bridge. While generally considered a four-lane roadway, it practically functions as a three-lane roadway much of the time due to the space requirements of the trucks, which constitute a large portion of the bridge traffic.

This original roadway was supplemented some years ago by the provision of a two-lane roadway for the exclusive use of passenger cars in space on the north side of the upper deck formerly occupied by street cars. Travel on this roadway is one-way, its direction being reversed to accommodate the preponderant traffic flow.

It is proposed to convert the south upper deck in a similar manner and the City is arranging to acquire the street railway line which now occupies that deck as part of its route between Manhattan plaza and a terminal on Flatbush avenue at Fulton street, Brooklyn. The consummation of this proposal would result in a bridge with four lanes for the exclusive use of passenger cars and four lanes for either truck traffic or mixed traffic, and a potential traffic capacity that will only be effective if adequate modifications are made at the bridge terminals.

The Manhattan plaza of the bridge adjoins the Bowery practically as its intersection with Canal street. The main streams of bridge traffic cross the Bowery, with its elevated structures, street car lines and heavy traffic flows, on their way to or from Canal street. The recently completed widening of Canal street has been very helpful in facilitating the movement of bridge traffic.

Observation of the traffic movements at this terminal show much congestion between the Bowery and the bridge, due in large part to the conflict between bridge traffic and street traffic in the Bowery and also due to a restriction in the roadway space between the plaza proper and the bridge, as shown on page 52. The widening of this space, and the removal of the elevated stairway from the roadway to the adjacent sidewalk would greatly facilitate the movement of bridge traffic and appears entirely practicable.

VIEWS SHOWING MANHATTAN TERMINALS OF THE BROOKLYN AND THE QUEENSBORO BRIDGES

View Along Park Row Towards Brooklyn Bridge Portals, Centre Street and Municipal Building in Background

View Looking Northwest Across the Queensboro Bridge. 2nd Avenue in the Background

A more difficult situation exists with respect to providing a new and independent connection between the proposed passenger car roadway on the bridge and the street system, which should naturally lead off towards the south. Unless such a connection can be developed, the provision of the additional capacity on the bridge is likely to add to, rather than relieve existing congestion.

The available areas in the Brooklyn plaza of this bridge and the alignment of its approach with Flatbush avenue are such that, with the removal of the street railway line from the bridge and plaza, ample opportunity will be afforded for arranging entrance and exit lanes co-ordinating the traffic capacity of the bridge and that of the adjoining streets.

The removal of pedestrian traffic now crossing the bridge traffic at both terminals, or its material reduction, by the provision of appropriate grade separation would remove a hazard and a serious obstruction to free vehicular movement.

The Brooklyn Bridge.

The roadway capacity of this bridge consists of two driveways, each slightly less than 17 feet in width and carrying a street railway track. The vehicular traffic over these four lanes is about 55 per cent. of that carried by the four lanes on the Williamsburg Bridge, due in large part to the restriction to movement offered by street cars and horse-drawn vehicles. Even if these were removed, the narrow roadways would not accommodate mixed traffic satisfactorily, although they would be wide enough for two lanes of passenger car traffic.

The terminal conditions are unfavorable, but offer limited opportunities for advantageous modification. On the Manhattan side, however, considerable relief would be afforded to both street and bridge traffic if the roadway of Centre street were straightened and widened on the west side, where there is more than ample sidewalk space adjoining City Hall Park. This situation is shown on the photograph on page 54.

Photo by Fairchild Aerial Surveys Inc, N.Y.C.

GENERAL VIEW IN MID-MANHATTAN

SECTION IV

PROPOSED NEW FACILITIES

The new facilities which should be given consideration from the standpoint of affording relief from present conditions and providing for future growth include additional traffic regulating devices, extensions to existing highways, new arterial surface highways, bridges, tunnels and elevated structures at various locations throughout the five Boroughs. This section of our report treats of those projects relating to the main arterial highway system.

THE PROPOSED TRIBOROUGH BRIDGE

A growing recognition of the desirability and manifest advantages of affording more direct means of vehicular communication between Queens and upper Manhattan and The Bronx has resulted in various proposals for its accomplishment, including a triborough bridge, a triborough tunnel, the utilization of the Hell Gate Bridge and approaches, and separate bridges or tunnels connecting Queens and Manhattan and Queens and The Bronx, respectively.

A triborough bridge, passing over Hell Gate, Ward's and Randall's Islands and the adjoining waterways, was first proposed in 1916. Initial appropriations for its study were made in 1923. Early in 1929, and during the course of our investigation, the City definitely committed itself to the execution of the project on a toll basis by appropriate legislation. The preparation of detailed plans is actively under way and the beginning of construction work is imminent.

The Present Situation.

The Queensboro Bridge is the only major vehicular connection between Queens and Manhattan, and the only one across the East River in the 6-mile stretch from the Williamsburg Bridge to the mouth of the Harlem River. Traffic over it has been growing rapidly, a week day count in October, 1928, showing some 72,000 vehicles per day.

North of the Queensboro Bridge, the only means of vehicular communication between the two Boroughs is afforded by the Astoria Ferry, with a week day traffic of only about 1,600 vehicles per day.

The only means of direct vehicular communication between Queens and The Bronx is afforded by the Clason Point Ferry, with an average week day traffic of about 2,300 vehicles per day. Demands for service on this ferry are growing rapidly, and particularly so on week ends and holidays.

As developed more fully later, about 20,000 vehicles per day moving between points in Queens, upper Manhattan and The Bronx must under present conditions travel via the Queensboro Bridge, accounting for almost one-third of its total traffic, and forming a very appreciable portion of the north-south traffic flow in Manhattan.

The resulting concentration of interborough traffic on the Queensboro Bridge is the outstanding cause of the serious traffic congestion existing on that bridge and in its approach areas. The large portions of the traffic moving to or from sections remote from the bridge heads add to and conflict with the heavy local flows and cause congestion in such areas as well, particularly in Manhattan.

Additional interborough connections are urgently needed to relieve the Queensboro Bridge and to afford relief to the street systems which it connects by providing routes that are either more direct or that do not pass through congested areas. The relief expectable from the 38th Street-East River Tunnel has been set forth elsewhere in this report, this section dealing primarily with that expectable from additional crossings farther north.

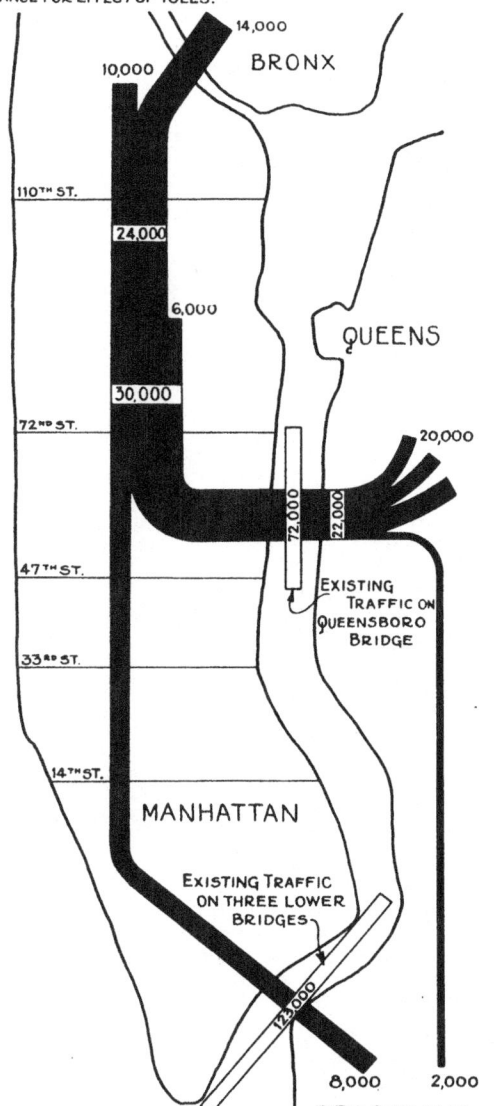

The application of the results of our studies of the origin and destination of East River bridge traffic to the 1928 counts shows that about 24,000 vehicles per day cross the East River on their way to or from points in Manhattan north of 110th street or in The Bronx. Of these about 16,000 vehicles per day now move over the Queensboro Bridge, mostly to or from points in the Borough of Queens. The remaining 8,000 vehicles per day travel throughout the entire length of Manhattan and move over the three lower bridges to or from points in Brooklyn.

In addition there are some 6,000 vehicles per day moving over the Queensboro Bridge between zones extending from 72d to 110th street in Manhattan and zones in the northern part of the Borough of Queens. This traffic now moves much longer distances over the streets of both Queens and Manhattan than would be necessary if a more direct interborough connection were available farther north.

The routes necessarily followed by this traffic under existing conditions result in delay and inconvenience to the traffic itself and add to the congestion on the bridges and streets traversed. It is particularly susceptible of diversion to the more advantageous routes which would be afforded by a direct connection, such as the Triborough Bridge, between Queens, upper Manhattan and The Bronx, in conjunction with improved north-south highway facilities through Brooklyn and Queens.

Based upon our study of the general traffic situation and of the various relief measures proposed, and with particular reference to needs having a bearing on Triborough Bridge, it is our opinion that

There is an urgent present need for relief of the nature and extent of that which would be afforded by an East River crossing in the general location proposed for the Triborough Bridge.

The relief afforded would extend to conditions on the Queensboro Bridge and in its approach areas, on the avenues of upper Manhattan and on the Harlem River bridges.

The need for relief of the nature which would be afforded by such a facility is growing rapidly, due both to increased development of the tributary areas and to increased traffic.

The Relief Afforded.

The Triborough Bridge, in conjunction with improved highway facilities in Brooklyn and Queens, by providing new routes between points in Queens, upper Manhattan and The Bronx would tend to reduce the number of vehicles now moving over the Queensboro Bridge and through upper Manhattan.

From the standpoint of time and convenience it would afford superior routing for about 30,000 vehicles per day. The distances traveled by the traffic originating in or destined for the Borough of Queens would be shortened considerably, and the delay and inconvenience now experienced by this traffic due to the necessity of moving through the congested Queensboro Bridge approach areas in both Manhattan and Queens, as well as on the avenues in upper Manhattan, would be eliminated. The traffic now moving over the three lower bridges between points north of 110th street in Manhattan and in The Bronx and points in Brooklyn would be enabled to avoid the delays and inconvenience resulting from passage through the most congested sections of Brooklyn and Manhattan.

Assuming that all of this traffic would use the Triborough Bridge instead of present routes, the nature and extent of the traffic relief afforded is shown diagrammatically on page 58.

The diagram on the left shows the present routing of the traffic considered as potential to Triborough Bridge, on the assumption that it would follow the most convenient routes based on time and for distance. The heavy black lines together with the figures indicate the daily volume of traffic now using the various existing facilities and the relative volumes originating in or destined for each district.

The diagram on the right shows the assumed future routing of this same traffic and the relief which would be afforded by the diversion from the existing bridges, their approach areas and the streets of Manhattan. The Queensboro Bridge and its approach areas would be relieved of about 30 per cent. and the Harlem River Bridges of about 7 per cent. of their present weekday burden. The complete removal of some 30,000 vehicles per day from the avenues above 59th street represents a reduction of about 10 per cent. in the present traffic flow on all avenues at that point.

The foregoing figures and statements are based upon 1928 weekday conditions, no allowance being made for any growth during or subsequent to the period of construction, or for expectable diversion from nearby ferries. If the growth of recent years continues, the interboro traffic will be increased about 50 per cent. by 1935. Sunday and holiday traffic between and through the districts considered is very heavy. Due to its strategic location, the proposed bridge when completed will undoubtedly experience special increases in traffic attributable to the 178th Street Bridge across the Hudson River, the Narrows Tunnel and to traffic induced by the more convenient means of communication afforded between the districts it will connect. Such factors will tend to increase both the traffic on the bridge and the measure of relief afforded.

Proposed Triborough Tunnel.

During the course of our study of this project, our attention was directed to two other means suggested for the accomplishment of the same general purpose of connecting The Bronx, upper Manhattan and Queens.

One of these involved the connection of the three boroughs by a system of vehicular tunnels, with substantially the same terminals as proposed for the Triborough Bridge. The main advantages suggested were more economical construction and the movement of traffic free from interruption by the elements and by the needs of navigation on the Harlem River and Bronx Kills crossings.

The distances across Ward's and Randall's Islands, the channel depths of the river crossings, and the topography at the terminals are factors which would result in long lengths of costly tunnel construction. A four-lane vehicular tunnel would have about one-half the capacity of the eight-lane bridge it is proposed to construct and would cost about twice as much to build and would be more expensive to operate. Further, the indications are that the traffic demand would exceed the capacity of the tunnel in relatively few years, thereby advancing the need of providing additional crossings to the south and to the east of the site.

In our opinion, the needs of the situation can be most advantageously and economically provided for by bridge construction.

Proposed Utilization of Hell Gate Bridge.

There was also brought to our attention the possibility of utilizing the Hell Gate Bridge and approaches belonging to the New York Connecting Railroad in providing a vehicular connection between the three boroughs.

One suggestion involves the addition for highway purposes of a second deck approximately 50 feet in width; and another involves adding a 30-foot or perhaps a 40-foot roadway on each side of the existing structures. Construction by the railroad and lease of the highway structure to the City, or construction by the City under rights purchased from or leased from the railroad, as well as construction and operation under private ownership, on terms to be negotiated, were among the suggestions submitted. The proposers claim lower initial expenditures, shorter time for construction, and general economic advantages through a better utilization of an existing structure rather than creating a new one.

We understand that these projects would require State Legislation granting additional charter rights to the railroad company and would involve negotiations and whatever municipal legislation would be needed to consummate them.

It is evident that in addition to questions concerning the practicability, the adequacy for present and future needs of the proposed highway construction, and the complications arising from the joint occupancy and use of such a structure, there is involved the important economic consideration of the compensation which would be asked by the railroad company for the use of its present structure and rights. This matter would probably not be definitely ascertainable until extended analysis and active negotiations between the City and the railroad company were undertaken.

In a report by the Chief Engineer of the Department of Plant and Structures submitted in 1927, it is stated that the possible use of the Hell Gate Bridge had been carefully investigated and that the roadway width that could be erected would be inadequate to care for traffic demands.

Under the circumstances set forth and in view of the definite commitment of the City to the immediate construction of the Triborough Bridge, complete analysis of these proposals was not undertaken.

Proposed Triborough Bridge.

The general description of the bridge and discussion of its traffic features which follow are based upon the preliminary plans set forth in the report of the Department of Plant and Structures under date of March 8, 1927, and upon later data made available to us during the course of our investigation. Further modifications undoubtedly have accompanied the detail planning and design now actively under way.

Location and General Features.

The general location of the bridge and its relation to the street systems it connects is shown on the map on page 62. It will connect a terminal near 2d and Hoyt avenues in Queens with a terminal at Cypress avenue near Southern boulevard, in The Bronx, and with a terminal in Upper Manhattan at 125th street, between 1st and 2d avenues. The main connection, between Queens and The Bronx, will have two four-lane roadways about 14,000 feet in length and the spur to Manhattan will provide one six-lane roadway, about 4,000 feet in length. The bridge is a composite structure consisting of a suspension span across Hell Gate, a fixed span across Little Hell Gate, draw bridges of the bascule type across Bronx Kills and the Harlem River and connecting viaducts and approaches.

The potential traffic capacity of the bridge, on the approximate basis of number of traffic lanes, will be one-third greater than that of either the Queensboro or the Manhattan Bridges, each of which at present has provision for six traffic lanes. Its great possibilities for traffic relief are accompanied by possibilities of creating new centres of traffic congestion at and near the terminals by reason of the heavy traffic flows expectable and for which bridge roadway capacity is being provided. The situation emphasizes the need of very careful consideration of features of design which will affect the freedom with which traffic can flow to and from, and over the bridge, and the extent of its interference with local traffic flows in the vicinity of the bridge terminals. This need is further emphasized when consideration is given to the many similarities in street and traffic conditions at the terminals of the proposed bridge and of the existing East River bridges, particularly the Queensboro Bridge, where most objectionable traffic congestion is encountered. Every effort should be made to avoid the creation of such new centres of congestion, and to enable traffic to flow freely by the provision, as far as practicable, of ample plaza areas and perimeters, ample street capacity in the vicinity of the plazas and the separation of conflicting traffic flows.

The Bronx Terminal.

The general relation of the bridge approach to the established street system in the vicinity, and particularly to the Southern boulevard is shown on page 62. The traffic flows to and from the bridge will create two distinct main streams at this terminal, one including movements between the bridge and areas to the north and west of the terminal and the other including movements along the Southern boulevard to or from areas to the northeast. The Southern boulevard at Cypress avenue carries a double-track street car line and a considerable volume of local and through traffic. Its importance as an arterial highway will undoubtedly be increased by contemplated improvements and extensions and by the construction of the Triborough Bridge, with resulting increases in the traffic flows to be accommodated.

The lines of flow of bridge traffic moving to or from the northwest, of necessity intersect the lines of flow of traffic moving past Cypress avenue on the Southern boulevard. The line of flow of onbound bridge traffic moving from the northeast via Southern boulevard also intersects that of the Boulevard traffic and that of the offbound bridge traffic moving to the northwest. The other main streams can readily merge with the local flows. With traffic streams of the magnitude expectable crossing each

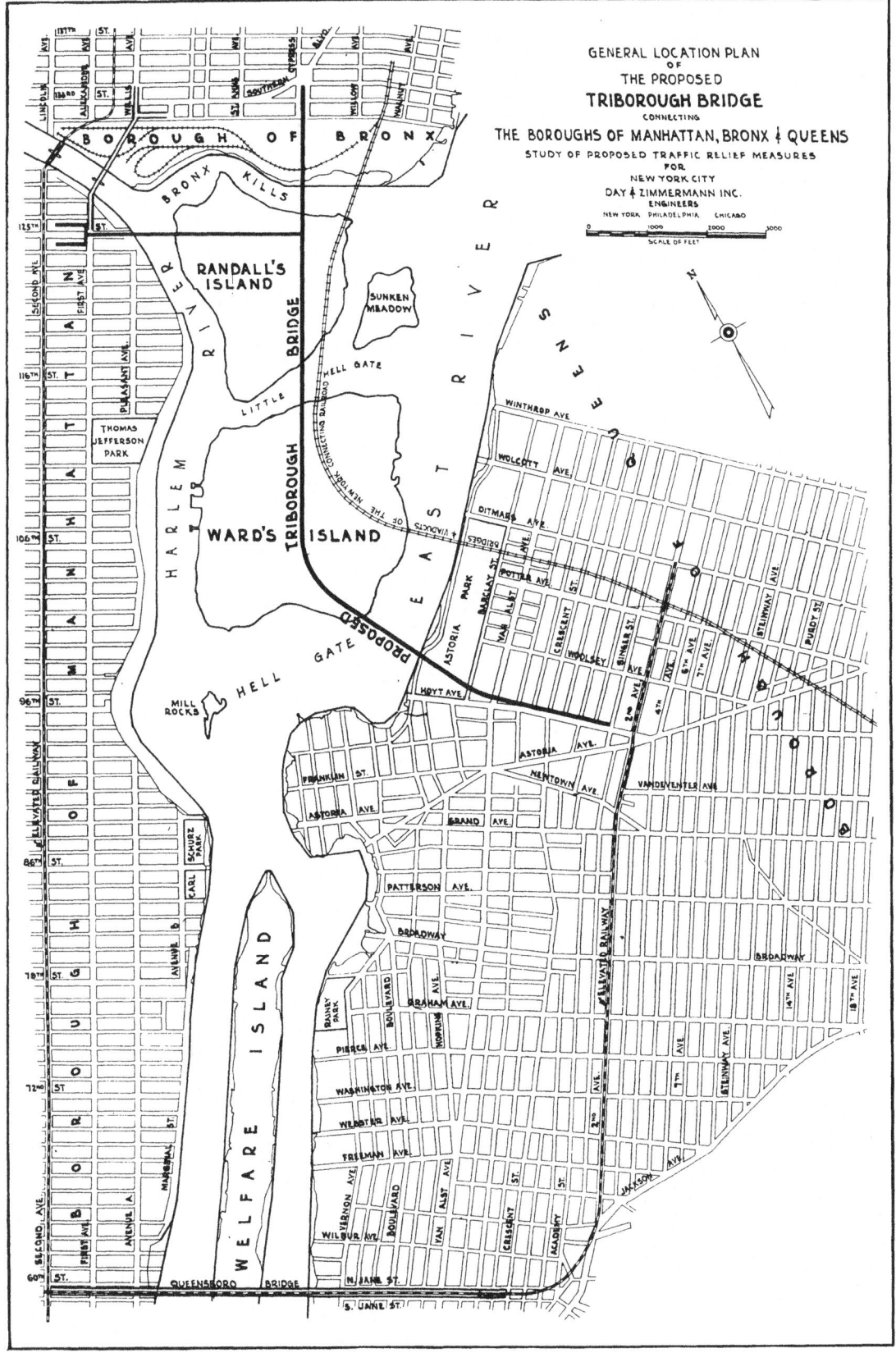

other at grade, delay and congestion is inevitable, even though liberal street widths and plaza areas are provided. Separation of grades for the intersecting streams will most fully ensure satisfactory traffic conditions and, in our judgment, should be provided.

The Manhattan Terminal.

The placing of the Manhattan terminal at 125th street as shown on page 62, has the advantage of affording a direct connection with a 100-foot wide crosstown street extending from the Harlem to the Hudson and at a point as far north as practicable. The flanking streets, 124th and 125th streets, although narrower, will also serve as direct approaches. 1st avenue, with its heavy traffic movements, attributable to the Willis Avenue Bridge, is to be crossed above grade by the approach structure, which then branches and comes to grade in plazas north and south of 125th street and east of 2d avenue.

An elevated railway structure and station, a double track street railway, and a heavy vehicular and pedestrian traffic in 2d avenue create decidedly adverse conditions to the free flow of bridge traffic quite similar to those at the Manhattan terminal of the Queensboro Bridge, which also has six traffic lanes.

The indications are that the main streams of bridge traffic will cross 2d avenue on 124th, 125th and 126th streets on their way to or from areas to the south, west and north of the terminal. Movements to and from 1st avenue will include relatively minor portions of the bridge traffic in addition to the local traffic.

The limitations and restrictions imposed upon the terminal design by the existing conditions, and the necessity of guarding against the duplication of the congestion found at the existing bridge terminals, create a most difficult situation. A widening of 2d avenue between 123d and 124th and between 126th and 127th streets, and of 1st avenue between 124th and 126th streets, would encourage a wider distribution of the bridge traffic streams across 2d avenue, and generally enable freer flows to and from the bridge. The maximum practicable plaza depths, an unusually liberal allowance of toll lanes and the elimination of pedestrian conflict with the main traffic streams by means of over or under passes, are further measures to offset the unavoidable features of the situation, which in our judgment should be provided.

The Queens Terminal.

The general relation of the bridge approach to the street system in the immediate vicinity and particularly to 2d, Hoyt and Astoria avenues, is shown on page 7350. The traffic flows to and from the bridge will create three rather distinct main streams near this terminal, one including movements between the bridge and areas to the northeast along the general line of Astoria avenue, and a second including movements to and from areas lying south and southeast of the terminal and moving in the general direction of Astoria avenue, to a junction with the proposed new north-south highway, through Brooklyn and Queens. Both of these streams must cross 2d avenue. The third stream includes movements to and from riverfront areas lying to the west of the terminal and for which easy access can be provided to Van Alst avenue and parallel streets.

The presence of street car lines, a fairly heavy local vehicular traffic, and an elevated line and station in 2d avenue in the vicinity of Hoyt avenue, creates extremely adverse conditions for the free movement of vehicles to and from an eight-lane bridge with its terminal just to the west of 2d avenue.

The local conditions and considerations of reasonable costs apparently preclude carrying the traffic streams across 2d avenue, and across each other at separate grades, and indicate the desirability of considering means for increasing the number of routes available to traffic between the bridge plazas and points of connection with the main highways well beyond 2d avenue, thereby spreading the traffic across 2d avenue rather than concentrating it.

Separation of on-bound and off-bound traffic streams, plaza locations further west of 2d avenue and easier distribution of the traffic would be facilitated by the use of a delta approach construction, similar to that proposed for the Manhattan terminal, with the plaza for off-bound traffic located between Hoyt and Astoria avenues, and that for on-bound traffic between Hoyt and Woolsey avenues. Such an arrangement, in conjunction with the necessary street extensions and widenings to enable traffic to flow to or from Potter, Woolsey, Hoyt, Vandeventer and Newton avenues, and via these streets to their junctions with Astoria avenue or with the proposed north-south highway, would reduce appreciably the potentiality of congestion and in our judgment should be provided.

The Bridge Roadways.

The Bridge will provide free routes of large capacity approximately 2½ miles in length, between the terminals. The advantages afforded to traffic by the Bridge will be much enhanced if traffic is enabled to move at high speeds and this consideration points towards the desirability of providing liberal roadway widths and the necessity of junction and turn out provisions which will avoid delay at these points.

The preliminary plans of the Bridge show two 36-foot roadways for the accommodation of eight lanes of traffic on the main connection between Queens and The Bronx, and one 53-foot roadway for six lanes of traffic on the Manhattan spur. We are advised that at the junction point provision will be made for avoiding conflict by carrying the Manhattan bound traffic across the traffic to and from The Bronx at separate grades. The provision of occasional space for crippled cars, towing and repair equipment, etc., and ramps for access to Ward's and Randall's Islands are also contemplated and will undoubtedly be planned to avoid the interference of turn outs across the main traffic flows such as now occur at the Welfare Island connection to the Queensboro Bridge.

The roadways will be subjected to mixed traffic, any separation of trucks and faster moving vehicles to be accomplished by regulation, with the probable aid of marked lanes. The general characteristics of the expectable weekday traffic on this bridge are quite similar to that on the existing East River bridges, which shows about 29 per cent. commercial car traffic between the hours of 7 a. m. and 7 p. m. The greater road space required for truck and motor bus traffic and its tendency to slow up mixed traffic due to its lower speed, cumbersomness and bulk is beyond question. The trend of the times is towards a wider use of motor trucks and busses and towards larger units, with resulting increased requirements for roadway space.

The roadway widths proposed for the main structure of the Triborough Bridge and for the Manhattan spur result in average lane widths of 9 feet and 8 feet 10 inches, respectively. These widths may be compared with average lane widths of about 8 feet 10 inches on the Queensboro Bridge, 8 feet 9 inches on the main deck of the Manhattan Bridge, 10 feet on the Williamsburg Bridge, 9 feet 6 inches on the Delaware River Bridge, and 10 feet on the Hudson River Bridge. The tendency on the larger bridges of more recent design is clearly towards average lane widths ranging between 9 feet 6 inches and 10 feet.

Our observations of traffic on existing bridges, the trend of practice, and consideration of the local factors set forth above, including the large traffic flows for which provision is being made, indicate the desirability of providing greater highway widths than shown on the preliminary plans and in our judgment, the plans should be suitably modified.

The Cost of the Project.

In its 1927 report of the Triborough Bridge, the Department of Plant and Structures, estimated the cost of the project, exclusive of land and of interest during construction, at $24,625,000, and stated the assessed value of the land required for terminals to be $2,810,000. Since that time changes have been made in the location of the bridge and of its Queens Terminal, and later estimates by the Department place the cost, exclusive of interest during construction, in the neighborhood of $36,000,000. On the basis of a four-year construction programme, allowing 12 per cent. for interest during construction would bring the total cost to a little over $40,000,000.

Our review of the costs of projects involving similar construction indicates that a bridge in the location and with the general features proposed would cost, exclusive of overheads, approximately $35,000,000. Allowing 20 per cent. to cover overhead costs such as interest, engineering, administration and similar costs during construction would bring the total cost of the project to substantially $42,000,000.

Using the larger figure, the annual cost, based on an allowance of 6 per cent. for fixed charges and on operating expenses estimated at $600,000 per year, would total $3,120,000 per year. This is substantially the revenue which would have to be collected each year in order to make the project self-supporting. On the basis of an average toll of 50 cents per vehicle, the volume of traffic required to yield this amount would be 6,240,000 vehicles, and on a 25-cent basis about 12,500,000 vehicles per year.

Tolls and Traffic.

The toll charges in effect on the Holland Tunnel are averaging about 55 cents per vehicle. The traffic during 1928, the first full year of operation totalled some 8,745,000 vehicles. Rapid and continued growth in traffic has been experienced from the beginning of operations, traffic in March, 1929, exceeding that in March, 1928, by 37 per cent.

Traffic on the East River bridges has also shown rapid and continued growth. If the growth of recent years continues, bridge traffic in 1935 will be about one and one-half times what it was in 1928. On the basis of the 1928 traffic counts and with no allowance whatever for growth during or subsequent to the period of construction, we find that there is a volume of traffic approximating 30,000 vehicles per day now using other routes which, from the standpoints of time and convenience, could more advantageously use the Triborough Bridge. Considering the general characteristics of this traffic, it would total substantially 11,000,000 vehicles per year, which is within about 12 per cent. of the traffic required to make the project self-supporting on an assumed average charge of 25 cents and materially in excess of that required on an assumed average charge of 50 cents per vehicle.

Conclusion.

In our opinion, the project under consideration constitutes an outstanding traffic relief measure, planned to relieve conditions rapidly becoming intolerable, and from the standpoints of both necessity and convenience, its construction is warranted.

There is no definite method of determining the actual number of vehicles which would use the bridge on a toll basis, although there is an existing volume of traffic which would be better served from the standpoints of time and convenience and which would make the project self-supporting on the basis of an average charge of 29 cents per vehicle.

PROPOSED 38TH STREET-EAST RIVER VEHICULAR TUNNEL.

The proposed 38th Street-East River Vehicular Tunnel project is designed to relieve the rapidly growing and burdensome congestion in mid-Manhattan, on the Queensboro Bridge, and its approach areas, as well as in other sections of the City. It was first officially proposed by the Borough President of Manhattan, early in 1926, and includes the construction of a vehicular tunnel extending under 38th street and the East River and connecting terminals located on the west and east sides of Manhattan with terminals in Queens and Brooklyn in the vicinity of Newtown Creek. Early in 1927, funds were appropriated for preliminary engineering studies to be made by the Department of Plant and Structures.

In response to a request from the Mayor we submitted under date of June 4, 1929, a preliminary statement with respect to the project, and under date of June 13, 1929, the Department of Plant and Structures submitted a report giving the results of its studies. Further hearings on the project were held by the Board of Estimate and Apportionment, followed on July 25, 1929, by appropriate legislation definitely committing the City to its execution and appropriating $2,000,000 towards its design and construction as a toll project.

The Present Situation.

The Queensboro Bridge is the only major vehicular connection between Queens and Manhattan, and the only one across the East River in the 6-mile stretch from the mouth of the Harlem River to the Williamsburg Bridge, which lies about 3 miles to the south. Its terminal is practically at the northern boundary of the highly developed and important mid-Manhattan area, the lower limits of which lie far to the north of the terminals of the Williamsburg, Manhattan and Brooklyn Bridges.

During the 20-year period since the newest of the four East River Bridges was opened to traffic, there has been not only a tremendous growth in and shifting of population, industry and business on both sides of the river, but also a complete change in the characteristics of vehicular traffic through the development and wide use of the automobile and the motor truck. Motor vehicle registration in New York City and vehicular traffic over the East River Bridges for 1928 are over three times as great as in 1920. If the growth of recent years continues, bridge traffic in 1935 will be about one and one-half times what it was in 1928, or substantially 300,000 vehicles per day.

The traffic congestion on the bridges, in the bridge head areas and in the streets of mid-Manhattan, resulting from the conditions outlined above, is evident to the most casual observer. The limited number of bridges and their locations result in concentration of traffic instead of distribution, in restricted flows instead of free flows and in inferior routing with respect to both time and distance.

General Traffic Flows and Distribution.

Much of the congestion on the streets of mid-Manhattan is due to the large portion of the traffic which moves over the bridges, and which on its way adds to and conflicts with the heavy traffic flows more local to Manhattan. The counts of week-day bridge traffic made in October, 1928, and our origin, destination and routing studies made this year indicate the following:

The traffic movements over the Queensboro Bridge amount to 72,000 vehicles for 24 hours, of which 48,000 occur during the 12-hour period between 7 a. m. and 7 p. m. 43 per cent. of the day time traffic moves to or from points north of 57th street and 57 per cent. to points south. Approximately 38 per cent. of the total traffic moves to or from the west side of Manhattan and for the most part uses crosstown streets in mid-Manhattan.

The combined traffic movements over the three lower bridges amount to 123,000 vehicles per 24 hours, of which 84,000 occur during the 12 hours between 7 a. m. and 7 p. m. Approximately 15 per cent. moves to or from points in Manhattan between 33d and 47th streets, and about 14 per cent. to points even further north.

The combined northbound and southbound flow on all avenues at about 51st street is substantially 211,000 vehicles in the 12-hour period from 7 a. m. to 7 p. m., and approximately 17 per cent. of these vehicles move over the East River Bridges.

The combined eastbound and westbound flows at 5th avenue on all crosstown streets between 30th and 59th streets, inclusive, are about 160,000 vehicles in the day time 12 hours, and of these approximately 11 per cent. move over the East River, chiefly via the Queensboro Bridge.

Of all the traffic crossing 5th avenue on the streets enumerated, approximately 8.5 per cent. moves on these streets from at least 9th avenue to at least 3d avenue, and in addition about 11.7 per cent. from at least 7th avenue to at least 3d avenue. If deductions are made for the East River Bridge traffic included in these portions, the respective figures become 5.2 per cent. and 7.4 per cent., which gives a measure of the extent of "long haul" crosstown traffic in this area.

Traffic Flows Subject to Inferior Routing.

The same studies show clearly that considerable Queensboro Bridge traffic moves through the congested midtown streets on its way farther down town and that at the same time much traffic coming over the three lower bridges moves long distances on Manhattan streets on its way to points in the midtown area and through that area on its way to points farther north, with obvious disadvantages to itself and to the other traffic in the districts through which it moves.

These movements are of particular interest because of the more advantageous routing which would be afforded them by the proposed 38th Street Tunnel. The application of the results of our origin and destination studies to the 1928 counts of weekday East River bridge traffic, show them to total substantially 38,000 vehicles per day, divided as follows:

A volume of traffic consisting of some 15,000 vehicles per day now moves over the existing facilities between points in Queens lying north of Newtown Creek and points on the west side of Manhattan below 33d street in New Jersey, and in the district in Manhattan lying east of Broadway between 14th and 33d streets. Of this traffic about 11,000 vehicles per day use the Queensboro Bridge and move through the congested area in mid-Manhattan. The remaining portion uses the three lower bridges, involving for the most part increased distances traveled and movements over the congested crosstown streets in Lower Manhattan.

About 11,000 vehicles per day now move over the existing facilities between points in Brooklyn and Queens lying south of Newtown Creek and points in Manhattan lying between 47th and 72d streets. Of this traffic some 7,000 vehicles per day use the three lower bridges and not only experience considerable inconvenience and delay in moving through the bridge approach areas on both sides of the river, but also must move over the congested streets of mid-Manhattan. The remaining 4,000 vehicles per day use the Queensboro Bridge, necessitating movements through the congested approach areas in both Manhattan and Queens.

Some 7,000 vehicles per day now move over the Queensboro Bridge between points in the outlying districts of Queens and points in Manhattan between 33d and 47th streets, and approximately 2,000 vehicles per day move over the three lower bridges between the outlying points in Brooklyn and points in the same section of Manhattan. The present routing of this traffic necessitates movements through the congested bridge approach areas and for considerable distances on the streets of Manhattan.

In addition there are about 6,000 vehicles per day moving for the most part over the Williamsburg Bridge between points in the section of Brooklyn bounded roughly by the Newtown Creek, Chauncey street, Atlantic avenue, Bedford avenue and the East River, and points in Manhattan between 14th and 47th streets. The portion of this traffic originating in or destined for the northern portion of the Brooklyn area, consisting of approximately 3,000 vehicles per day now moves for considerably longer distances than would be necessary if an interborough connection were available in the vicinity of Newtown Creek.

The Relief Afforded.

The relief which would be afforded by the 38th Street-East River Vehicular Tunnel, together with adequate north and south highways through Brooklyn and Queens, is in most part distinct from that which would be furnished by authorized or proposed interborough connections farther to the north or to the south. The facilities would provide new routes which would tend to reduce the number of vehicles passing through and the distances they have to travel in congested areas. The aforementioned interborough traffic now passing through congested areas on its way from points of origin to points of destination lying outside of such areas would be enabled to avoid them and that going to or coming from points within such areas would be afforded a much shorter and more direct route.

Superior Routing.

The 11,000 vehicles per day moving over the Queensboro Bridge between points in Queens and points below 33d street in Manhattan would be relieved of the difficulties and delays now experienced in moving through the Queensboro Bridge approach areas in both Manhattan and Queens, and in addition would be able to move below the surface of the streets in mid-Manhattan, completely avoiding the necessity of surface movements through this congested area. The 4,000 vehicles per day now using the three lower bridges and moving between these same areas would be provided with a much more direct route and since most of this traffic moves to or from the west side of Manhattan, the use of the tunnel would eliminate delays now experienced in crosstown movements on the surface.

Of the 11,000 vehicles per day moving between points in Brooklyn and Queens below Newtown Creek and points in Manhattan between 47th and 72d streets, the portion now using the three lower bridges would be provided with a route by the proposed tunnel which would considerably shorten the distances now traveled over the streets of Manhattan and avoid the difficulties of passing through the midtown area. The portion now using the Queensboro Bridge would be enabled for the most part to shorten the length of its journeys as well as avoid much delay now experienced in moving through the bridge approach areas in both Manhattan and Queens.

The 9,000 vehicles per day moving between outlying points in Brooklyn and Queens and points in Manhattan lying between 33d and 47th streets would by the use of the new routes be enabled to avoid the bridge approach areas and to shorten the distances now traveled on the streets of Manhattan, especially the portions of this traffic moving to or from the west side.

In addition the tunnel would provide a more direct and more accessible route for approximately 3,000 vehicles per day which now move mostly over the Williamsburg Bridge between points in the northern section of Brooklyn and points in Manhattan lying between 14th and 47th streets.

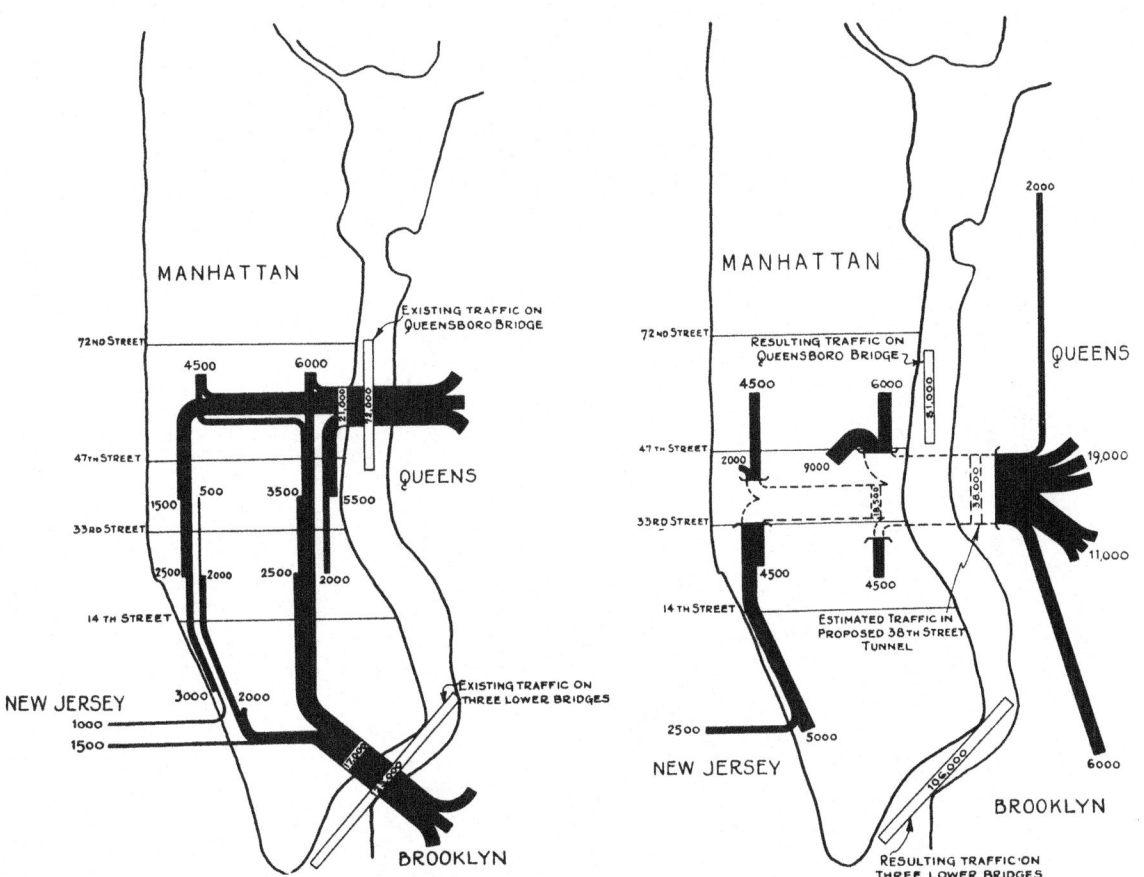

Diversion of Traffic.

Assuming that all of the traffic enumerated, totalling 38,000 vehicles per day, would use the tunnel instead of the East River bridges, the nature and extent of the traffic relief afforded is shown diagrammatically on the chart on page 68.

The diagram on the left shows the present routing of the traffic considered as potential 38th Street-East River Vehicular Tunnel traffic, under the assumption that it would follow the most convenient route based on time and/or distance. The heavy black lines together with the figures indicate the facilities now used and the relative volumes moving to or from each district.

The diagram on the right shows the assumed future routing of the same traffic and the relief which would be afforded by its diversion from the existing bridges, their approach areas and the streets of Manhattan.

The Queensboro Bridge and its approach areas would be relieved of about 29 per cent. and the three lower bridges and their approach areas of about 14 per cent. of their present traffic burdens. The reduction in crosstown surface movements and in traffic on the east side avenues is clearly evident. The removal of some 18,000 vehicles per day, or about 6 per cent. of the total crosstown flow at 5th avenue on all streets between 30th and 59th streets, inclusive, from these streets will not only relieve them but will also reduce materially the interference between east and west and north and south traffic flows.

Similar studies of the origin and destination of local crosstown traffic in mid-Manhattan indicate that some 13,000 vehicles per day could move to better advantage if the crosstown section of the new tunnel were available for their use. The diversion of this volume of local traffic from the surface of the streets, not shown on the diagram, would constitute an additional reduction of about 6 per cent. in the total vehicular movements on 30th to 59th streets, inclusive.

Approximately 29 per cent. of the East River bridge traffic during the daytime hours and approximately 20 per cent. of the crosstown traffic at 5th avenue between 30th and 59th streets is commercial. The new crosstown tunnel would offer opportunities of great relief through the removal of much of this commercial traffic from the surface. Furthermore the proposed improvements in freight facilities along the west side will undoubtedly increase greatly the number of trucks desiring to move towards the east side of Manhattan and to Brooklyn and Queens, and the uninterrupted routes that would be furnished by the new facility would not only afford a great saving in time for the truck traffic, but by its removal from the surface a greater facility of movement for the traffic remaining.

Additional tunnels under the Hudson River are in contemplation, and one in the vicinity of 38th street is of particular interest in that if constructed it would add materially to the volume of traffic desiring to cross mid-Manhattan, in which event the measure of relief afforded by the 38th Street-East River Tunnel would be much greater than under present conditions.

The foregoing figures and statements are based upon 1928 week day conditions, no allowance being made for any growth during or subsequent to the period of construction. It is general experience in similar situations that additional traffic is induced by the provision of improved means of communication. Such factors would tend to increase both the traffic through the tunnel and the measure of relief afforded.

Description of the Project.

The project as originally proposed is outlined on a plan entitled "Study for a Vehicular Tunnel between Manhattan, Queens and Brooklyn," made by the Bureau of Engineering of the Borough of Manhattan under date of January 23, 1926, and showing a four-lane vehicular tunnel under 38th street extending across Manhattan and continuing under the East River to portals located in Queens and in Brooklyn, in the general vicinity of and to the north and to the south of Newtown Creek. The location of the river crossing is about one mile below the Queensboro Bridge and about two miles above the Williamsburg Bridge.

Original Proposal.

The suggested location of the tunnel and of its terminals and their relation to the neighboring facilities and street systems is shown on the location plan on page 70. The main tunnel would begin at 38th street and 10th avenue, Manhattan, with approach tunnels in 10th avenue, with north and south portals near 42d and 34th streets, respectively, and extending across Manhattan as a two-deck tunnel in 38th street to a junction with approach tunnels on the east side of Manhattan at 3d avenue. The north and south portals of the 3d avenue approaches would be near 47th and 28th streets, respectively.

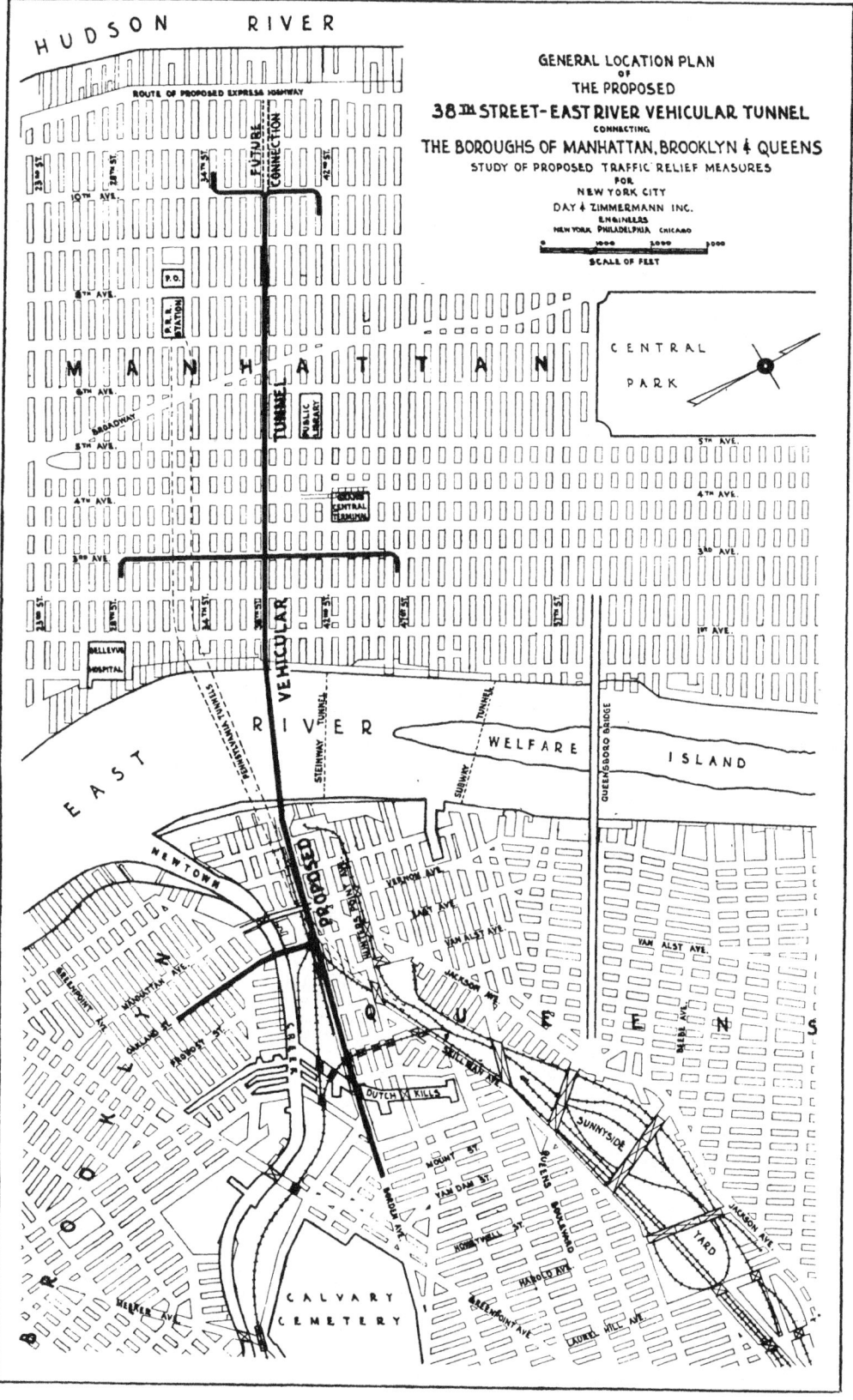

The main tunnel would continue under 38th street to the East River, which would be crossed by twin tubes from 38th street to Borden avenue, Queens, in which Borough the tunnel would be built in Borden avenue, passing under the Dutch Kills to a portal in the vicinity of Mount street. A junction would be made at about East and Borden avenues with a south approach tunnel passing under Newtown Creek, an important waterway, to a portal near Oakland and Huron streets, Brooklyn.

Separate roadways, 20 feet in width between curbs, would be provided for eastbound and for westbound traffic, with maximum adverse grades on the approaches not in excess of $3\frac{1}{2}$ per cent. The magnitude of the project may be gauged by the fact that it includes about five and one-half miles of main tunnel and approaches, with four lanes of roadway space, six entrance and exit plazas and will require about six ventilating tower buildings and appurtenant equipment.

Special features to be noted are the proposed double-deck construction and the provision of branch tunnels leading to the portals, both of which features, as far as we can ascertain, are unique in vehicular tunnel practice.

The capacity of the tunnel, on the basis of mixed traffic with general characteristics similar to that through the Holland Tunnel and over the East River bridges, is estimated at about 38,000 vehicles per day or about 19,000,000 vehicles per year, of which total 6,000,000 represents the estimated capacity available for crosstown traffic local to Manhattan.

Alternate Proposals.

We believe that by placing the eastern terminals in the vicinity of Borden avenue and Van Alst street, and providing additional bridge and street capacity in this vicinity to enable tunnel traffic to get across Newtown Creek and across Dutch Kills, the resulting construction cost could be materially reduced with no substantial loss in the effectiveness of the tunnel as a traffic relief measure.

The Department of Plant and Structures in its report giving the results of its investigations affirms the feasibility of the general project, and stresses the importance of careful design of the plazas and of the junctions between the approach tubes and the main tunnel. Study plans and estimates of cost covering several alternate schemes are presented.

The first scheme differs from the original proposal, in that the Brooklyn-Queens terminals are located slightly farther east and in the omission of the approach tunnels on the west side of Manhattan, the main tunnel terminating in plazas located on either side of 38th street between 9th and 10th avenues and between 10th and 11th avenues, respectively.

In connection with the second scheme, it is stated that improved grades and a considerable reduction in costs could be obtained by locating entrance and exit plazas at East avenue and 3d street in Queens, with street widenings and viaducts over the nearby railroad yards to provide connections to the main highways to Queens and via Borden avenue and the Greenpoint Avenue Bridge to Brooklyn.

The third and fourth schemes provide for twin tube crossings of the East River, located respectively on about the lines of 38th street and of 45th street, but without provision of a tunnel across Manhattan.

The Queens-Brooklyn Terminals.

The major questions involved centre around the suggested omission of the tunnel sections under Newtown Creek and under Dutch Kills and the establishment of terminals in the vicinity of Borden and either Van Alst or East avenues. As far as their general relation to the street system or to expectable traffic streams are concerned, these sites may be considered as identical.

Our traffic studies indicate that about one-half of the tunnel traffic will be attributable to outlying areas in Queens and Brooklyn, in general well to the east of the Sunnyside Yards, about one-third of the traffic to Brooklyn areas lying to the south of Newtown Creek, and about one-sixth to areas in Queens to the north of the tunnel and skirting the East River.

The latter traffic in large part would move along streets near to and generally paralleling the waterfront, such as Van Alst avenue, and would be afforded more convenient and direct access to the tunnel if the terminal location were modified as suggested. Carrying the two other main traffic streams across Newtown Creek and Dutch Kills, respectively, by means of tunnels, thereby avoiding interruption due to navigation requirements, is almost ideal from the tunnel traffic viewpoint, but rather costly.

Borden avenue affords a natural and advantageous outlet to the east due to its favorable connections with the main highways well beyond the Sunnyside Yards and the approach areas of the Queensboro Bridge. The only obstacle to its use as a surface street by the main stream of tunnel traffic is the drawbridge crossing over the Dutch Kills, which ends about 1,600 feet to the north and which is also crossed by a bridge in the line of Hunters Point avenue. The provision of a wider bridge of more modern type would reduce considerably the obstruction offered to the free flow of traffic, and, together with the possibilities of limiting the hours during which the bridge would be opened for navigation, would add correspondingly to the possibilities of securing adequate connections to the east without extending the tunnel construction under Dutch Kills.

The tunnel traffic to and from Brooklyn must cross Newtown Creek. Under existing conditions, if the terminals were located in the vicinity of Borden and East avenues, it could do so by using the Manhattan Avenue Bridge, located about 1,000 feet to the west or the Greenpoint Avenue Bridge, located much farther to the east. Either of these routes involves superimposing the tunnel traffic upon the local traffic and delays due to bridge openings for navigation, and in the case of the Greenpoint avenue route involves a considerable detour. In our judgment, the situation would require the provision of facilities affording additional and more direct routes across Newtown Creek in order to develop adequately the possible advantages of the main project.

A viaduct in effect extending Van Alst avenue across the railroad yards and by a bascule bridge over Newtown Creek at relatively high level to reduce the number of openings for navigation, with suitable ramp connections to the tunnel plazas near Borden avenue, would add materially to the possibilities of securing adequate connections to the south without extending the tunnel construction under Newtown Creek. It would also provide an additional route for the movement of local traffic between the adjoining waterfront sections of Brooklyn and Queens, which would not be true of a tunnel crossing.

The Manhattan Terminals.

A valuable feature of the project as originally proposed is the number and wide separation of the Manhattan terminals and their general location with respect to the areas of greatest traffic congestion, which, assuming the provision of entrance and exit facilities at each terminal, would result in an advantageous distribution of the tunnel traffic and a shortening of the distances it would have to move on the surface streets. Approximately one-half of the existing interborough traffic which could more advantageously use the tunnel moves to or from the west side of Manhattan.

The arrangement offers similar advantages with respect to local crosstown traffic moving between the west side and the east side of mid-Manhattan, the existing volume of which justifies every effort to encourage its diversion from the surface to the tunnel.

In addition to increasing the cost of the project, the provision of branch tunnels imposes burdens of design with respect to the junction chambers in order to give the flexibility of turnout movements necessary to avoid undue reduction in the capacity of the tunnel and in the continuity of traffic flow. The requirements of toll collection, together with the high land values involved and the heavy traffic flows in the streets surrounding the proposed terminals, require special recognition in the design of the entrance and exit plazas in order to ensure the maximum obtainable freedom of movement to and from the tunnel, and the minimum of congestion in the adjoining streets.

With respect to the suggested omission of the approach tunnels in 10th avenue, with terminals in the vicinity of 42d and 34th streets, consideration should be given to two factors. The first is the effect of the evident movement westward of intensive building development, the authorized changes in freight yards and terminal facilities along the west side, and the construction of the West Side Express Highway upon future traffic conditions in this vicinity. There appears to be every likelihood of conditions quite comparable to those now existing in the vicinity of the east side portals and equally justifying the provision of separated terminals.

The second factor is the desirability of direct connection with a tunnel extending under the Hudson River to New Jersey, in case one should be built in this vicinity. The advantages of enabling traffic to move between such a tunnel and points on the east side of Manhattan or on Long Island via the 38th Street Tunnel without adding to the surface traffic are evident, as is the necessity of carefully co-ordinated designs of the two projects to ensure advantageous distribution of their terminals and hence of their traffic upon the surrounding street system. In our judgment, the general situation indicates the desirability of providing two separated terminals at the western end of the 38th Street-East River Tunnel.

The Cost of the Project.

Our review of the costs of projects of a similar nature indicates that as originally proposed the project will cost substantially $87,000,000, exclusive of interest, engineering and similar overhead costs during construction.

On the basis of a modified plan, locating the eastern terminals in the vicinity of Borden and Van Alst avenues and providing added bridge and street capacity in this vicinity to enable tunnel traffic to get across Newtown Creek and across Dutch Kills, the resulting construction cost would be reduced to approximately $72,000,000.

Allowing 20 per cent. to cover interest during construction, engineering, administrative and similar overhead costs, would bring the total cost of the project as proposed to practically $103,000,000 and of the modified project to $86,000,000.

The report of the Department of Plant and Structures gives the estimated cost of the project, with tunnels extending under Newtown Creek and Dutch Kills and the western terminal on the line of 38th street, as $80,650,000, exclusive of interest during construction and of the cost of land with an assessed valuation of some $5,822,000. For a modified project, with an eastern terminal in the vicinity of Borden and East avenues, special Y construction at the 3d avenue junction in Manhattan, and provision for connection with a tunnel to New Jersey, the corresponding estimate is $65,000,000 and the assessed value of land required is $6,835,000.

If, in order to enable comparison of the estimates, the cost of acquiring the necessary land is taken as about twice the assessed valuation, and 12 per cent. is allowed for interest during construction, as was done in our estimates, the total costs based on the estimates of the Department of Plant and Structures would become $103,400,000 and $88,100,000, respectively. With respect to the close agreement of the two estimates, it must be recognized that, considering the preliminary status of the plans, they can only be reasonable approximations of the probable costs of the project.

The annual cost, based on an allowance of 6 per cent. for fixed charges and on operating expenses estimated at $2,620,000 and $2,340,000, respectively, would total $8,800,000 for the project as originally proposed and $7,500,000 for the project if modified. These are the amounts of revenue which would have to be collected in order to make the project self-supporting. Assuming an average toll of 50 cents, the respective volumes of traffic required to yield these amounts would be 17,600,000 and 15,000,000 vehicles per year.

Tolls and Traffic.

The toll charges in effect in the Holland Tunnel are averaging about 55 cents per vehicle. As developed above, the volume of traffic which could advantageously use the tunnel, amounting to approximately 19,000,000 vehicles per year, is in excess of that required to make the project self-supporting on the basis of an average charge of 50 cents per vehicle.

Factors to be considered in this connection are that a willingness to pay tolls has been expressed by many interests favoring the tunnel, and, moreover, even with the benefits resulting from the construction of the added facilities under consideration the expectable growth in traffic will create conditions resulting in an added volume of traffic willing to pay tolls in order to move more freely than possible on the surface.

Conclusion.

In our opinion the project under consideration constitutes a well conceived traffic relief measure designed to relieve conditions rapidly approaching unmanageable proportions and from the standpoints of both convenience and necessity its construction is warranted. There is no definite method for determining the actual number of vehicles which would use the proposed facilities on a toll basis, although there is an existing volume of traffic which would be better served from the standpoints of time and convenience and which is in excess of the total required to make the project self-supporting on the basis of an average charge of 50 cents per vehicle.

THE PROPOSED NARROWS VEHICULAR TUNNEL CONNECTING RICHMOND AND BROOKLYN.

The construction of a vehicular bridge or tunnel across the Narrows between Brooklyn and Richmond (Staten Island) has been vigorously urged as a means of terminating the practical isolation of Richmond from the other boroughs of New York City and thereby stimulating its development for housing and industry, as well as affording traffic between points in Brooklyn, Queens and outlying sections of Long Island and points in southern New Jersey, a short and direct route which avoids the congestion encountered in moving by way of Manhattan.

In March, 1929, the Board of Estimate and Apportionment directed the Department of Plant and Structures and the Board of Transportation to jointly prepare the

necessary plans for the construction and equipment of a vehicular tunnel connecting the Boroughs of Brooklyn and Richmond, and, subject to approval of the plans, to begin its construction. In response, a preliminary report dated June 7, 1929, and giving the results of an engineering investigation of the project was submitted to the Board of Estimate and Apportionment.

Following consideration of the project and public hearings, the Board on July 25, 1929, by appropriate legislation definitely committed the City to the construction of the tunnel as a toll project and appropriated $3,000,000 towards its design and construction.

The General Situation.

The Borough of Richmond, co-extensive with Staten Island, ranks third among the Boroughs of New York City in area, but last in population. Within its limits large areas are available for development of housing, industry and shipping, which has been retarded by the relative isolation of the island from the other boroughs, and, until recent years, from New Jersey.

Present Connections and Traffic.

Ferry service affords the only means of direct communication for vehicles or persons with Manhattan and with Brooklyn. It is about five miles from the northern end of Staten Island to the Battery, but only about a mile across the Narrows to South Brooklyn. A railroad bridge at Elizabethport, ferry lines at Perth Amboy, Carteret, Elizabethport and Bergen Point, and vehicular toll bridges at Elizabeth, Perth Amboy and Bayonne (under construction) connect the island with New Jersey.

The vehicular traffic flows over the facilities enumerated, based on 1928 week day conditions, average approximately 2,900 vehicles per day to Manhattan, 1,800 to Brooklyn and 4,600 to New Jersey. Sunday flows are much greater, particularly in the warmer months. Traffic between points in Elizabeth and farther south and points in Brooklyn and Queens represented only a very small fraction of the week day flow through the Holland tunnel. A measure of the relative magnitude of these flows is afforded by comparison with the average week day traffic movements of about 23,000 vehicles per day through the Holland Tunnel and about 72,000 over the Queensboro Bridge.

The Need for Improved Connections.

There are certain disadvantages inherent in ferry service under present day conditions, the outstanding ones being the limitations in capacity, the intermittent nature of the service, the relatively long time required for passage, and in many situations the frequency of delays due to fog and weather conditions. As a result of the wide use and increased importance of motor vehicle transportation and the accompanying emphasis placed upon speed and time, there has been a countrywide tendency during recent years to provide vehicular connections across wide waterways by the construction of bridges or tunnels in situations where heretofore only ferry service was available. Illustrations of this tendency, aside from the projects now under consideration in New York City, are furnished by the vehicular tunnel between Oakland and Alameda in California, the tunnel and the bridge under construction at Detroit, Michigan, the Delaware River bridges at Philadelphia, the proposed tunnel connecting Boston and East Boston, the Holland Tunnel and the 178th Street Bridge crossings of the Hudson, and others.

A similar situation exists with respect to Staten Island, which is separated from the other Boroughs of New York and from New Jersey by the Upper Bay, the Narrows and tributary waters. The relative location of major existing and proposed vehicular bridges and tunnels is shown diagrammatically on the map on page 74 which also indicates the isolation referred to above.

The completion of the bridges leading to Perth Amboy and Elizabeth, and the pending completion of the bridge to Bayonne, mark the first steps in furnishing improved means of communication between Staten Island and neighboring areas. The growth in traffic on the completed bridges has been marked, and their importance will become even greater when more convenient means of communication are established with Brooklyn and through it with the other sections of the City and points beyond.

The advantages which would be afforded by such a connection are not to be measured solely in terms of present day traffic but also in terms of future conditions. Any well planned facility providing easier communication with the other Boroughs would be an effective means of stimulating development within rather than without the City limits and of bringing about a fuller utilization of the vast unused resources of Richmond in land and waterfront.

A vehicular tunnel across the Narrows would afford more convenient and quicker routes for traffic moving from Brooklyn and Queens to Staten Island and to New

STATEN ISLAND AND THE NARROWS

Jersey. The routes now available involve either a slow ferry trip or passage over the East and Hudson Rivers and through the congested sections of Brooklyn or Queens, Manhattan and Jersey City. It would greatly facilitate the heavy traffic movements on week-ends and holidays to or from the recreational centers on Long Island and Staten Island and along the New Jersey coast.

In connection with the Triborough Bridge, the proposed highways through Brooklyn and Queens, the Staten Island highways and the bridges leading to New Jersey, such a tunnel would be an essential link in a through route by-passing Manhattan on the east, traversing Long Island, and affording a very direct connection between points in south Jersey and points in New England or in Westchester County. This route has been included in the proposals of the Regional Plan for the development of the arterial highway system in the metropolitan area.

A vehicular tunnel across the Narrows would also offer substantial possibilities for improved passenger transportation service between Richmond and the other Boroughs through the development of bus lines operating on Staten Island and through the tunnel to a connection in South Brooklyn with the 4th Avenue Subway Station at 86th street and perhaps to more distant terminals.

The Development of the Project.

Needs and advantages such as outlined above, and the successful completion of the Holland Tunnel have led to the development of the project under consideration.

Some years ago, after an exhaustive study, a tunnel location connecting St. George, Staten Island, with the Bay Ridge section of Brooklyn was selected as the best location for a railroad and rapid transit tunnel. Shafts were constructed at each end and then work was discontinued. The utilization of this location, and of the completed work, for the construction of a vehicular tunnel was investigated by the departments to which the matter had been referred by the Board of Estimate and Apportionment.

In their report they point out that this is the most advantageous location for the future provision of through railroad connections between New York and New Jersey and rapid transit connections between Staten Island and Brooklyn, or both, and that its utilization for a vehicular tunnel would undoubtedly be adverse to the future development of the New York side of the port. Furthermore, the length of the tunnel, the necessity of enlarging the shafts, the unfavorable topographical conditions at its terminals, and the increased ventilation problems, are factors that would add greatly to the cost of the project and be adverse to its utilization for purposes of a vehicular tunnel. For the foregoing reasons, this location was rejected by them.

A project for constructing a bridge across the Narrows was developed by private interests and vigorously urged by them as the best solution of the problem. It was opposed with equal vigor by advocates of tunnel construction on the grounds of the great span involved, foundation problems, and possible interference with access to the port in time of war. In view of the decision of the City to proceed with the construction of a tunnel, and the lack of substantial differences as far as vehicular traffic flows are concerned, further discussion of this bridge project would serve no useful purpose in this report.

At a meeting of the American Society of Civil Engineers held in New York on December 19, 1928, a paper was presented dealing with the proposed construction of a bridge across the Narrows. In the resulting discussion, the Chief Engineer of the Holland Tunnel presented the results of a study made by him of a vehicular tunnel crossing, in which he suggested a location substantially the same as the one now under consideration.

As previously stated, the Department of Plant and Structures and the Board of Transportation were directed in March, 1929, to prepare plans and, upon their approval, to proceed with the construction of a vehicular tunnel connecting Richmond and Brooklyn. The results of an investigation and study made by the Chief Engineers of these two bodies were set forth in a preliminary report transmitted to the Board of Estimate and Apportionment under date of June 4, 1929. This report was accompanied by plans showing the recommended location of the tunnel and its terminals and the type of construction proposed, and presents a discussion of the major problems involved in des'gn and construction, with estimates of the cost on various bases.

Description of the Project.

The following description is based upon the prel'minary report and plans to which reference has just been made. The location recommended for the tunnel and its terminals is shown on the plan on page 78.

General Features.

The tunnel consists of two tubes, each providing for two lanes of traffic moving in the same direction. The distance between ventilating shafts placed at the pierhead

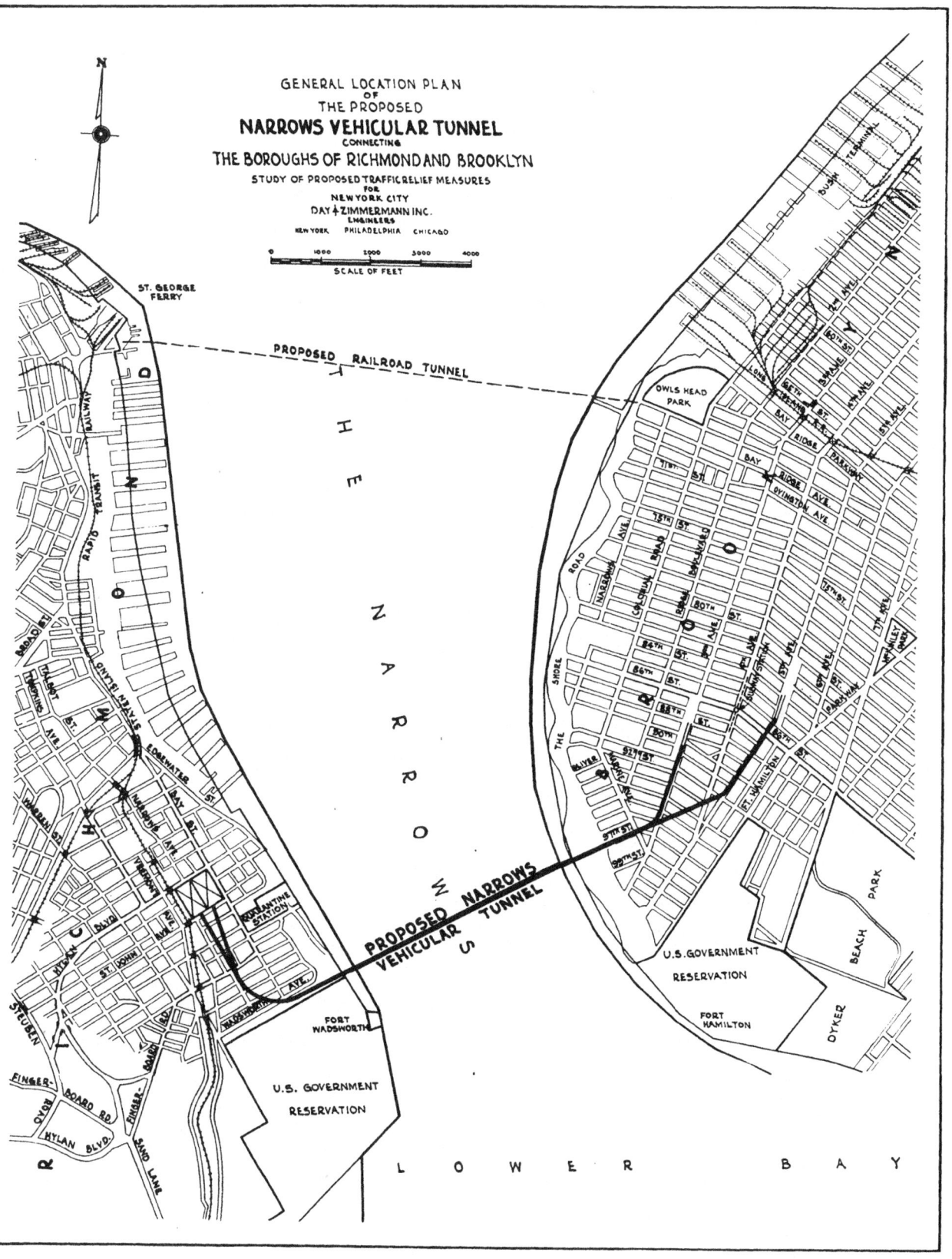

lines is 4,700 feet, or about 1,300 feet greater than the corresponding distance for the Holland Tunnel. The length between portals of the tube for westbound traffic is 11,100 feet and that of the eastbound tube is 12,800 feet. These dimensions are about one-third greater than those of the Holland Tunnel. The comparisons are cited to establish the greater magnitude of the project, with its bearing upon design and costs.

The increased distance between ventilating shafts adds materially to the ventilation problem. The greater space requirements for air ducts indicates that for the main sections of the tunnel the tube diameters will have to be about 32 feet, as compared with 29½ feet developed in the Holland Tunnel and here proposed for the approach sections. The roadway space will provide a vertical clearance of 13½ feet and widths of 21 feet in the main sections and 20 feet in the approach sections.

The profile shown on the plans provides for maximum adverse grades of three per cent. extending from the pierhead lines to the surface on the exit approaches and maximum descending grades of 4 per cent. on the entrance approaches.

The Staten Island Terminals.

The plans contemplate the collection of all tolls on the Staten Island end of the tunnel and the provision of a plaza approximately 750 feet square for the accommodation of both entering and leaving traffic. The location selected lies between the Hylan boulevard and St. John's avenue and between Bay street and the right-of-way of the Staten Island Rapid Transit Railway.

Bay street leads past the extensive municipal pier development to St. George. The Hylan boulevard extends along the south shore of the island to Tottenville and affords a favorable connection with the Outerbridge Crossing leading to Perth Amboy. The Hylan boulevard, Bay street and Tompkins avenue all afford more or less direct connection with Clove road and other main highways leading to the northern side of the island and to the Elizabeth and the Bayonne crossings.

The Brooklyn Terminal.

On the Brooklyn end of the tunnel, there will be no need of plaza space for toll collection and it is planned to have the entrance located in a suitably widened section of 3d avenue at 88th street, and the exit similarly placed in 5th avenue at 83d street. The separation of these terminals and their location relative to 4th avenue and to 86th street, both main thoroughfares, will enable a favorable distribution of traffic.

3d, 4th and 5th avenues afford direct and favorable connection with the business section of Brooklyn, with the proposed West Street-Hamilton Avenue Tunnel, and via the proposed north-south highway through Brooklyn and Queens with the Triborough and intervening East River bridges or tunnels to Manhattan. The Fort Hamilton parkway is a main traffic artery leading to the Prospect Park, Flatbush avenue and Jamaica sections, and in connection with other existing and proposed main highways to the Triborough Bridge and other more distant points in Queens and in Long Island. 86th street and 92d street afford favorable connections with Coney Island and the sections of Brooklyn and Queens adjoining Jamaica Bay.

The Cost of the Project.

The report of the Chief Engineers sets forth the basis upon which their estimates of cost were prepared, and states that if the tunnel is constructed by the shield method, the estimated cost complete, including an allowance of 15 per cent. for engineering, administration and contingencies, but exclusive of interest during construction, is $77,900,000.

If the grades on the exit approaches are increased from 3 to 3½ per cent. the estimated cost would be reduced about $4,000,000, and if the trench method of construction is used on the sections between the pierhead lines, the estimated cost can be further reduced by from $5,000,000 to $9,000,000.

The range in the foregoing estimates is from $64,900,000 to $77,900,000. The time required for construction and equipment of the tunnel is estimated at five years. On this basis, using an allowance of 15 per cent. for interest during construction, the range in total costs would be from $75,000,000 to $90,000,000 in rounded figures.

Using the lower figure for purposes of illustration, the annual cost, based on an allowance of 6 per cent. per annum for fixed charges and $1,700,000 per year as the estimated cost of operation, would be $6,200,000. This is a measure of the revenues which would have to be collected each year in order to make the project self-supporting. On the basis of an average toll of 50 cents per vehicle, the volume of traffic required to yield this amount would be 12,400,000 vehicles per year.

The development of the project in steps, limiting the initial construction to a single tube through which traffic would flow in both directions, offers a means of reducing the costs involved, which merits careful study and consideration.

Potential Traffic.

The general advantages which would be afforded to local and to through traffic by a vehicular tunnel connecting Richmond and Brooklyn have been set forth in presenting the needs for such an improvement. There is no definite method by which the actual number of vehicles which would use the proposed facility on a toll basis can be determined. However, by a consideration of the present traffic flows and of the changed conditions which would result from the establishment of a new and improved means of communication, it is possible to set up a measure of the traffic considered potential for such a facility.

Present Flows.

In the development of the potential traffic from this viewpoint, 1928 traffic data has been taken as indicative of the volume of present flows and the results of our origin, destination and routing studies of weekday traffic as indicative of its distribution.

The traffic on the ferries connecting Staten Island and South Brooklyn amounts to approximately 650,000 vehicles per year. Practically all of this traffic is attributable to Brooklyn and Queens, and about 20 per cent. moves to or from points in New Jersey. With the exception of horse drawn vehicles amounting to less than 2 per cent. of the total, all of this traffic would be afforded quicker and more convenient routes by the proposed tunnel.

The traffic on the ferry connecting Staten Island with the Battery on Manhattan amounts to about 1,100,000 vehicles per year, with approximately the same proportion of horse drawn vehicles. The distribution of week day traffic indicates that about 52 per cent. moves to or from points in Manhattan below 14th street, 28 per cent. between 14th and 72d streets, 13 per cent. north of 72d street, and about 7 per cent. to or from points on Brooklyn and Queens. Approximately 88 per cent. of the traffic is attributable to Staten Island, the remaining 12 per cent. to points in New Jersey or beyond. The portion of this traffic now moving over Manhattan streets and the East River bridges to or from points in Brooklyn and Queens, amounting to about 77,000 vehicles per year, would be greatly advantaged by the use of the proposed tunnel.

Under present conditions, the proposed tunnel would not afford much advantage to the remaining portion of the traffic now using the Staten Island-Battery Ferry. However, the situation would be entirely changed if the proposed north-south highway through Brooklyn and Queens were considered available in conjunction with the proposed Narrows Tunnel.

Under such conditions, much of this traffic would be afforded more advantageous routes than those now available. The time required for crossing the bay, and that now used in moving over Manhattan streets would both be materially reduced, as would also the inconveniences of movement through congested areas. The completion of the Triborough Bridge and the 38th Street-East River Tunnel, and of the proposed West Street-Hamilton Avenue Tunnel would still further increase the advantages indicated.

The traffic through the Holland Tunnel in 1928, totalled 8,745,000 vehicles, and represents about 80 per cent. of the traffic crossing the Hudson below Canal street. The portion of this traffic moving between points in the vicinity of or to the south of Elizabeth and points in Brooklyn or Queens would be afforded more direct, quicker, and more convenient routes by the proposed Narrows Tunnel. Based on the distribution of week-day traffic, its volume is approximately 280,000 vehicles per year.

It therefore appears that the volume of traffic now using other routes which, from the standpoints of time and convenience, could more advantageously use the Narrows Tunnel is somewhere between one and two million vehicles per year.

Future Conditions.

The present flows stated above are based on 1928 data and made no allowance for growth during or subsequent to the period of construction. For the three-year period ending with 1928, the average annual increase in vehicular traffic on the Staten Island-Battery Ferry has been 5 per cent., on the East River bridges 6 per cent., on the Harlem River bridges 8 per cent. and on the Hudson River ferries and tunnel 20 per cent. With one exception, similar figures for 5-year and for 8-year periods show even greater average annual increases. Traffic through the Holland Tunnel has grown rapidly and consistently since its opening late in 1927, traffic in March, 1929, showing a 37 per cent. increase over that in March, 1928. On the basis of an increase of 6 per cent. each year, traffic volumes would double in about 12 years. The estimated time required to construct and equip the proposed tunnel is five years.

The establishment of a new or materially improved vehicular connection between two districts is usually accompanied by a marked increase in the traffic between them, due to movements induced by the increased convenience of travel. An illustration is afforded by the great increase in vehicular traffic between Manhattan and New Jersey immediately following the opening of the Holland Tunnel late in 1927. The total traffic across the Hudson was some 13,700,000 vehicles in 1926, 16,100,000 in 1927, and 20,700,000 in 1928. The tunnel officials estimate that approximately 45 per cent. of the traffic through the tunnel was new traffic induced by the improved convenience of crossing afforded and the remaining 55 per cent. was diverted from ferries. In our judgment, this effect would be very pronounced in the case of the Narrows Tunnel, particularly with reference to pleasure traffic desiring to move from points in Brooklyn and Queens to the beaches and resorts on Staten Island and along the Jersey Coast and from points in the vicinity of and south of Elizabeth to the beaches and resorts on Long Island.

Reference has been made to the absence of rapid transit connections between Staten Island and the other boroughs, and to the possibilities for improved passenger transportation offered by the establishment of bus lines operating on Staten Island and through the tunnel to a connection with the 4th Avenue Subway at the Brooklyn terminal of the tunnel. On the basis of 1926 data, the passenger traffic between Staten Island and Manhattan is about 26,000,000 and to Brooklyn about 2,000,000 passengers per year. All of this traffic could hardly be handled satisfactorily in the manner suggested, but to the extent that such bus lines could be developed with advantage, they would add to the potential tunnel traffic.

It is evident that the effects such as set forth above cannot be definitely evaluated. In our judgment they require particular consideration in this situation and indicate that the potential traffic for the proposed Narrows Tunnel is much greater than that estimated on the sole basis of present flows and present conditions.

Summary and Conclusions.

The proposed vehicular tunnel connecting Richmond and Brooklyn would afford quicker and more convenient routes for between one and two million vehicles per year, now in most part dependent upon ferry service. The use of the new routes would reduce the number of vehicles passing through, and the distances traveled on the streets of the congested areas, although the relief thus afforded would be relatively minor. The extent and nature of the relief afforded, if measured solely in terms of present day traffic, would place the project in a group with others scheduled for future development.

However, as we view the project, its relative importance should be determined on far broader aspects, and with a view to the greater demands and advantages of the future. The general growth in traffic in and between the boroughs of the City, and between the City and adjoining sections of New York State, New England and New Jersey should be considered as well as the special growth induced by the provision of new and improved routes. An extensive system of highways and interborough bridges and tunnels is being planned to improve traffic conditions in all parts of the City, including circumferential through routes in Richmond, Brooklyn and Queens, in which the proposed tunnel would be an essential link.

Furthermore, the development of Richmond has been retarded by the lack of convenient means of communication with the other boroughs. It contains within its limits, and therefore within the limits of the City of New York, extensive areas suitable for housing, industry and shipping. The utilization of these valuable assets would be stimulated by the proposed tunnel, the City as a whole benefiting by development within, rather than without its limits. It is upon considerations such as those enumerated above that final judgment as to the project should be reached.

THE PROPOSED MANHATTAN-BROOKLYN VEHICULAR TUNNEL FROM WEST STREET, MANHATTAN, TO HAMILTON AVENUE, BROOKLYN (BATTERY TUNNEL).

A project to provide an additional traffic connection between lower Manhattan and Brooklyn by means of a vehicular tunnel with portals in the vicinity of Cedar and West streets, Manhattan, and extending under West street, Battery Park and Governors Island to a terminal at about Hamilton avenue and Hicks street in Brooklyn, is outlined in a letter from the Commissioner of the Department of Plant and Structures to the President of the Brooklyn Chamber of Commerce under date of January 23, 1929, accompanied by a location plan dated January 15, 1929.

Description of Project.

The suggested location of the tunnel and its relation to the existing bridges and street systems is shown on the map on page 82. The length of the proposed tunnel is approximately 12,000 feet. By carrying the line of the tunnel under Governors Island, the distances between possible ventilation shaft locations are brought

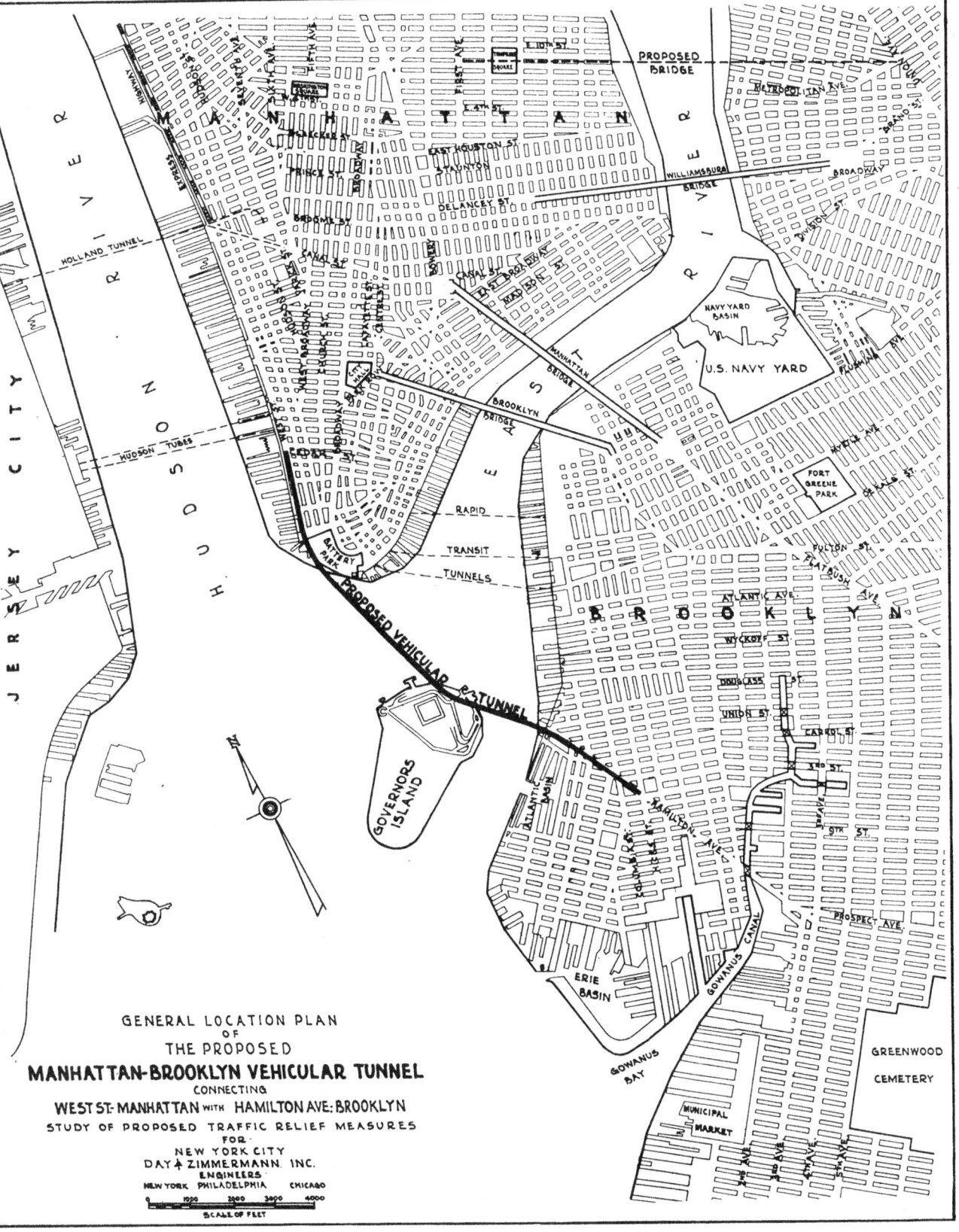

within limits proven practicable by the Holland Tunnel, and at the same time construction conditions secured making for rapidity and economy in construction.

Provision by the City of elevator service between the tunnel roadway and the surface of Governors Island has been suggested as a basis upon which the Federal Government would probably give the necessary easements. In any event, permission to construct the tunnel and shafts and to erect and maintain one or more ventilating tower buildings on the island is an essential element of the project.

Although the general knowledge of conditions available as a result of the successful construction of transit tunnels in this vicinity and other data point towards the entire feasibility of the proposed construction, final determination of the location and detailed features of the tunnel must rest upon the results of borings and preliminary studies not yet made.

It is to be assumed that the general features and proportions of the tunnel will embody the proven elements of the Holland tunnel, and that it will provide for two traffic lanes in each direction, of widths and grades suitable for mixed traffic. The arrangement and exact location of portals and toll plazas and any modification in street plans necessary to absorb the tunnel traffic without congestion have not yet been developed, but seem to present no unusual problems.

Manhattan Terminal.

The suggested approximate location of the Manhattan terminal in West street near Cedar street lends itself admirably to the service of traffic moving between New Jersey, the lower west side districts of Manhattan and the southern districts of Brooklyn. It is about one mile south of the terminals of the West Side Express Highway and of the Holland Tunnel, with favorable street conditions for traffic flows between them. The width of some 250 feet between the bulkhead line and the house line of West street seemingly invites the placing of the portals in the street, with the entrance and exit portals separated longitudinally to avoid congestion and planned to co-ordinate with the ramps of the contemplated extension southward of the West Side Express Highway. On this basis all toll collection facilities would probably be located at the Brooklyn terminal.

Brooklyn Terminal.

The suggested location of the Brooklyn terminal along Hamilton avenue in the vicinity of Hicks street is also a very favorable one from the traffic viewpoint. It is about one-half mile distant from the East River waterfront and from the Gowanus Canal. It would afford easy and direct access for traffic moving to or from points along the important waterfront and industrial sections surrounding it and to traffic from the more central sections of Brooklyn.

Traffic attributable to the extensive waterfront, industrial and residential sections of Brooklyn lying to the south and southeast of the Gowanus Canal would have to cross the canal and would tend to move largely along Hamilton avenue on its way to or from main arteries such as 3d, 4th and 5th avenues and the general street system farther east. There is now a considerable flow of traffic in this direction and reinforcement of the local street system and of the drawbridge capacities across Gowanus Canal will undoubtedly be required in order to ensure favorable traffic conditions and the maximum benefits from the tunnel.

The plaza areas required to enable adequate toll collection facilities and the local street and traffic situation point towards the necessity of locating them outside of the present street lines and the desirability of a reasonable separation of entrance and exit plazas.

Present Situation.

Much of the congestion in lower Manhattan and in the bridge approach areas in Brooklyn is due to the concentration of heavy interborough traffic flows on the three lower East River bridges. About 123,000 vehicles per day moved over these bridges in October, 1928, approximately two-thirds of them using the Brooklyn and the Manhattan Bridges. Study of the distribution of this traffic on the basis of its points of origin and destination disclosed that nearly 90 per cent. of it is attributable to areas in Brooklyn lying east and south of the bridge terminals and a slightly lesser percentage to Manhattan areas south of 47th street, and that about one-half of the total traffic moves to or from the west side of Manhattan. The rate of growth in traffic over these bridges during recent years has been only slightly less than that experienced on the Queensboro Bridge.

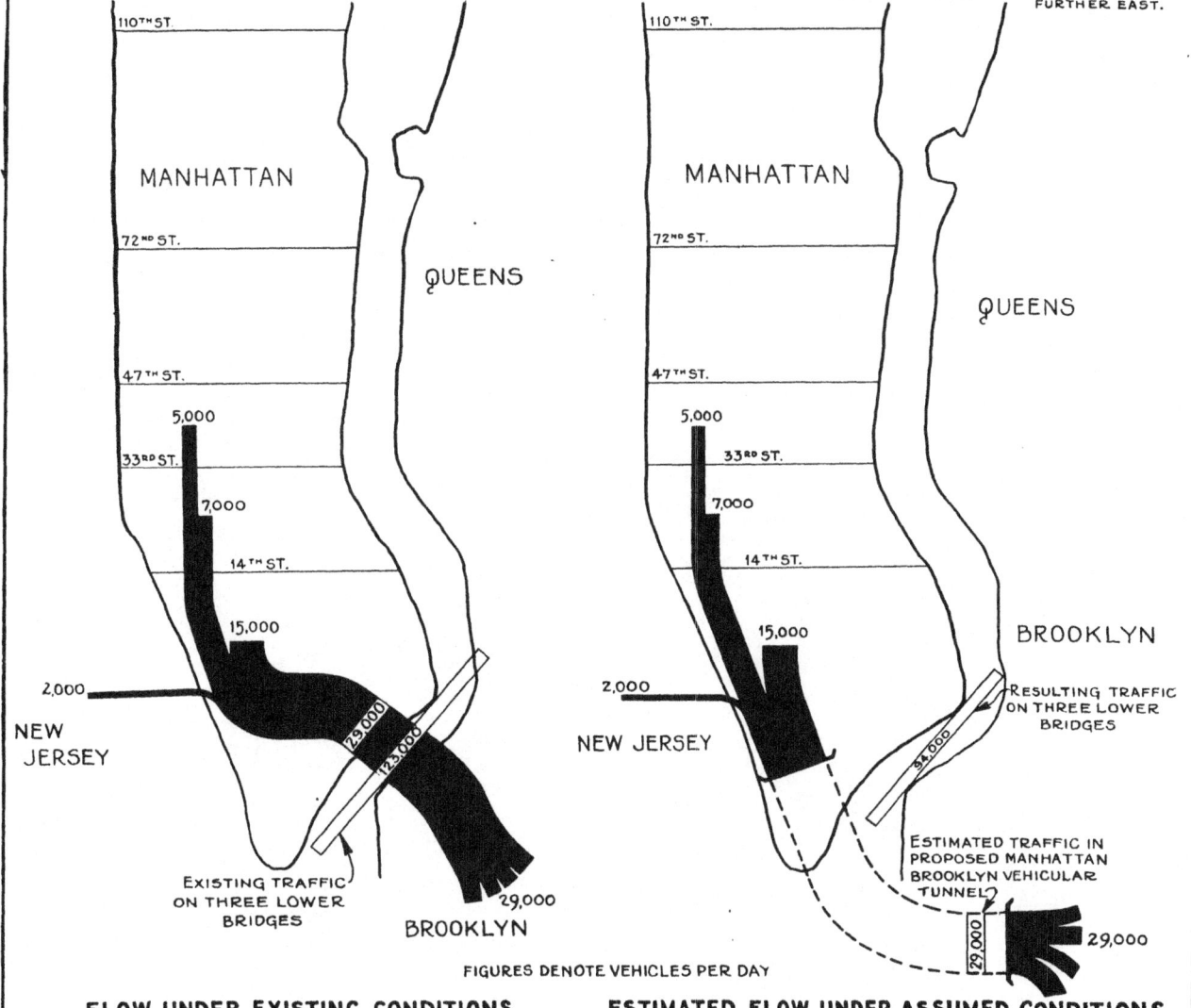

In lower Manhattan, the three bridge terminals all fall within a mile at points located from one-third to one-half of the way across the island, imposing their traffic upon the irregular and heavily used street system with resulting conflict of flows and congestion. The interference between the heavy flows of east and west traffic in Canal street and of north and south traffic in Lafayette street is an outstanding example of this cause of delay.

On the Brooklyn side the terminal of the Williamsburg Bridge is well to the north of the Manhattan and Brooklyn Bridge plazas, which are within about one-quarter mile of one another and so located that all traffic reaching them must travel through areas where the traffic flows and congestion are quite comparable with those of lower Manhattan and which extend at least as far east as the intersection of 4th, Flatbush and Atlantic avenues.

The heavy traffic flows over the individual bridges and the limitations and restrictions placed upon entering and leaving traffic by the structures and traffic in the streets immediately adjoining the bridge plazas, create further points of congestion and add to the delays being experienced by interborough traffic.

The conditions outlined above clearly indicate the necessity of avoiding further concentration of interborough traffic in these areas and of seeking present relief and provision for the greater requirements of the future by the establishment of new routes which will enable a considerable portion of the traffic to pass around instead of through the most congested areas, and with sufficient directness to result in an appreciable saving of time.

There is a considerable portion of the traffic in question that would be particularly advantaged by such diversion. It moves between points in New Jersey and in Manhattan west of Broadway and south of 47th street and points in Brooklyn located roughly south of the line of Atlantic avenue and beyond the bridgehead areas. The application of the results of our origin and destination studies to the 1928 counts of East River bridge traffic indicate that its volume is substantially 29,000 vehicles per day.

The present routing of this traffic necessitates movements through the most congested area of Brooklyn, extending from the Manhattan and Brooklyn Bridge plazas to the intersection of Atlantic and Flatbush avenues. The traffic also moves over the crosstown streets of lower Manhattan, mostly using Canal street. The use of these streets not only results in delay and inconvenience to the traffic itself, but also adds greatly to the serious interference with the movement of north and south bound traffic in lower Manhattan.

Relief Afforded.

Considering all of the traffic which could use the tunnel to better advantage than the East River bridges, the nature and extent of the traffic relief afforded by the proposed tunnel is shown diagrammatically on page 84.

The diagram on the left shows the present routing of the traffic considered as potential to Manhattan-Brooklyn Vehicular Tunnel, on the assumption that it would follow the most convenient routes based on time and/or distance. The heavy black lines together with the figures indicate the daily volume of traffic now using the existing facilities and the relative volumes originating in or destined for various districts.

The diagram on the right shows the assumed future routing of this same traffic and the relief which would be afforded by its diversion from the existing bridges, their approach areas and the streets in both Brooklyn and Manhattan. The three lower bridges would be relieved of about one-fourth of their present combined traffic burden. More detailed studies indicate that the Williamsburg Bridge would be relieved of about 6 per cent., the Manhattan Bridge of about 36 per cent. and the Brooklyn Bridge of about 24 per cent. of their present traffic. The congested area of Brooklyn as well as the crosstown streets of lower Manhattan would be relieved of some 29,000 vehicle movements per day.

Of the traffic moving over the three lower bridges to and from zones on the west side of Manhattan, it has been found that about 32 per cent. now uses Canal street. On this basis the diversion of traffic by the proposed Manhattan-Brooklyn Vehicular Tunnel from Canal street alone would be some 9,000 vehicles per day, which represents a reduction of substantially 38 per cent. in the present traffic burden on this street. Such a relief to this important crosstown artery would materially reduce its present interference with the movements of north and southbound traffic in lower Manhattan.

The estimates given above are based on 1928 traffic counts, no allowance being made for the growth in traffic due to general causes. Also no consideration has been given to the induced traffic which would no doubt result from the provision of this more convenient means of communication between the important waterfront districts

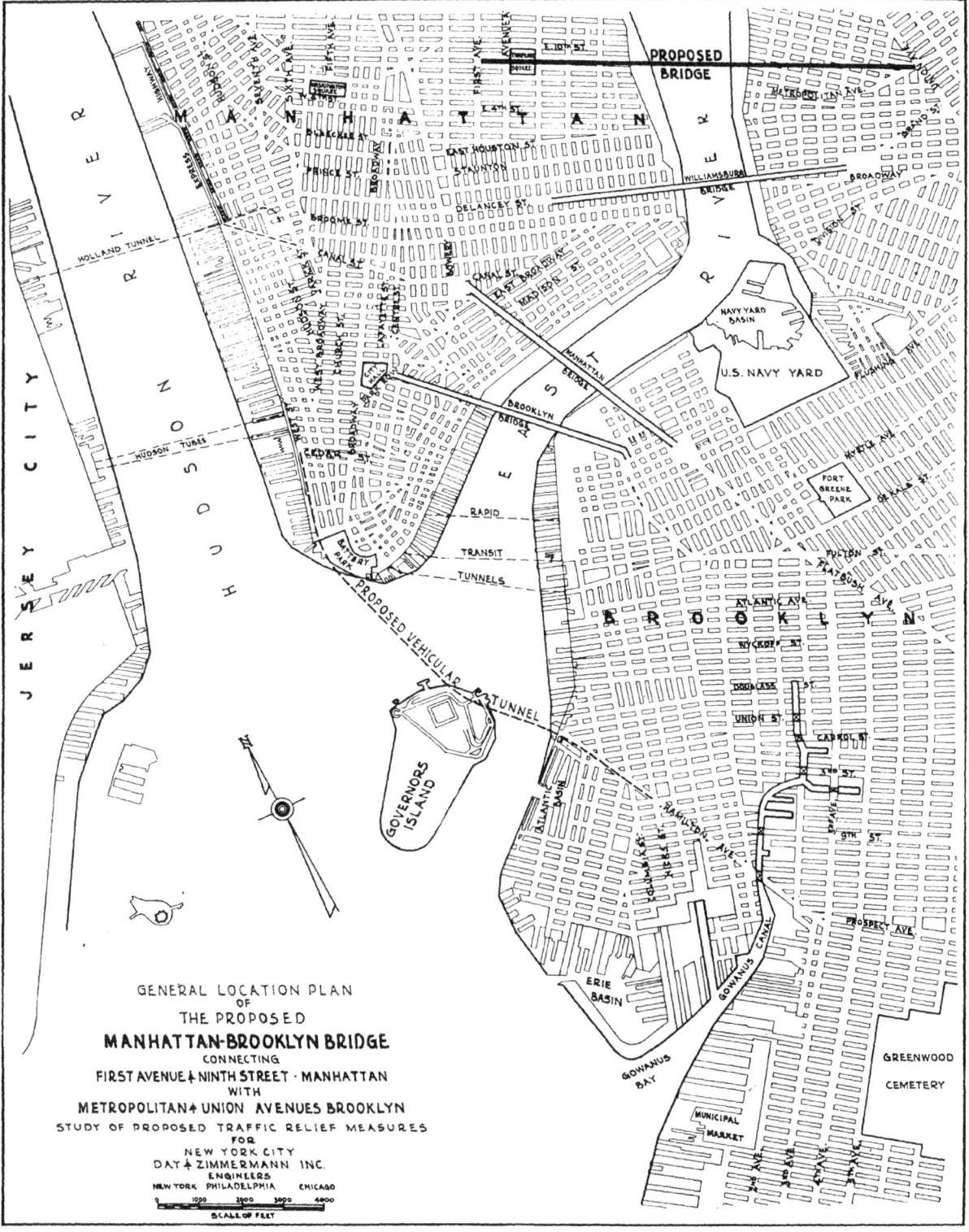

in South Brooklyn and the west side of Manhattan and New Jersey. These factors would tend to increase both the tunnel traffic and the relief afforded.

Cost of the Project.

As previously set forth, the project has not been advanced to a point where the results of investigation and preliminary studies would be available as an aid in estimating its probable cost. Our review of the costs of projects of a similar nature indicate that a vehicular tunnel in the general location and of the general features described would cost in the neighborhood of $55,000,000, exclusive of interest, engineering, administration and similar costs during construction. Allowing 20 per cent. to cover such overhead costs would bring the total cost of the project to practically $66,000,000.

The annual cost, based on an allowance of 6 per cent. for fixed charges, and on operating expenses estimated at $1,700,000, would total $5,660,000 per year. This is substantially the amount of revenue which would have to be collected each year in order to make the project self-supporting and on the basis of an average toll of 50 cents per vehicle, the volume of traffic required to yield this amount would be some 11,300,000 vehicles per year.

Tolls and Traffic.

A measure of the volume of traffic which could advantageously use the proposed tunnel has been developed above on the basis of 1928 traffic counts, without allowance for growth during the period of construction or subsequently. Considering the general characteristics of this traffic, it would total substantially 10,000,000 vehicles per year, or within practically 10 per cent. of the volume required to make the project self-supporting on an assumed average charge of 50 cents per vehicle.

Conclusion.

In our opinion the project under consideration constitutes an outstanding relief measure which would afford extensive relief of the burdensome traffic conditions now existing in the important business sections of Lower Manhattan and Brooklyn and on the three lower East River bridges and their approaches, and from the standpoints of both convenience and necessity its construction is warranted.

There is no definite method for determining the number of vehicles which would use the proposed tunnel on a toll basis, although there is an existing volume of traffic which would be better served from the standpoints of time and convenience and which is within 10 per cent. of the volume required to make the project self-supporting on the basis of an average charge of 50 cents per vehicle.

THE PROPOSED BROOKLYN-MANHATTAN BRIDGE CONNECTING 1ST AVENUE AND 9TH STREET, MANHATTAN, WITH METROPOLITAN AND UNION AVENUES, BROOKLYN (10TH STREET BRIDGE).

A new bridge across the East River located about one-half mile north of the Williamsburg Bridge is one of the major measures proposed for the relief of traffic conditions on the East River bridges, particularly the Williamsburg, Manhattan and Brooklyn Bridges, and in the areas which they connect.

In a report under date of December 28, 1922, the Department of Plant and Structures submitted preliminary plans and estimates for such a bridge, definitely fixing its type and location, and recommended approval of the project and appropriations for borings and the preparation of detail plans. The project failed of approval at that time.

In its recommendation of traffic relief measures made public early in 1929, and in the hearings held by the Board of Estimate prior to the approval of the 38th Street-East River Vehicular Tunnel, the Brooklyn Chamber of Commerce urged the construction of a bridge in practically the same location as proposed by the Department of Plant and Structures.

The general public discussion of this and similar projects developed suggestions for the provision of a vehicular tunnel in the same general location, rather than a bridge.

Description of the Project.

The plans of the Department of Plant and Structures show a bridge extending from 1st avenue between 8th and 9th streets, Manhattan, to a plaza at the intersection of Metropolitan and Union avenues in Brooklyn, with a branch approach towards the intersection of Manhattan and Nassau avenues in the Greenpoint section of Brooklyn. The general location proposed, and its relation to the existing bridges and street systems is shown on the map opposite this page.

The preliminary plans call for a suspension bridge with a main span about 1,800 feet long, and with a cross section providing a total roadway width of 118 feet for vehicular traffic, divided into four roadways, as well as space for transit lines. We are advised that under present day conditions the Department of Plant and Structures would recommend a cross section similar to that planned for the Triborough Bridge, which provides two four-lane roadways for vehicular purposes totalling 72 feet in width, with no provision for transit lines.

Extensive changes proposed in the street plans in order to provide adequate terminals include a new street, 206 feet in width, extending from 1st to 4th avenues in Manhattan, a new diagonal street 120 feet in width extending from the Brooklyn plaza to Bushwick avenue, and the extension of Meeker avenue from its present terminal at Manhattan avenue to the bridge plaza.

On both sides of the East River the bridge approaches would extend inland about three-quarters of a mile, although traversing areas of relatively low land values and building development. The Manhattan terminal would be about one-half mile to the north of the Williamsburg Bridge and about one mile south of the nearest portal of the 38th Street-East River Vehicular Tunnel. Bridge traffic would be superimposed upon the street traffic as far west as 1st avenue, with 14th street the nearest wide crosstown street extending from river to river. On the Brooklyn side the terminals are advantageously located for the service of bridge traffic attributable to the Greenpoint and Williamsburg sections of Brooklyn. Metropolitan avenue, together with the proposed new diagonal streets, would afford convenient routes for traffic moving between the bridge and outlying points in Queens and Brooklyn.

The Brooklyn Chamber of Commerce proposed a bridge extending from the vicinity of 1st avenue and 10th street, Manhattan, to a point just north of Metropolitan avenue in Brooklyn, with a total roadway width for 16 lanes of traffic and with branch approaches at each end of the bridge to afford a wider distribution of the traffic. This location, as far as its effect upon traffic flows is concerned, may be considered identical with that proposed by the Department of Plant and Structures.

The suggestions for the construction of a vehicular connection in the same general location by tunnel rather than by a bridge were very general in their nature and as far as we are advised, no specific studies have been made or plans prepared for such a project.

The advantages urged in favor of a tunnel included the lesser volume of traffic to be absorbed by the adjoining street systems, the lesser encroachment of approach structures upon the streets, and the reduction in the amount of property removed from private ownership for plazas and approaches, as well as the possibilities of extension across Manhattan in order to reduce crosstown surface traffic and afford more or less direct connection with existing or proposed tunnels under the Hudson River.

Such general knowledge of conditions affecting construction as is available indicates that it is feasible to construct a vehicular tunnel across the East River in this location. Due to the net work of rapid transit tunnels, particularly on the west side of Manhattan, detailed studies would be required to determine the feasibility of its extension across the island in the line of 9th or 10th streets. The conditions for such an extension appear much more favorable in the vicinity of 18th street, and as developed more fully later, such a location for the Manhattan end of the crossing would be more advantageous from the viewpoint of traffic relief. Although the East River widens appreciably above 10th street, the widths would not be so great as to preclude a diagonal crossing in order to reach a favorable terminal area on the Brooklyn side, as for example, that lying to the southwest of McCarren Park.

The Present Situation.

The distance between the Queensboro Bridge and the Williamsburg Bridge, the nearest of the three lower bridges, is about three miles. In lower Manhattan, the three bridge terminals all fall within a mile at point located from one-third to one-half of the way across the island, imposing their traffic upon the irregular and heavily used street system with resultant conflict of flows and congestion.

On the Brooklyn side, the terminal of the Williamsburg Bridge is about one and one-half miles to the northeast of the Manhattan and Brooklyn Bridge plazas, which are within about one-quarter mile of one another, and so located that all traffic reaching them must travel through areas where the traffic flows and congestion are quite comparable with those of lower Manhattan and which extend at least as far east as the intersection of 4th, Flatbush and Atlantic avenues. Traffic from the southern sections of Brooklyn endeavoring to move over bridges farther north causes and experiences conflict in moving through these areas.

Vehicular traffic over the three lower bridges is characterized by its division into two main streams. The first stream moves between points in southern Brooklyn and along its waterfront and points in Manhattan below 47th street, using chiefly the Manhattan and Brooklyn Bridges and passing through the approach areas on both sides of the river. The second stream moves between points in the northern sections of Brooklyn and points in lower Manhattan, using chiefly the Williamsburg Bridge, and is more local in its nature.

The concentration of vehicular traffic on the three lower East River bridges resulting from their location relative to the districts between which the traffic moves is responsible for much of the congestion in the streets of lower Manhattan and of the bridge approach areas in Brooklyn.

The counts of weekday bridge traffic made in October, 1928, and our origin, destination and routing studies made this year indicate the following:

The traffic on the Williamsburg, Manhattan and Brooklyn Bridges was, in round figures, 41,000, 60,000 and 22,000 vehicles per day, respectively.

Dealing with the combined traffic over the three bridges, about 54 per cent. of the total moves between the bridges and points in Manhattan south of 14th street, about 32 per cent. to points between 14th and 47th streets, and about 14 per cent. to points north of 47th street. Approximately one-half of the total traffic moves to or from districts on the west side. On the Brooklyn side about 95 per cent. of the traffic is attributable to districts lying south of Newtown Creek.

Traffic using the three lower bridges represents approximately 30 per cent. of the combined traffic on all the avenues at 14th street and about 7 per cent. of that at 51st street.

About 90 per cent. of the traffic on the Manhattan Bridge is attributable to Brooklyn areas lying to the east and to the south of the bridge, and in general quite distinct from those to which the Williamsburg Bridge traffic is attributable. On the Manhattan side, about 85 per cent. of the total traffic is quite uniformly distributed between eastside and westside districts lying to the south of 47th street.

On the Brooklyn side, about 53 per cent. of the Williamsburg Bridge traffic moves to or from points in the districts directly adjoining and to the east and north of the bridge, only small portions coming from districts north of Newtown Creek or from the southern sections of Brooklyn. The distribution on the Manhattan side shows a similar concentration, about 57 per cent. of the total traffic moving between the bridge and points south of 14th street, and about 30 per cent. to points between 14th and 47th streets.

About 80 per cent. of the Brooklyn Bridge traffic moves to or from Brooklyn districts to the south and east of the bridge, with an even greater concentration on the Manhattan side, where about two-thirds of the total traffic is attributable to the sections below Canal street.

The conditions outlined above clearly indicate the need of avoiding further concentration of interborough traffic in these areas and of seeking relief from present conditions and providing for the greater requirements of the future by additional bridges or tunnels across the East River. Further, the capacity of such connections should be limited to the traffic volumes which the adjoining street systems can readily absorb, and the locations should provide new routes enabling considerable portions of the traffic now using existing facilities to reduce the distances traveled on Manhattan streets and to move around instead of through congested areas, and with sufficient directness to result in an appreciable saving of time.

Relief Afforded.

Consideration of the present traffic flows as developed by our origin and destination studies and application of the results to the 1928 counts, indicates that in general the interborough traffic which would be offered more advantageous routing by the proposed connection, in conjunction with the north-south highway through Brooklyn and Queens, would be included in the following movements over the existing bridges to or from points in Manhattan below 47th street and in New Jersey:

(a) A flow of about 10,000 vehicles per day between points in Manhattan below Canal street and in New Jersey and points in Queens above Newtown Creek and in Brooklyn lying between the East River, Newtown Creek and Flushing avenue.

(b) A flow of about 9,000 vehicles per day between the district in Manhattan bounded by Canal and 14th streets and the Queens and Brooklyn districts stated in the preceding paragraph.

(c) A flow of about 40,000 vehicles per day between districts in Brooklyn and Queens lying to the south of Newtown Creek and Manhattan districts between 14th and 47th streets.

Superior Routing.

(a) *Traffic to or from Points South of Canal Street.*

About 35 per cent. of this traffic now uses the Queensboro Bridge, traveling long distances on Manhattan avenues between 59th street and points south of Canal street and of necessity passing through and adding to the midtown congestion. The use of the proposed bridge and north-south highway through Brooklyn and Queens would enable this traffic to avoid the crowded Queensboro Bridge and approach areas and to materially shorten the distances travelled on Manhattan streets, thereby affording a quicker and more convenient route.

The remainder of the traffic now moves over the three lower bridges, chiefly via the Williamsburg Bridge, and is subject to the delays imposed by the existing conditions along such routes. The portion of the traffic attributable to the Brooklyn area between the proposed bridge and Newtown Creek and moving to the west side of Manhattan or New Jersey approximates 1,500 vehicles per day. The proposed bridge would afford this traffic a route more direct and more favorable for crosstown movements than the routes offered by the existing facilities.

On the foregoing basis, about one-half of this traffic flow, or some 5,000 vehicles per day would be afforded more advantageous routing by the proposed facilities.

(b) *Traffic to or from Points Between Canal and 14th Streets.*

About 4,000 vehicles per day move between points in Queens lying north of Newtown Creek and points in Manhattan between Canal and 14th streets. Approximately two-thirds of this traffic uses the Queensboro Bridge, the remainder in most part using the Williamsburg Bridge. The use of the facilities under consideration would afford all of this traffic more direct routes and by enabling it to avoid the congestion on and in the vicinity of the existing bridges would afford it more favorable entry and exit. The portion now using the Queensboro Bridge would in addition be benefited by not having to move through mid-Manhattan and by greatly reduced distances it would have to move on Manhattan avenues.

Of the 5,000 vehicles per day moving to or from the section of Brooklyn, lying between the East River, Newtown Creek and Flushing avenue, about 93 per cent. now use the Williamsburg Bridge. The portion of this traffic attributable to the area north of the proposed bridge, approximately 2,500 vehicles per day, would be afforded the same general advantages of more favorable entry by the proposed facilities and in addition a shorter total journey between points of origin and destination.

The considerations set forth indicate that in this group about 7,000 vehicles per day would be afforded more advantageous routing as to time and convenience by the use of the proposed facilities.

(c) *Traffic to or from Points Between 14th and 47th Streets.*

The traffic to or from the section of Brooklyn surrounding the Brooklyn and Manhattan Bridge plazas, totals about 5,500 vehicles per day, 94 per cent. of which move over these two bridges. The directness of access and routing afforded by the existing bridges, and the location of the proposed north-south highway at the eastern end of the district, indicate that the use of the proposed bridge would not offer superior routing for any appreciable portion of this traffic.

There are about 3,800 vehicles per day moving to or from the section of Brooklyn lying between the East River, Newtown Creek and Flushing avenue, of which number about 11 per cent. now use the Queensboro Bridge and 84 per cent. the Williamsburg Bridge. The routes made available by the proposed bridge would advantage all of this traffic by shortening the distances now moved on Manhattan avenues, by furnishing more favorable conditions of entry and exit, and for most of it by shortening the total length of journey.

The district lying to the east of the one referred to in the preceding paragraph and between Chauncey street, Flushing and Atlantic avenues, accounts for about 3,000 vehicles per day, of which number 71 per cent. use the Williamsburg Bridge and 20 per cent. the Manhattan Bridge. The use of the proposed bridge and the north-south highway would enable this traffic to avoid the congestion existing on the bridges now used and in the downtown sections of Brooklyn and Manhattan, to shorten the distances moved on Manhattan avenues and for most of it to decrease the total length of journey.

About 4,000 vehicles per day move to or from outlying areas in Brooklyn and Queens to the south of a line through Newtown Creek and to the east of Chauncey street. Of these, approximately two-thirds use the Queensboro Bridge and most of the remainder the Williamsburg Bridge. The routes made available by the proposed facilities would not appear to offer any material advantages to the traffic now using the Queensboro Bridge, but would afford the advantages of shortened travel on Manhattan avenues and more favorable conditions of entry and exit to the traffic now using the lower bridges, or to about 1,400 vehicles per day.

The sections of Brooklyn lying generally to the south and east of Atlantic avenue and between the waterfronts and a line through Fresh Creek Basin, account for about 24,400 vehicles per day, of which approximately 81 per cent. now use the Manhattan Bridge and about equal portions of the remainder the Brooklyn and the Williamsburg Bridges. The larger portion of the Brooklyn Bridge traffic is attributable to the areas between 9th avenue and the Upper Bay, and of the Williamsburg Bridge traffic to the sections to the north and east of Flatbush avenue.

The concentration of traffic from this vast area upon the Manhattan Bridge is a natural result of the convergence of the main highways upon a small area in the vicinity of the intersections of 4th, Flatbush and Atlantic avenues, and the direct route from there to the bridge afforded by Flatbush avenue. The route of the proposed north-south highway passes a short distance to the east of the same intersection and would, therefore, offer opportunity for intercepting large portions of the traffic under discussion.

The traffic moving to or from the waterfront sections to the west of the Gowanus Canal, would find little advantage in the use of the proposed facilities, as the more direct access and routing would be afforded by the existing facilities. With respect to the remainder of the traffic, some 23,000 vehicles per day, comparison of the routes which would be made available with those now used by this traffic indicates that the advantages offered by the new routes are not as great or as sharply defined as was the case in connection with the other East River crossings under consideration, creating a doubt as to which one of several available routes would be the most attractive from the standpoints of time and convenience.

The routes now used by the bulk of this traffic, although quite direct, involve passage through the downtown sections of Brooklyn and Manhattan, use of the crowded Manhattan Bridge, and use of Manhattan avenues between Canal street and about 33d street. The new routes, while somewhat longer, would have the advantages of movement over a special highway with relative freedom from delays due to intersecting traffic streams, and over a bridge in a location such as to approximately cut in half the distance traveled on Manhattan avenues. Under existing conditions, the outstanding advantages would be the movement around, instead of through, the congested areas enumerated.

The considerations set forth indicate that on the basis stated, about 31,000 vehicles per day in this group would be afforded more advantageous routing by the use of the proposed facilities.

Summarizing the indications set forth in the preceding paragraphs, the use of the proposed bridge and the north-south highway would appear to afford relief by superior routing to approximately 43,000 vehicles per day, but with respect to about one-half of this traffic there is an important qualification.

It is evident that if the present traffic flows over the three lower bridges could be reduced by approximately one-third, there would be such a marked improvement in traffic conditions on these bridges and in their approach areas as to place the routes presently used by some 23,000 vehicles per day more nearly on a parity with those which would be afforded by the proposed bridge, and which under present conditions were considered superior. The result would be to reduce materially the value of traffic advantaged by use of the proposed bridge.

Relief Afforded to Streets and Bridges.

Assuming that all of the traffic enumerated, totalling some 43,000 vehicles per day, would use the proposed bridge instead of the existing East River bridges, the nature and extent of the relief afforded is shown diagrammatically on page 92.

The diagram on the left shows the present routing of the traffic considered as potential for the proposed bridge, on the assumption that it would follow the most convenient route based on time and/or distance. The heavy black lines together with the figures indicate the daily volume of traffic now using the existing facilities and the volumes moving to or from various districts.

The diagram on the right shows the assumed future routing of the same traffic and the relief which would be afforded by its diversion from the existing bridges, their approach areas, and the streets of lower Manhattan.

The most striking relief effect is the removal of traffic approximating 36,000 vehicles per day from the three lower bridges and the downtown sections of Brooklyn and Manhattan. The Manhattan Bridge would be relieved of about 19,000 and the Williams-

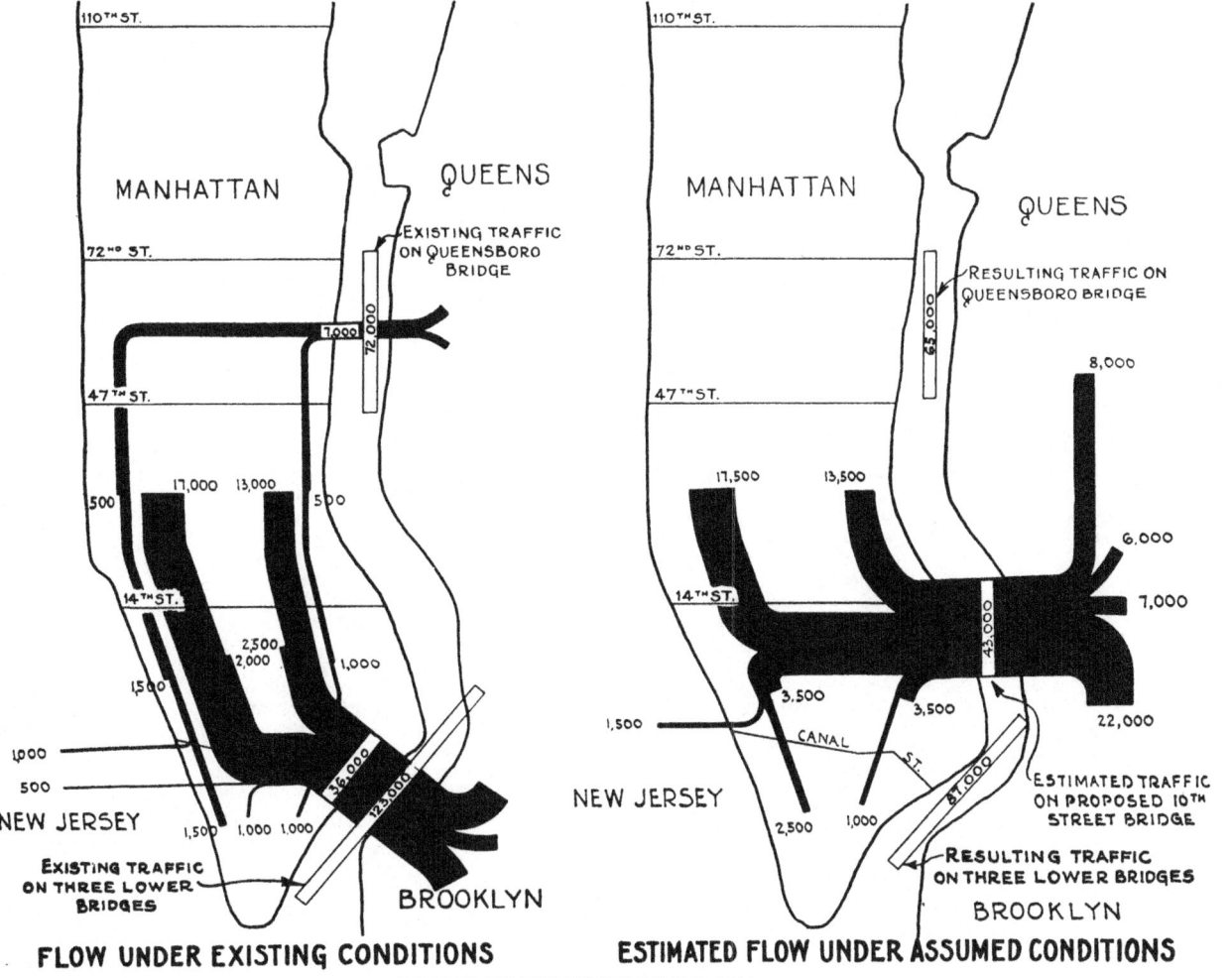

burg Bridge of about 16,000 vehicles per day. These figures are 32 per cent. and 39 per cent., respectively, of their present traffic burdens.

About three-quarters of this traffic moves to or from points between 14th and 47th streets, and the assumed diversion would practically cut in half the distances it now moves on Manhattan avenues, thereby affording substantial relief of this nature. A location somewhat farther north would increase the relief afforded this portion of the traffic and to the streets of Manhattan, although decreasing the relief afforded the smaller portion moving to points south of 14th street.

The diversion of about 7,000 vehicles per day, or 10 per cent. of its present traffic from the Queensboro Bridge to the proposed facility would afford substantial traffic relief in its approach areas and on the avenues of Manhattan, particularly in the midtown section.

On the other hand, the diagram also shows that about two-thirds of the assumed bridge traffic is attributable to districts on the west side of Manhattan, and as it would have to continue to move over crosstown streets on its way to or from the bridge, there would be no relief due to reduction in the volume of crosstown surface movements or in its interference with north and southbound traffic at street intersections.

Effect of Other Proposed Relief Measures.

The foregoing statements of the extent of relief afforded are subject to an indeterminate reduction due to the improvement which the assumed diversions would make in present traffic conditions along existing routes. Further, they are based upon the assumption that only the existing facilities, the proposed bridge, and the proposed north-south highway would be available, and make no allowances for the effect of other proposed traffic relief measures upon the situation.

Similar analyses of the distribution of present interborough traffic result in an assumed diversion from the three lower bridges and the downtown areas of Brooklyn and Manhattan of 8,000 vehicles per day to the Triborough Bridge, 17,000 to the 38th Street-East River Vehicular Tunnel and 29,000 to the proposed West Street-Hamilton Avenue Vehicular Tunnel, a total diversion of 54,000 vehicles per day or about 45 per cent. of the 1928 traffic on these bridges.

Included in the assumed diversion of 43,000 vehicles per day to the proposed bridge in the vicinity of 9th street is traffic moving between Manhattan points lying west of Broadway between 14th and 47th streets and Brooklyn points lying roughly south of the line of Atlantic avenue and beyond the bridgehead areas, and amounting to about 12,000 vehicles per day. Both the present routing and that here proposed involve surface movements across Manhattan, resulting in delay and inconvenience to the traffic in question and to the north and south bound traffic movements with which it conflicts at street intersections.

Comparison of the routes made available by the proposed bridge and by the proposed West Street-Hamilton Avenue Vehicular Tunnel shows that the latter offers greater and more definite advantages to the traffic in question. The outstanding advantages are the directness of the routes and the greater convenience resulting from direct communication with the west side of Manhattan. The use of the vehicular tunnel instead of the proposed bridge by this traffic would afford equal relief to the three lower bridges and to the downtown sections of Brooklyn and Manhattan, and in addition would reduce greatly the traffic on crosstown streets in lower Manhattan.

There is also included in the assumed diversion of 43,000 vehicles per day, traffic moving between points on the west side of Manhattan below 47th street and in New Jersey and points in Queens and in the northern sections of Brooklyn, amounting to about 11,000 vehicles per day. Both the present routing and that via the proposed bridge involve surface movements across Manhattan.

The routes made available to this traffic by the 38th Street-East River Vehicular Tunnel would be superior from the standpoints of time and convenience to those afforded by the proposed bridge. The tunnel routes would be in general more direct, travel through congested areas would be shorter, and above all crosstown movements would be under ground rather than on the surface. The portion of the traffic moving to or from points well to the south of 34th street would be further advantaged by the use of the West Side Express Highway now under construction.

If this traffic used the 38th Street Tunnel rather than the proposed bridge, the relief to the existing bridges and their approach areas and to the midtown section would be just as great. In addition there would be the relief due to the reduction in crosstown surface movements and in the conflict with north and south bound traffic at street intersections.

Assuming that the 38th Street-East River Tunnel, the West Street-Hamilton Avenue Vehicular Tunnel and the proposed bridge were all made available, and disregarding the indeterminate reduction referred to above, the traffic considered potential for the proposed bridge would be reduced from 43,000 to 20,000 vehicles per day, with corresponding reduction in the relief afforded by it to existing streets and bridges. Three-quarters of the remaining traffic is attributable to the section of Manhattan between 14th and 47th streets. On this basis, the total assumed diversion from the three lower bridges would be 71,000 vehicles per day, or about 58 per cent. of the 1928 traffic, of which number 17,000 would be attributable to the proposed bridge.

The estimates given above are based on 1928 traffic counts, no allowance being made for any growth in traffic during or subsequent to the period of construction.

Capacity and Type of Structure.

For the purposes of this discussion, the capacity of a bridge or tunnel may be considered as proportional to the number of traffic lanes provided by its roadways. The Queensboro and Manhattan Bridges have six lanes each, the Williamsburg Bridge has four lanes and the Holland Tunnel has four lanes. The combined traffic over the three bridges mentioned was 173,000 vehicles per day in October, 1928.

The suggestions under consideration include a 16-lane bridge, an 8-lane bridge and a 4-lane vehicular tunnel. The provision of a 16-lane bridge would concentrate in one crossing a potential capacity equal to that of the Queensboro, Williamsburg and Manhattan Bridges, and four times that of the Holland Tunnel. The difficulty of absorbing potential traffic flows of such magnitudes in restricted sections of the City is evident, and even with special approach structures and extensive additions to the adjoining street systems, there would be created conditions in its terminal areas similar to those now encountered at the existing bridges and from which relief is being sought. We believe a 16-lane bridge in this situation would tend to defeat its purpose and would not be an appropriate traffic relief measure.

An 8-lane bridge, which would have a capacity about one and one-third times that of the Manhattan Bridge, would also necessitate special approach structures and extensive street additions in its terminal areas in order to enable a more favorable distribution and absorption of its traffic than is now afforded at the terminals of the existing bridges.

A 4-lane vehicular tunnel would have a capacity about one-half that of an 8-lane bridge and would present terminal problems of the same general nature and importance but of much lesser magnitude. Provision for adequate distribution and absorption of its traffic would involve far less encroachment upon existing streets and upon property now in private ownership and far less extensive additions to the street systems in its terminal areas.

Assuming a continued growth in traffic, the less the capacity of the crossing provided, the sooner will expenditures for additional crossings become necessary. Our analysis of the present interborough traffic flows and of the effect of the various bridges and tunnels proposed as traffic relief measures indicates a potential week day traffic for this crossing of about 20,000 vehicles per day. This flow is slightly less than one-half of the capacity of a 4-lane vehicular tunnel for mixed traffic and about one-eighth that of a 16-lane bridge. If this traffic should continue to grow at the rate at which East River bridge traffic has been growing during recent years, it would equal the capacity of the tunnel in about 15 years. A vehicular tunnel would appear to offer ample reserve capacity.

From the view point of traffic relief, a location somewhat to the north of that proposed for the bridge would be more advantageous, but due to the widening of the East River would add appreciably to the length of the main span of the bridge and proportionally more to its cost. For the distances here involved, tunnel costs would not be increased in as great a measure. A tunnel would offer more flexibility in the location of terminals, and the outstanding advantage of the possibility of affording additional relief by its later extension across Manhattan. These and other advantages afforded by vehicular tunnels such as lesser encroachment upon streets and private property, smaller possible concentrations of traffic, and less effect upon traffic conditions in terminal areas, in our judgment would outweigh considerations of the greater costs of construction and operation in the present situation, and indicate the desirability of having the results of thorough preliminary investigations and studies of the tunnel project made available for use in planning the future development of these sections of the City.

The Cost of the Project.

In its 1922 report, the Department of Plant and Structures estimates the cost of construction of the bridge and its approaches at $27,000,000, and states the assessed valuation of property required for the approaches to be $6,172,000, and for the extensive changes in the adjoining street systems to be $8,648,000. The bridge as then proposed includes provision for rapid transit and bus or trackless trolley lines, in addition to four roadways with space for practically 12 lanes of vehicular traffic.

Under present conditions, we are advised the Department would recommend an 8-lane structure in general similar to that proposed for the Triborough Bridge and without provision for transit purposes. Our review of the costs of projects of a similar nature indicates that the total cost of such a bridge in this location would be about $40,000,000, exclusive of the cost of major street extensions.

The co-ordination of the capacity of the adjoining street system with that of an 8-lane bridge in order to enable adequate distribution of the traffic would require either extensive street changes or special approach structures, or both, the cost of which might readily be in the vicinity of $10,000,000.

As previously stated, the project to construct a vehicular tunnel rather than a bridge has not advanced to the point where the results of detailed investigation and preliminary studies would be available as an aid in estimating its probable cost. Our review of the actual and estimated costs of similar projects indicates that a 4-lane vehicular tunnel crossing the East River in the general location described, planned to enable future extension across Manhattan, would cost approximately $55,000,000. Extension of the tunnel to suitable terminals and connections on the west side of Manhattan would cost about $35,000,000 additional, or a total cost approximating $90,000,000 for a combined river crossing and crosstown tunnel.

The annual cost for the bridge project, based on an allowance of 6 per cent. for fixed charges and on operating expenses estimated at $400,000 per year, would be $2,800,000 per year.

The annual cost for the tunnel project, exclusive of the extension across Manhattan, based on the same allowance for fixed charges and on operating expenses estimated at $1,600,000, would be $4,900,000 per year.

These are substantially the amounts of revenue which would have to be collected each year in order to make the projects self-supporting. On the basis of an average toll of 50 cents per vehicle, the volume of traffic required to yield these amounts would be some 5,600,000 vehicles per year for the bridge and 9,800,000 vehicles per year for the tunnel. On the basis of an average toll of 25 cents per vehicle, the respective yearly traffic volumes would be some 11,200,000 and 19,600,000 vehicles.

Conclusions.

The provision of a vehicular connection across the East River in the general location proposed would be desirable from the point of view of convenience. The measure of the relief to be afforded, assuming the construction of the Triborough Bridge, the 38th Street-East River Tunnel, the north-south highway, and the Battery Tunnel, would not in our judgment be sufficient to make the project self-supporting on any reasonable toll basis. Moreover, the general improvement in traffic conditions expected from the creation of the new facilities enumerated above will so materially affect the situation with respect to this project, that, in our judgment, its construction should be deferred until the results of actual experience are available.

The construction of the facility will undoubtedly be warranted at some time in the future, in which event the question of the use of a tunnel rather than a bridge should be given serious consideration, as in our judgment a tunnel at this particular location would have certain marked advantages as hereinbefore set forth.

THE PROPOSED NORTH-SOUTH HIGHWAY THROUGH BROOKLYN AND QUEENS.

There has been general recognition of the desirability of additional highway facilities in the western sections of Brooklyn and Queens to enable a freer movement of traffic in a direction roughly paralleling the East River.

The additional traffic relief possibilities of such a highway in diverting traffic from the crowded avenues of Manhattan to the Long Island side of the East River, where provision can be more readily made for its accommodation, have been developed in our presentation of the various bridge and tunnel projects under consideration.

The matter has been the subject of much study by the City and Borough officials, the Queens Planning Commission, the Chambers of Commerce of Brooklyn and of Queens, and others interested, and various solutions have been proposed.

There is general unanimity of opinion concerning the need of such a highway, with some differences of opinion as to its specific location, the type of highway

GENERAL VIEW OF NAVY YARD SECTION IN BROOKLYN

required and the extent to which right-of-way should be obtained by the widening of existing streets or by the cutting through of new and more direct routes.

Effect of Street Plans upon Traffic Flows.

The barrier imposed by the East River upon vehicular communication with Manhattan has had a marked influence upon the development of Brooklyn and Queens and of their street and highway systems. The most noticeable result is the convergence of main highways leading from the more remote sections upon rather small areas back of the terminals of the Queensboro and of the Williamsburg, Manhattan and Brooklyn Bridges. Another result is the large number of different "checkerboard" street systems which have been developed along or between the radiating main highways. This is particularly true of the sections nearer the East River, the areas of uniformity becoming much greater in the outlying sections. There is also a marked absence of direct or continuous through highways traversing these Boroughs in a north and south direction near to and in general parallel to the East River.

These conditions and the limited number of crossings over natural barriers such as Newtown Creek and over artificial barriers such as the Sunnyside yards of the Long Island Railroad greatly restrict the free flow of traffic between and in the important industrial and shipping sections of Brooklyn and Queens, as well as that of traffic moving across the East River bridges to or from Manhattan.

The heavy concentrations of East River bridge traffic in the area immediately back of the Queensboro Bridge, and for example in the vicinity of the intersection of 4th, Atlantic and Flatbush avenues, result in densities of flow substantially equal to those found in the most congested sections of Manhattan and create further barriers to free north and south bound movements.

The street plan of Manhattan, with the exception of the downtown area, is laid out on a uniform checkerboard system. Its avenues run roughly parallel to the East River and by their width and number facilitate movement in a north and south direction. Near its southern end, the closely spaced Williamsburg, Manhattan and Brooklyn Bridges afford connection with the street system of Brooklyn and connection with that of Queens is afforded by the Queensboro Bridge at 59th street.

Interborough Traffic Flows and Effects.

Much of the congestion in the streets of Manhattan is due to the limited number of bridges, their location and the heavy flows of interborough traffic, which add to and conflict with the more local traffic flows as they move over the crosstown streets and along the avenues of Manhattan. An indication of the relative proportions of these traffic flows and of the distances traveled in a north and south direction through congested areas is afforded by the following figures, based on 1928 counts of week-day street and bridge traffic and on the results of origin, destination and routing studies made this year:

Traffic on the Queensboro Bridge totals 72,000 vehicles per day, about 70 per cent. of which move during the 12-hour period 7 a. m. to 7 p. m. Approximately 21 per cent. of this traffic moves to or from points lying north of 110th street and about 10 per cent. to points south of 14th street.

The combined traffic on the three lower bridges totals 123,000 vehicles per day, about 32 per cent. of which move to or from points lying between 14th and 47th streets and 14 per cent. to points north of 47th street.

The combined north bound and south bound flow on all avenues at about 51st street is about 211,000 vehicles during the period 7 a. m. to 7 p. m., and approximately 17 per cent. of this traffic moves over the East River bridges.

On the Long Island side of the East River, the bulk of the traffic using the Queensboro Bridge moves to or from points in Queens, only a minor portion being attributable to Brooklyn areas. The bridge head area and the Flushing districts account for 59 per cent. of the total. About 95 per cent. of the traffic over the three lower bridges moves to or from districts in Brooklyn and Queens lying to the south of a line through Newtown Creek, with the greatest concentration in the districts along the bay and river fronts and in the vicinity of, and to the south of, Prospect Park.

Nature of Relief Needed and Afforded.

Consideration of the origin, destination and routing of East River bridge traffic, briefly outlined above, develops clearly the controlling influence of the characteristics of the highway systems of Brooklyn and Queens upon the distribution of traffic between the Queensboro Bridge and the three lower bridges. Traffic now follows the converging main highways to the bridge most accessible from its point of origin on the Long Island

GENERAL VIEW IN QUEENS SHOWING NEWTOWN CREEK AND EAST RIVER

side, which bridge for much of the traffic is not the one affording the most direct entry to its Manhattan destination. A new or improved through highway enabling such traffic to move more freely in a north and south direction between the converging main highways, would afford the traffic a superior routing and by its diversion from, and the reduction in the distances traveled on Manhattan streets, afford relief where it is most needed and most difficult to obtain.

In its broader aspects, the street plan of Manhattan has been given a fixed status by the intensive building development, particularly in the areas where additional street capacity would be most helpful in relieving traffic congestion. Under existing conditions, the opening of new north and south avenues would involve a destruction of buildings and resulting costs of such magnitude as to demand that other relief measures be first sought for and tried out. The West Side Express Highway and the proposed marginal way along the East and Harlem Rivers are among the projects intended to provide additional street capacity in Manhattan for north and south movements of traffic. The project under consideration, in connection with the various existing and proposed bridges and tunnels across the East River, aims to provide for such movements on the Long Island side of the East River, where in general the development is less advanced, and property values much lower than in Manhattan.

The provision of additional bridges or tunnels across the East River will relieve conditions on the existing bridges and in their approach areas and due to the greater number of points of entry and exit, afford general relief to the street system of Manhattan. The full measure of the relief which such new facilities can afford will be obtained only if convenient and advantageous routes are provided between their terminals and the various districts of Brooklyn and Queens. In our presentation of these projects, we have based our conclusions as to the measure of relief which they would afford, upon the assumption that the proposed north-south highway would be available to furnish the necessary convenience of access.

Based on a combination of the various flows of traffic which were assumed to use such a highway in estimating the potential traffic on the proposed East River bridges and tunnels, the potential interborough traffic in sections of the highway between the limits stated is approximately as follows:

    Between Flatbush avenue and Broadway, 15,000 vehicles per day.
    Between Broadway and Borden avenue, 33,000 vehicles per day.
    Between Borden avenue and Queens boulevard, 20,000 vehicles per day.
    Between Queens boulevard and Astoria avenue, 12,000 vehicles per day.

If the estimated effect of the proposed bridge at 9th street upon the distribution of interborough traffic is taken into consideration, the traffic in the first section would be increased to 24,000, and in the portion of the second section lying between Broadway and Metropolitan avenue would be increased to about 48,000 vehicles per day. The estimates are based upon 1928 data, no allowance being made for growth during or subsequent to the period of construction. The flow stated for the section between Broadway and Borden avenue is substantially equivalent to the week day flows on 5th avenue at 42d street and along the western sections of the Queensboro boulevard.

In addition to the advantages afforded interborough traffic, it is evident, from a consideration of the character of the districts which would be connected and the characteristics of the existing street systems and traffic flows, that such a highway would offer large volumes of local traffic more convenient and quicker routes than are now available and in so doing afford material traffic relief in Brooklyn and Queens.

General Requirements of the Project.

In order to afford relief of the nature and extent desired, the proposed highway must offer to traffic using it, marked advantages in convenience and in time required for specific journeys, and to do so under the surrounding circumstances, the plans for the highway should be based upon meeting, as far as local conditions will permit, the following general requirements:

    The direction followed by the highway should be in general parallel to the East River and the avenues of Manhattan.

    The location of the highway should be somewhat to the east of the plazas of existing and proposed East River bridges and tunnels in order to enable connection with their main approaches beyond the areas of greatest traffic concentration and also to enable traffic to move between the highway and the plazas without reversals in its general direction of flow.

    The highway should intersect the line of the principal highways connecting outlying points in Brooklyn and Queens with the bridge and tunnel plazas in order that it may function as a "header" for the collection and distribution of interborough traffic. At or in the immediate vicinity of these intersections, provision should be made for easy interchange of traffic.

Subordinate to the requirements set forth above, the location should be as near the river front as possible in order to make the highway of greatest service to the important traffic flows attributable to the shipping and industrial areas in this section of the City.

The route of the highway should be as direct as the surrounding circumstances and a reasonably economical development will permit. The disadvantages of long diagonal intersections should be recognized and considerations of traffic flow as well as cost indicate the desirability of utilizing as far as practicable sections of existing streets, obtaining any additional right-of-way required by appropriate widenings.

The cross section of the highway should reflect its primary purpose by providing a separate roadway or roadways for the use of through traffic, with service roaddays on either side where needed for access to adjoining property or for the requirements of strictly local traffic. The main roadway widths should provide amply for the heavy traffic flows indicated as potential under present day conditions, with liberal allowance for future growth.

There should be a separation of grades where the proposed highway intersects the main highways leading to the plazas of existing or proposed East River bridges or tunnels, in order to enable traffic on the proposed highway to move with a minimum of interruption due to cross traffic and at high average speeds, and also by eliminating similar interference to facilitate the heavy flow of traffic to or from the East River crossings.

The planning of the highway and the design of the grade separations should recognize that the greater demands of the future may readily require added roadway capacity and more complete separation of grades, and the possibilities offered in these respects by a wide right-of-way and the future provision of an elevated highway similar in its characteristics to the West Side Express Highway now under construction in Manhattan.

Description of the Project.

Our presentation of this project is based upon our study of the various plans and suggestions placed before us by the representatives of the two boroughs, the Queens Planning Commission and the Chambers of Commerce of Brooklyn and of Queens, supplemented by the results of our field and office study of this and relative projects.

The various plans for the project are still rather general and preliminary in nature and for this reason we have elected to present a "suggested location" as a basis for discussion and as indicative of a route which in our judgment is in reasonable conformity with the general requirements set forth above. In doing so, it is fully recognized that sections of the route, or even considerable portions of it may be subject to change for reasons of cost or expediency developed as detailed studies and designs are completed by the various borough officials charged with this duty.

The map opposite this page shows the location suggested for the proposed highway and its relation to major existing and proposed streets, bridges and tunnels. Existing facilities are shown in black, proposed new facilities in red and proposed widenings, etc., in red and black.

At one end of the map is shown the proposed Narrows Tunnel connecting Brooklyn with Staten Island and through it with New Jersey. At the other end is shown the proposed Triborough Bridge connecting Queens with upper Manhattan and with The Bronx and main land routes to New York and New England. The sections of the main highways leading from outlying points in Brooklyn and Queens towards the East River crossings show clearly this tendency to converge upon the areas back of the existing bridges, and hence the possibilities of better distribution of interborough traffic offered by the proposed highway. The conflicting checkerboard arrangements of streets through large sections of the area traversed is clearly evidenced by the base map.

South Brooklyn Section.

The street plan of the section of Brooklyn between Fort Hamilton and Atlantic and Flatbush avenues is quite favorable to the predominant traffic flows, which move in a north and south direction and increase in density towards the north. 4th avenue, the prinicpal through highway, has a roadway width of 60 feet unencumbered by car tracks. It is flanked throughout its length by 3d and 5th avenues, somewhat narrower streets, each with a double line of car tracks, but affording considerable potential capacity for future support of 4th avenue.

Oversized Foldout

The reduction in the number of through streets in the area between Greenwood Cemetery and the waterfront creates a bottle neck which may require relief in the future. Although the building of the Narrows Tunnel and the proposed West Street-Hamilton Avenue Tunnel may, by stimulating development in South Brooklyn, change the situation, there does not appear to be any need for fundamental additions to the street system under consideration for some time to come.

Mid-Brooklyn Section.

The most unfavorable conditions for the free movement of traffic in a north and south direction, and probably the worst traffic congestion in Brooklyn, are found in the general vicinity of the intersection of 4th avenue with Atlantic and Flatbush avenues. The long diagonal crossings, the indirect routes resulting from the conflicting street plans, street railway loops in Times plaza, and the heavy traffic flows on the converging main highways are the outstanding factors adverse to such movements. Separation of the conflicting traffic streams, either by diversion or by grade separation, is the only remedy commensurate with the importance and acuteness of this situation.

The tentative plans of the Brooklyn Borough officials show a broad, new highway extending from the Grand Army Plaza along Vanderbilt and Clinton avenues, suitably widened, to Willoughby street. From this point on, a new diagonal highway cuts through to a point on Flushing avenue just east of the Naval Hospital, where it connects with a widening of Rutledge street extending to Union avenue.

The proposed route would enable traffic to avoid the congested areas referred to above. The circle around the Grand Army Plaza would offer more favorable conditions for carrying north-south traffic across the east-west traffic in Flatbush avenue, but would make no material change as far as that in Atlantic avenue is concerned. The plan would add another to the main highways now converging on the plaza and add correspondingly to the heavy traffic volumes now moving around it. While it offers an advantageous point for the diversion of north-south traffic coming from the east and southeast, the location would involve considerable detour for traffic naturally moving on 4th and adjoining avenues.

A second suggestion for the separation of the conflicting traffic flows involves the construction of a vehicular tunnel extending from portals in the vicinity of 4th avenue under Flatbush and Atlantic avenues and Fulton street to portals located in the general vicinity of Cumberland street and DeKalb avenue. Topographical conditions north of Fulton street, the rapid transit and railroad subways under Flatbush and Atlantic avenues and the proposed subway under Fulton street, and the necessity of locating much of the tunnel under private property are adverse factors. While such preliminary studies as we have made indicate that the conditions referred to can be overcome, it would require much detailed investigation and the preparation of preliminary plans to satisfactorily establish the practicability of the proposed construction and the costs involved.

From the viewpoint of traffic relief, the advantages of the tunnel as part of the proposed north-south highway would be largely restricted to traffic attributable to south Brooklyn areas as it would be very difficult and costly to establish advantageous connections with the tunnel for the use of traffic moving via Flatbush and Atlantic avenues. Without such connections, traffic between these main highways and the proposed north-south highway would have to move over surface streets towards the north, with resulting conflicts at main intersections.

The Brooklyn Chamber of Commerce proposed that a new diagonal street be cut through from 4th avenue and DeGraw street to 5th avenue and Park place, connecting at this point with a 60-foot wide viaduct passing over Flatbush and Atlantic avenues and, due to the elevated railway structure on Fulton street, brought to grade at a point in Cumberland street just south of Fulton street. From this point on, a new diagonal highway would be cut through to a point just east of the Naval Hospital.

In order to make the proposed viaduct fully effective for traffic moving to or from points to the east, suitable ramp connections would have to be provided for traffic moving west on Flatbush avenue and desiring to move to the north, and for traffic moving south on the proposed highway and desiring to move to the east on Atlantic avenue. The construction of such ramps and of the long crossings over the railroad yards and over several wide streets will offer certain difficulties, but as far as can be determined by a general study of the situation, the proposal offers a practical solution of the problem.

On the south side of Flatbush avenue, the ground slopes away to the west and better grades could be obtained if the approach structure were located more nearly parallel to 6th avenue as shown on the map, terminating in a plaza in the vicinity of Park place. It also appears to us that the widening of Park place and perhaps an adjoining street to form a header crossing 5th, 4th and 3d avenues would encourage and enable a better distribution of traffic than would a diagonal street leading only to 4th avenue. All things considered, a viaduct along the general lines set forth would seem to best meet the needs of the situation.

Considering the street plan and the traffic flows in the area traversed, we believe the proposed diagonal street leading towards the Naval Hospital would afford a superior route to one obtained by widening existing streets, as for example Lafayette and Classon avenues.

North Brooklyn Section.

The continuation of the highway northwards from the Naval Hospital as proposed by the Brooklyn Chamber of Commerce involves a new diagonal street extending to the intersection of Division and Keap streets, a widening of Keap street to its intersection with Union and Metropolitan avenues, and another new diagonal street connecting with Meeker avenue at its intersection with Manhattan avenue, just to the east of McCarren Park. This gives practically a direct route between the Naval Hospital and the Meeker Avenue Bridge over Newtown Creek but creates a large number of long diagonal intersections.

The tentative plans of the Brooklyn Borough officials show a route following the lines of Rutledge street, Union avenue, Bedford avenue and Oakland street to a point of connection with the Brooklyn terminal of the proposed 38th Street-East River Tunnel. All of these streets would require widening. For the connection through Queens to the Triborough Bridge, the plan proposes a branch from Union avenue along the line of Bayard street, Engert and Meeker avenues to Newtown Creek. All of these streets would require widening and the provision of a new bridge over Newtown Creek, for which plans have been authorized, would be essential to the project. This route is reasonably direct, is in harmony with the street plans and traffic flows in the area traversed, and appears to us to offer the more advantageous solution.

Queens Section.

For this section of the highway, the suggested route extends from the Meeker Avenue Bridge over Newtown Creek along the Laurel Hill boulevard to Borden avenue, thence along 43d street to the Northern boulevard and thence along 12th avenue to Astoria avenue, which in turn connects with the Triborough Bridge. All of these streets would require widening, the development in general being favorable to such a program. The use of 13th and 14th avenues, each about 30 feet between curbs, as tentatively suggested by the officials of Queens, would seem to be an inadequate provision for a highway of the type and importance of the one under consideration.

The northern end of the highway has been shown as ending at its junction with Astoria avenue. The most favorable connections with the Triborough Bridge can best be developed concurrently with the plans for the bridge terminal, and as set forth in our presentation of that project, we believe advantageous use can be made of streets on either side of Astoria avenue, such as Potter, Woolsey, Vandeventer and Grand avenues.

The relative location of the terminals of the Queensboro and Triborough Bridges, their main approach highways, and the Sunnyside Yards of the Long Island Railroad, is such as to force a location of this branch of the proposed highway as far east as shown, with the result that it would be of little use to north-south traffic in the area near the East River waterfront. For such traffic, Van Alst avenue and adjoining streets would afford ready connection with the Triborough Bridge on the north and with the main section of the north-south highway on the south.

Grade Separations.

The effectiveness of the proposed highway as a traffic relief measure will be largely dependent upon the extent to which its design will enable traffic to move over it freely, continuously and at high average speeds, and at the same time not interfere with intersecting traffic flows. To attain the desired result, the frequency and duration of interruptions caused by cross traffic or by traffic control lights must be minimized.

The route of the proposed highway intentionally intersects the heavily used main highways leading towards the East River crossings and also intersects many streets of intermediate or minor importance. Complete separation of grades would be ideal, and although hardly warranted by present requirements, should be recognized as a probable ultimate development. Separation of grades at intersections with the existing main highways is a present necessity if the proposed highway is to offer north-south traffic routes superior to those now available and if the flows of east-west traffic are to be facilitated rather than obstructed.

Certain of the intersecting highways, now relatively unimportant, will become principal traffic arteries in the future, as conditions are changed by the general growth in traffic and by the provisions of additional East River connections and other highway facilities. In such situations, the design of the highway, and as far as expedient, the acquisition of property, should reflect the probable need of future separation.

The separation of grades at Flatbush and Atlantic avenues will be taken care of by the proposed viaduct construction, which should be designed to facilitate its extension across Fulton street as soon as the proposed removal of the elevated railway structure from that street permits. We believe that provision should also be made for the separation of grades as part of the initial development of the highway at its intersections with Flushing avenue, Broadway, Metropolitan avenue, Bayard street and Manhattan avenue, in Brooklyn and with Borden and Roosevelt avenues, Queens boulevard, Skillman avenue, Northern boulevard and Astoria avenue, in Queens.

Type and Width of Roadway.

The arrangement and widths of the roadway space provided will also be important factors influencing the effectiveness of the proposed highway as a traffic relief measure. In general, the primary purpose of the highway will be best served if a separate roadway or roadways are provided for the use of through traffic, with service roadways on either side where needed for access to adjoining properties or for the requirements of strictly local traffic. The nature of the highway also emphasizes the importance of providing liberal widths for present requirements and for the greater demands of the future.

For the greater portion of the route suggested, the provision of an adequate cross section will require extensive widening of existing streets, and variations in development, lot depths, and street widths along different sections of the highway will naturally be reflected by variations in the additional right-of-way and highway cross section as detailed plans are developed.

A center roadway 60 feet wide, separated by 10-foot strips from service roadways between 25 and 30 feet wide, would require a right-of-way width totalling between 160 and 180 feet. Two 30-foot roadways for through traffic would be preferable to a single 60-foot roadway for this type of highway.

A more desirable arrangement in many respects would be the provision of two 40-foot roadways for through traffic and suitable service roadways where needed, for which a right-of-way width of from 200 to 210 feet would be required. Such a width would enable ample roadway capacity, afford a maximum flexibility in the matter of present and future grade separations. It would also enable a clearance between the building line and the structure of an elevated highway, if one should become necessary in the future, great enough to eliminate the most objectionable features ordinarily urged against such a structure.

Certain collateral advantages in the way of boulevard and park treatment of the highway could also be obtained, with the wider right-of-way. On the basis of the existing street widths and lot depths, it would be necessary in many instances to acquire one and one-half lots or three-quarters of a block in order to obtain a 210-foot right-of-way, and under such conditions it might prove desirable to acquire the entire block at slightly greater cost and obtain a right-of-way 320 feet wide. Traffic considerations alone could hardly justify such widths.

A right-of-way width of about 160 feet fits local conditions for the longer sections of the highway and is particularly adaptable for these locations where the block depth is 200 feet and the street width 60 feet. It would permit the separation of through from local traffic, would facilitate the separation of grades at important intersections, and permit the future construction of an elevated highway, six lanes wide, no portion of which would need to come closer than 50 feet to the abutting properties. Added widths, up to a total street width of about 185 feet, would be necessary wherever longitudinal ramps were needed to get on and off the structure.

The Cost of the Project.

The project involves the construction of approximately nine miles of special highway, of which about two miles is obtained by cutting through new streets and the remaining seven miles by widening existing streets. Such plans and estimates as are available are very tentative and preliminary. By far the largest element of cost is that incident to the acquisition of property, an item difficult of estimation and subject to much modification depending upon the route selected and the widths considered necessary.

The Brooklyn Chamber of Commerce estimated the cost of the section of the highway, as proposed by it, as approximately $30,000,000. This provided for a 60-foot roadway on viaduct and 80-foot roadways where the highway would be at grade. It did not provide for grade separations except in the viaduct section or for the branch connecting with the 38th Street-East River Tunnel. We have reviewed that estimate and some tentative figures for sections of the highway furnished us by the Borough officials of Brooklyn and of Queens in an effort to establish an approximate measure of the cost of the project.

On the basis of the suggested location shown on our map, with a right-of-way in general about 160 feet wide, providing space for 60 feet of roadway for through traffic as well as space for service roadways and sidewalks where needed, with grade separations at the important intersections enumerated, we estimate the cost of the project to be in the order of $70,000,000.

Conclusion.

An adequate north and south highway through Brooklyn and Queens near the East River is essential to the full development of the traffic relief possibilities of the major bridges and tunnels recently authorized or under consideration and in this respect would greatly benefit traffic conditions in all the Boroughs.

In addition it would provide an urgently needed route for the free movement of traffic in and between the important shipping and industrial sections extending along the Upper Bay and the East River from the lower section of Brooklyn towards the Astoria section of Queens.

In our opinion the project constitutes an essential and outstanding traffic relief measure, and from the standpoints of both convenience and necessity its immediate construction is warranted.

WEST SIDE MARGINAL HIGHWAY, MANHATTAN.

The West Side Marginal Highway project as here considered contemplates the creation of an arterial highway along the Hudson River from Canal street to the mouth of the Harlem Ship Canal at the northern extremity of Manhattan, including the construction of a bridge over the Harlem Ship Canal to connect with a continuation of the marginal highway into The Bronx, all as indicated on the map opposite this page.

Proposed Route.

The route of the proposed marginal way extends from Canal street on the south in a northerly direction along West street, 11th avenue, 12th avenue, 13th avenue to 59th street and from there over and along the tracks of the New York Central and Hudson River Railroad to the Harlem Ship Canal, with a connection to Riverside drive at 72d street. The total distance from Canal street to Harlem Ship Canal is approximately 12 miles.

Development of Project.

At the present time the section between Canal street and 22d street is under construction, and an agreement has been reached between the City and the railroad company relative to the location and construction of the highway where the railroad tracks are affected, which involves the section from about 60th street to the northern end of the project.

From a traffic standpoint the project has two aspects in that the section extending from Canal street to 72d street will afford a substantial local relief in the areas of the City mostly in need of same, and that the entire project will provide a through route for long haul traffic, which should induce a large volume to leave the central and highly congested avenues of the City.

Although the City is committed to the entire improvement, its execution is tied up with the relocation of the tracks of the New York Central and will undoubtedly extend over a considerable period.

Description of Facilities.

The project as now proposed calls for a 60-foot roadway with a division curb in the centre throughout the entire length. From Canal street to 72d street the roadway will be carried by an elevated structure over the existing highways and railroads. The elevated highway as proposed at present is to be a single deck structure designed for the future construction of a second deck, at which time the upper deck will be used for southbound traffic and the lower deck for northbound traffic. Between 62d and 72d streets the two roadways will be at the same level, one leading to the connection with Riverside drive and the other continuing to the north over the tracks of the railroad as heretofore described. Ramps for access to the elevated highway are to be provided at the Canal street end of the highway and in the vicinity of 22d, 40th and 57th streets and at 72d street and Riverside drive.

The highway will be supported on a steel structure of good appearance, and will be centrally located between the wharves and the abutting properties on the east side

Oversized Foldout

of the street. The outside width of the structure is to be 70 feet between ramps and 99 feet at the ramps. Across the width of the structure there will be three rows of columns and at the ramp locations five rows of columns which will provide separate unobstructed north and south routes beneath the structure on the existing marginal street. The minimum clearance beneath the elevated highway to the street grade is to be about 14 feet. The spacing between columns along the length of the structure varies from 40 to 100 feet, with wider spacings being provided in certain sections in order to reduce obstruction to cross flows at more important points and intersections.

At ramp locations the structure is widened and the roadways are carried on either side of the ramps. There are four single lane ramps, two for entering and two for leaving traffic, each 10 feet in width and with grades averaging approximately 5½ per cent. The distance between the northbound and southbound entrances to the ramps at street grade is approximately 100 feet. The arrangement is such that it is believed no additional ramp capacity will be needed in the event that a second deck is constructed.

The section of the marginal way to the north of 72d street, known as the Hudson River Express Highway, is in most part located at the foot of a steep slope in Riverside Park and entrance and exit connections between it and Riverside drive and crosstown streets are to be provided at 79th street, 96th street, 121st street, 137th street, 158th street and at Dyckman street. There has also been discussion of a connection in the vicinity of the 178th Street Bridge. These connections are approximately one mile apart through a section where the present traffic along Riverside drive is heaviest.

Relief Afforded.

It will be seen that the project will provide a special highway of large capacity on which traffic will be able to move at high speeds and without interruptions due to cross traffic. The combined flow on all of the avenues in mid-Manhattan is approximately 27,000 vehicles per hour during the periods of greatest flow. The capacity of the proposed highway has been estimated to be between 5,000 and 7,200 vehicles per hour, and, assuming the provision of adequate facilities at the connections with the street system, may be safely considered to be 6,000 vehicles per hour for the present purposes. On this basis the single deck of the proposed highway would provide a capacity for almost one-quarter of the vehicles now using the surface avenues.

The results of the origin and destination studies made of avenue traffic crossing 51st street furnish a measure of the amount of traffic which could advantageously use such a highway. Dealing only with the distances moved by such traffic in a north and south direction and disregarding any distances moved across town or in other boroughs, the analysis developed the following distribution:

> About 39 per cent. of the total avenue traffic crossing 51st street traveled between districts involving north and south movements in Manhattan ranging from 5 to 8 miles and averaging 6¼ miles and about 31 per cent. of the total traffic involved movements ranging from 2½ to 3½ miles and averaging practically 3 miles.
>
> About 21 per cent. of the avenue traffic crossing 51st street moves to or from points in The Bronx and 27 per cent. to or from points south of 14th street.

These figures are indicative of the large proportion of the present traffic which travels distances long enough to justify using such a marginal highway. The provision of the highway would not only benefit the traffic using it, but it would relieve conditions on the avenues and on the crosstown streets in the more centrally located portions of the City.

Conclusions.

We are of the opinion that the West Side Marginal Highway as proposed is a well conceived traffic relief measure in that it is a very practical method of providing additional highway capacity for north and south bound traffic which is urgently needed. Every effort should be made to complete the project at the earliest possible date, particularly the section extending from Canal to 72d streets.

In the event that the Battery Tunnel is constructed, the extension of the marginal highway south from Canal street would be highly desirable, as it would materially increase the advantages afforded by both facilities.

EAST SIDE MARGINAL HIGHWAY, MANHATTAN.

It is proposed to create a continuous marginal highway of varying width from the Battery along the East River waterfront and the Harlem River to an intersection with the proposed West Side Marginal Highway at Dyckman street, all as shown on the map on page 107.

Photo by Fairchild Aerial Surveys Inc., N. Y. C.   GENERAL VIEW IN MANHATTAN ALONG EAST RIVER

Proposed Route.

The proposed route will extend along South street from the Battery to Montgomery street; thence along a new highway from Montgomery street north along the East River front to 125th street; thence along the Harlem River front to a point of connection with the Harlem River driveway; thence along the driveway to Dyckman street; thence along Dyckman street to a point in the proposed West Side Marginal Highway a total distance of approximately 15 miles. In the section extending from Montgomery street to the Harlem River driveway there are a number of short disconnected existing streets which will be utilized. Other portions of this section are to be located on land now under water and at some points outside the present bulkhead lines.

Development of Project.

No part of this project has yet been formally authorized. The greatest need for the facility at the present time exists in the midtown and uptown sections, and from our investigation and study of traffic flows we believe that the logical procedure in creating this facility would be as follows:

(a) The initial construction along the East River should be between 23d and 54th streets, as traffic from lower Manhattan could move over East Broadway, Essex street, which is now being widened, Avenue A and the new construction and continue over Avenue A above 54th street as far as 93d street, thereby affording relief to the midtown traffic.

(b) Coincident with the East River construction the section along the Halrem River extending from 7th avenue to the Harlem River driveway should be built, as this would provide a direct route from the Harlem to the Dyckman street sections of Manhattan. It would also provide a low level connection leading to the Hudson River Bridge, now under construction, obviating the present necessity of using the ramp approaches to the Macombs Dam Bridge, the 155th Street Viaduct and the side hill road connection to the Harlem River driveway or of circulating through the street system of Washington Heights.

(c) The portion of the Harlem River section extending from 7th to 2d avenue should be built concurrently with the Triborough Bridge in order to provide an arterial highway connection with the west side facilities such as the Hudson River Bridge and the through highway leading north through The Bronx.

(d) The two remaining sections extending from Montgomery street to 23d street and from 54th street to 2d avenue, which are necessary to complete the marginal highway, are more City-wide in importance and do not afford the same measure of local relief as do the other sections. From the standpoint of the project as a whole these sections should be constructed concurrently with the others, but from the standpoint of local relief afforded their construction could be deferred.

The project has not developed to the stage of detailed plans and specifications, and various proposals have been made for over-all widths ranging from 60 to 80 feet, which would result in roadway widths varying from about 30 to 50 feet. Considering the type of highway contemplated, it appears to us that more liberal widths should be provided consistent with reasonable costs. Another consideration is the possibility of adding an elevated roadway in the future.

Relief Afforded.

As in the case of the West Side Marginal Highway, the project is designed to act as a by-pass, enabling traffic to avoid the congested areas of Manhattan. Assuming the completion of the West Side Marginal Highway the initial advantage of this project would principally be local to the midtown and Harlem River districts. The advantage of ultimately encircling the island with an adequate marginal highway is obvious.

Conclusion.

In our judgment the proposed East Side Marginal Highway as proposed is a well conceived traffic relief measure. Considering the various aspects of the project, including its relation to other projects under construction or imminent, we are of the opinion that the section covered by sub-paragraphs a, b and c above should be given early consideration and that the construction of the sections covered by sub-paragraph d above could well be deferred.

THE NORTH-SOUTH VEHICULAR TUNNEL IN MANHATTAN.

Various proposals have been made for the construction of a north-south vehicular tunnel in Manhattan, some with a view to affording traffic relief in the more central sections of the island and others with a view to providing a through highway extending the lengths of Manhattan, in which vehicles could move long distances at high speeds and with a minimum of interruptions. The most definite of these proposals is that of the City Committee on Plan and Survey for the construction of express underground streets on each side of Central Park, extending from 59th street to 110th street. The remaining proposals are very general in their nature and the project as a whole is in such a preliminary stage that its various aspects must necessarily be presented in general terms.

Development of the Project.

The project would lend itself to progressive development, beginning with a section passing under the midtown area where relief is most needed and gradually extending the tunnel to the north and to the south as conditions warranted.

The tunnel would be most effective as a relief measure and afford a maximum of convenience to traffic using it, if it were located under one of the more central avenues, with ramp approaches about every mile leading to conveniently placed entrance and exit plazas on each side of the tunnel. Additional convenience would be afforded if the tunnel were placed close to the surface in order to shorten the length of the approach ramps. A deep level position would result in longer ramps, but would reduce the disturbance to traffic and business during the period of construction.

Central Park and the street system to the north of it offers some flexibility in the route of a centrally located vehicular tunnel, but south of Central Park the only available route to the downtown section appears to be under 5th avenue. It would require extensive detailed studies to establish its availability or that of sections of adjoining streets, and the possibilities with respect to the elevations at which the tunnel structure could be placed.

As to the deep level position, the Board of Transportation in its comprehensive planning for subways has generally placed the north and south subways on the first or upper level and assigned the east and west subways to the second level. Thus it appears that a deep level tunnel position would probably be in the third level except where some intermediate position could be found. A tentative study indicates that after allowing space for utilities and two levels for transit subways, then the upper and lower decks of a vehicular tunnel would be about 67 and 87 feet, respectively, below the street surface.

The ramps required to reach the greater depth, if built on $3\frac{1}{2}$ per cent. grades, would be approximately 2,500 feet in length. Straight line approches at right angles to a 5th avenue location would require east and west side plazas to be at about 2d and 8th avenues, respectively. If a high level position should be found practicable, then the length of ramps could be materially shortened. For both high and low level locations the positions of existing and planned subways and railroads would limit freedom in the location and construction of ramps. In such situations, or in order to obtain flexibility in the location of entrance or exit plazas, the ramps might be looped.

For the deep level position the approximate length of a pair of ramps at junction points would be slightly less than one mile, and if spaced at intervals of about one mile, then approximately two miles of tunnel construction would be required for every north and south mile of main tunnel. A high level position would reduce the construction per mile of main tunnel to approximately 1.6 miles.

Ventilation buildings for housing the equipment necessary to remove vitiated air and supply fresh air to the tunnel would be required at appropriate intervals. Plazas of adequate area to receive and distribute traffic and to provide for toll collection, if tolls should be charged, would also be required. These appurtenances to the tunnel would require the taking of considerable real estate and the acquisition of easements in areas with high assessed valuations.

The length of ramps required for a deep level position, the costly areas needed for plazas and approaches, and the probable difficulties of keeping clear of subway and railway structures, especially at the ramps, in a central location, suggests consideration of a location near the East River which might avoid or at least minimize such difficulties. In such a location the cross-river tunnels would probably allow a high level position for a north and south vehicular tunnel, resulting in shorter ramps, but with loop construction a necessity at practically all junction points on account of the proximity of the river. Entrance and exit plazas would be between 2d and 3d avenues.

An east side location would not afford the convenience of a more central location and moreover the through route which it would provide could be more economically developed by an elevated highway along the East River front.

A location between the central avenues, involving easements and construction through or under existing buildings, has also been suggested and in certain sections would appear to offer possibilities meriting study when the project reaches the stage of detailed investigation. Another factor entering into the question of available locations and deserving careful consideration is the possible future need of underground routes for rapid transit purposes.

Two tentative routes were developed in the course of our study, one for a central location and the other for an east side location. They are as follows:

Route "A"—This route is approximately ten miles in length and its northern terminal would connect with the Grand Boulevard and Concourse at 161st street, in The Bronx. After crossing the Harlem River, it continues southward under 7th avenue to Central Park, which would be traversed in appropriate location to near the southeast corner of the park, where the route would enter 5th avenue and continue southward, passing under Washington Square to a southern terminal near the intersection of Canal street and West Broadway.

Route "B"—This route is approximately 8½ miles in length and would have its northern terminal near the intersection of Lincoln avenue and 138th street in The Bronx. After crossing the Harlem River, it continues southward under 1st avenue to 23d street, where the tunnel turns eastward to Avenue B, and then continues southward on that avenue and on Clinton street to a southern terminal near the intersection of Grand street and East Broadway. This location is near the East River and it would be necessary to turn practically all of the ramps to the westward and approach the main tunnel by means of loops.

As previously stated, it would require extensive detailed investigation of the underground conditions and other factors in order to definitely establish the practicability of these routes, and they have been presented merely as indicative of the possibilities.

Cost of the Project.

Under the circumstances, any cost estimates of the structure itself can only be the most general approximations, and this is even more true of the estimated cost of land and easements. On the basis of a four-lane vehicular tunnel, with ramps spaced at intervals ranging up to 1½ miles, the indications are that the cost per mile of main tunnel, without allowance for interest during construction, would be between $20,000,000 and $25,000,000 for the central location and somewhat less for the east side location. This would indicate a cost for the entire project approximating $200,000,000.

If the project were undertaken, it would appear probable that it would be developed progressively, in which event the initial construction might be from about Washington Square to Central Park, for which the approximate cost indicated would be about $70,000,000, also exclusive of interest during construction.

On the basis of an average cost of $20,000,000 per mile of main tunnel, the fixed charges and costs of operation on a toll basis would be about $3,000,000 per mile of route per year, or an annual cost for the entire project in the order of $30,000,000 per year.

Relief Afforded.

The capacity of a four-lane vehicular tunnel for passenger car traffic is in the neighborhood of 4,800, and for mixed traffic about 3,800 vehicles per hour. In more general terms, it could handle approximately one-seventh of the combined north and south traffic now flowing on all the avenues in the vicinity of 51st street.

Under existing conditions, the average speed of traffic on the more centrally located avenues ranges from 7 to 12 miles per hour and frequently less, or about one-third of the practical speed on a through highway such as would be afforded by a vehicular tunnel. On this basis, the tunnel would offer a potential saving in time for a trip of five miles of approximately 18 minutes.

An indication of the large amount of long haul traffic and its distribution is afforded by the results of our study of the origin and destination of the total avenue traffic in the vicinity of 51st street, set forth in detail in a later section. Dealing only with the distances moved by such traffic in a north and south direction and disregarding distances moved across town or in other boroughs, the analysis discloses the following distribution:

About 39 per cent. of the total avenue traffic crossing 51st street travels between districts involving north and south movements in Manhattan ranging from 5 to 8 miles and averaging 6¼ miles, and about 31 per cent. of the total traffic moves distances ranging from 2½ to 3½ miles and averaging practically 3 miles.

About 21 per cent. of the avenue traffic crossing 51st street moves to or from points in The Bronx and 27 per cent. to or from points south of 14th street.

The foregoing statements and more general considerations of the advantages of such a through highway, either in its entirety or as a short section through the midtown area, indicate that the project has very material potentialities as a traffic relief measure.

Conclusions.

The construction of such a tunnel would be desirable from the point of view of convenience but the measure of relief it would afford, assuming the construction of the West Side Marginal Highway and the other highways and major bridges and tunnels either authorized or under consideration as measures to relieve the traffic conditions in the central sections of Manhattan, would not in our judgment be sufficient to make the project self-supporting on a reasonable toll basis. Moreover, the general improvement of traffic conditions expected to result from the creation of the new facilities referred to will so materially affect the situation with respect to this project that, in our opinion, further consideration should be deferred until the effect of the new facilities has been established by actual experience.

EXTENSION OF PARK AVENUE FROM 96TH STREET TO GRAND BOULEVARD.

It is proposed to extend Park avenue above 96th street by the construction of a vehicular viaduct over the elevated tracks of the New York Central & Hudson River Railroad, to continue across the Harlem River into The Bronx to a connection with the Grand Boulevard and Concourse.

The tracks of the New York Central Railroad are on a viaduct in the centre of Park avenue from 96th street to the Harlem River, crossing the river on a steel drawbridge and on a fill above the grade of the street system to a point above 138th street in The Bronx, where the tracks are below the grade of the street system and continue in this way to the Westchester County line.

A highway built above the railroad viaduct would afford a through route free from intersections. Such construction would about double the height of the present elevated structure in the centre of Park avenue and be an additional cause for depreciation in the properties along Park avenue in this section. Consideration should be given to decking over Park avenue north of 96th street above the railroad tracks from building line to building line, which would create a structure about four stories above the present street level. The lower four floors might be utilized for basement storage, kitchens, garages, etc. The construction of such a highway would probably be quickly followed by the erection of high class buildings such as now exist on Park avenue below 96th street.

The connection of this extension in Park avenue to the Grand Boulevard and Concourse would continue over the tracks of the New York Central Railroad to about 153d street and Mott avenue.

There are proposed projects in The Bronx, discussed elsewhere in this report, for the continuation of the Grand Boulevard and Concourse southward to about 153d street by the widening of Mott avenue and for the decking over of the tracks of the New York Central Railroad continuing this route to Fordham road or beyond.

As the proposed northerly extension of Park avenue would later be continued northward over the New York Central tracks through The Bronx to Fordham road or beyond, we are of the opinion that the proposed extension of the Concourse southerly over the widened Mott avenue and via a high level bridge over the Harlem River to the vicinity of Lenox or 7th avenue in Manhattan, should also be given consideration at this time, as a future additional north-south, Manhattan-Bronx route.

We believe this project should be given early study and consideration as many important features would have to be worked out with the railroad company. The project as outlined above would not only tend to improve the territory which it traverses but would also provide an arterial highway connection with other routes proposed in The Bronx.

LOWER MANHATTAN HIGHWAY EXTENSIONS.

There are a number of projects for providing more direct access to the congested areas of Manhattan, consisting principally of extensions of certain avenues to the southward, the removal of obstacles to traffic flow, such as elevated structures and surface car tracks and the widening of the roadways of certain streets and avenues.

Most of the projects for the removal of obstacles to traffic flow are either to remove elevated structures along certain routes or for the rearrangement of elevated columns or street car tracks at particular locations. All of these are excellent measures for traffic relief and are more needed at certain particular locations than at others. The elevated structures, are a particular hindrance to the flow of traffic when the supporting columns are in the roadway, the worst condition being when the roadway is not wide enough to allow one parking and one moving lane of traffic between the row of elevated columns and the curb line.

The outstanding projects at present for traffic relief of this nature, are for the removal of the 6th avenue elevated line from 53d to Morris street, and for the removal of one set of street car tracks along Park Row and a section of the Bowery. Both of these projects, if accomplished, would certainly help the flow of traffic along these streets. Where elevated structures have been removed in the past, great activity has occurred in the development of properties situated along such routes, for instance, along 42d street from Park to 3d avenue and on 6th avenue from 53d street to 59th street.

Material increase in capacity would accompany the elimination of the elevated structures, but it will undoubtedly be many years before the transit situations permit such removal, and relief from this source will be very gradual.

The City has adopted a policy of widening roadways along the streets and avenues of Manhattan as the development of properties takes place and repaving becomes necessary. A standard width of roadway has been adopted for each width of street and where the roadway is made wider, special study and consideration is first given to the particular situation. A number of roadways have been widened on Manhattan mostly by removing sidewalk encroachments or narrowing parking areas and setting back the curb lines. The most notable of these roadway widenings are along such important north and south avenues as Park, 5th, Madison, 8th and Amsterdam avenues, along many of the crosstown streets in the area between 23d street and 59th street and Lexington and 8th avenues, and along certain downtown streets.

There are a number of projects for roadway widening at particular locations, of which the widening of the roadway of 4th avenue between 12th and 14th streets seems particularly urgent. Here, a roadway, 70 feet wide both above and below this location is narrowed to 45 feet in width. Because of the narrowness of the street in these two blocks, arcaded sidewalks would be necessary. Such a roadway widening at this point would eliminate the existing bad condition of a bottle neck just below a main crosstown street.

The various projects now being considered for the extension of the avenue routes to the southward are indicated on the map on page 107 and are discussed as follows:

Sixth Avenue, Carmine Street to Fulton Street.

This project includes the extension of 6th avenue southerly from Carmine and Minetta streets to Canal street at about Sullivan street, thence southerly to Church and Franklin streets, via a widened Church street to Fulton street. This extension is being carried on in conjunction with the building of the new 8th Avenue Subway along this route and is nearing completion. It will provide a most desirable connection from a main north and south avenue to lower Manhattan at Fulton street, and when completed will afford a direct route via Church street and 6th avenue from below Fulton street in lower Manhattan to midtown Manhattan.

Canal Street, Mulberry Street to the Bowery.

The widening of Canal street from Mulberry street to the Bowery is about completed, affording a continuous 60-foot roadway from the Manhattan Bridge, head on the east side to West street on the west side of Manhattan. The approach to the Manhattan Bridge will be greatly improved upon the completion of this project.

Essex Street, Houston to East Broadway.

This project is under construction and provides for the widening of Essex street from Houston street to East Broadway, in connection with subway construction. The improvement constitutes an extension of Avenue A southerly to East Broadway and will provide a desirable connection from lower Manhattan via East Broadway and Avenue A to the area about 23d street. The facility provided by this route is somewhat the same as the extension of 2d avenue by the widening of Allen street except that this route is further east, a little longer than the Allen Street Route and traffic moving along it must cross the bulk of the traffic from the Williamsburg Bridge along Delancey street.

Chrystie Street, Houston street to Canal Street.

This project includes the extension of 2d avenue, southerly, by widening Chrystie street, from Houston to Canal street. It has been under consideration for some time due to collateral questions of parking and housing upon which the City has only recently reached a decision.

The improvement when completed will create a direct route from the Manhattan Bridge head through 2d avenue to middle and upper Manhattan.

Madison Avenue Extension, 23d Street to Franklin Street.

There are a number of projects collectively providing for the extension of Madison avenue southerly from 23d street to Union square, via Union Square East, a widened roadway along University place and a new connection between University place and Greene street to Greene street at 8th street, thence via a widened Greene street across Canal street to Franklin street.

The improvement as outlined above would provide an additional direct route from lower Manhattan via Church street at the south end to upper and middle Manhattan via Madison avenue at the north end.

We believe that the widening of the roadway on University place from Union square to 4th street should be accomplished as soon as possible, giving consideration to the present roadway widths along Madison avenue above 23d street. The widened roadway would provide an improved route for the existing traffic on University place below Union square, and extend its usefulness as far south as 4th street.

That portion of the project providing for the widening of Church street from Franklin to Canal street would not only be a step in the widening of the route of the extension of Madison avenue southerly, but would provide a shorter route for traffic moving northward on Church street bound for the Manhattan Bridge. Should the "Battery Tunnel" be built the necessity for this widening of Church street from Franklin to Canal would not be as great as if this facility were not provided.

We consider the extending of Madison avenue from 23d street south to Union square, the connecting of University place to Greene street at about 8th street and the widening of Greene street from 8th to Canal street as the final sections of this project to be provided.

Allen Street, Delancey to East Broadway.

This project provides for the extension of 1st avenue by widening Allen street from Delancey to East Broadway. 1st avenue has been extended by widening Allen street from Houston to Delancey street and is now used extensively by traffic bound to or from the Williamsburg Bridge.

We believe the extension of 1st avenue southerly would provide a desirable connection to lower Manhattan via East Broadway, but as the Essex street widening for the extension of Avenue A is now under way, and is a parallel route to the eastward, the urgency is not as great as it otherwise would be. This route is in some respects more desirable than the Essex street route, as it is nearer the congested area of lower Manhattan, is a more direct route avoiding some of the flow of the Williamsburg Bridge traffic along Delancey street, and continues along 2d avenue, which extends northward to the Harlem River, whereas Avenue A ends at about 26th street. However, if the section of the East Side drive from 23d street to 54th street is built, Avenue A will be continued as far northward as 93d street.

Lexington Avenue Extension.

It is proposed to extend Lexington avenue (Irving place) across Gramercy Park from 20th to 21st street and southerly from 14th street to Astor place. This project will provide more direct access between middle and upper Manhattan and lower Manhattan via a route along Lexington avenue, 4th avenue and the Bowery. The opening of the route will be more effective at such a time when the elevated structure is removed from the Bowery, and possibly when the surface car tracks are removed from Lexington avenue and the Bowery.

Lexington avenue is one of the narrower avenues on Manhattan extending from Harlem River to 14th street, where its dead end is objectionable, when considering traffic flow in that section. The development along Lexington avenue in the 42d street section has been most active in the past few years, a number of super-skyscrapers having been erected in that vicinity. Gramercy Park is privately owned by the owners of the properties facing on the park and the development of these properties in the past few years has been mostly by the building of high apartment houses. The most practicable method of extending Lexington avenue across this park would be at grade.

When considering these extensions as links in a Lexington Avenue-4th Avenue-Bowery Route, consideration should be given to the widening of the area of roadway between 8th and 10th streets where this route and the Lafayette Street-4th-Park Avenue Route are contiguous. In view of the present layout of streets and the proposed extension of Lexington avenue in this area, the widening of the roadway should be made on the west side of Astor place, which would continue the line of Lafayette street straight through to 4th avenue.

5th Avenue, 120th to 124th Street.

The proposed extension of 5th avenue through Mount Morris Park from 120th to 124th street would continue 5th avenue as an unobstructed route from Washington square to the Harlem River. This extension through Mount Morris Park would be desirable, relieving traffic along 5th avenue of making a number of turns in order to get around the park, as at present. This extension could be made by tunneling through the natural rock of the park and would little interfere with the use of the park for park purposes.

MISCELLANEOUS ARTERIAL HIGHWAY PROJECTS IN MANHATTAN, BRONX, BROOKLYN, QUEENS AND RICHMOND.

In the preceding sections we have dealt with projects involving the construction of major vehicular connections between the boroughs and of certain arterial highways which appear to us to be of more City interest and directly related to the relief of the congested areas of Manhattan. In addition there is a large number of projects involving the improvement of or extensions to the arterial highway systems throughout the five boroughs, the execution of which we believe to be very desirable from a traffic standpoint. In view of their nature and location and the local aspects involved, it is impractical for us to develop a definite schedule of procedure, but in this connection we have endeavored to set forth the particular advantages which would be afforded by the individual projects.

MANHATTAN.

The various projects for the improvement of the arterial highway system of Manhattan are indicated on the map on page 119 and are discussed in part as follows:

Riverside Drive, 155th Street to The Bronx.

This is a project to extend Riverside drive above 155th street to The Bronx, including the construction of viaducts at 155th street and across Dyckman street and a high level bridge across the Harlem River connecting with Riverdale avenue or with the proposed Riverside drive in The Bronx. It continues the present facility below 155th street through the territory above 155th street as a continuous unobstructed route along the Hudson River from 72d street to The Bronx and connects with the West Side Elevated Highway at 72d street, thereby forming a section of the West Side marginal way along Manhattan. Because of the present and proposed nature of the development along this section of the Hudson River shore, there is and will be little flow of traffic across this drive, except at certain crosstown street intersections, where the streets now lead to wharf or ferry locations or will connect with the proposed West Side marginal highway over the New York Central tracks, paralleling this drive a few hundred feet to the westward.

This project has been completed as far as Dyckman street with a connection to Dyckman street at Broadway, enabling traffic to flow to and from points in Yonkers and other Westchester County areas via Broadway and the Broadway Bridge and the Fordham road and University Heights Bridge.

The section of this project extending Riverside drive over Dyckman street, through Inwood Park and across the Harlem River by the proposed Hudson Memorial Bridge, we believe an excellent additional facility to connect the West Side marginal way with points in The Bronx, but it is a parallel route to the present Broadway route and in our opinion should not be made until after the 178th street Hudson River Bridge is completed.

West Side Improvement Plan.

The West Side Improvement Plan, which for years has been studied by the engineers of the New York Central Railroad and the West Side Improvement Engineering Committee has been generally advocated. For the area below 72d street it includes the removal of the railroad tracks in sections of Hudson, Canal and West streets, of 10th, 11th and 12th avenues; the removal of a number of sidings into warehouses at the grade of existing streets; the elimination of the present freight terminals at Hudson and Laight streets and at 32d and 36th streets on 10th avenue; the construction of new tracks on an upper or lower level over private right-of-way, including new sidings into warehouses and a new terminal at Spring and West streets, and the reconstruction of the terminal yards at 34th street and 10th avenue, and at 60th street and 12th avenue. For the area above 72d street this plan includes the construction of the Hudson River Express Highway as a deck above the tracks of the New York Central from 72d street to The Bronx, with the attendant realignment and changing of grade of certain sections of track, new viaducts at 125th street and Dyckman street, rearrangement of freight yards and a new bridge across the Harlem River.

The portion of this plan for the area below 72d street has already been commenced and we believe its completion will prove to be most important in providing traffic relief. The improvement should not only greatly facilitate the movement of traffic, by the removal of such obstacles as grade crossings and tracks along the avenues and streets and also by the erection of new warehouses along the new elevated or depressed tracks with loading and unloading facilities within the building lines, but should also change the flow of a considerable amount of trucking because of the elimination of the present freight terminal below Canal street and other smaller terminal yards along 10th avenue.

Manhattan Approach to Hudson River Bridge.

This project includes the construction of bridge plaza from Pinehurst avenue to Broadway between 178th and 179th streets, street connections to Riverside drive, each accommodating four lanes of traffic and a new traffic facility below grade from the center roadway of the bridge to Highbridge Park with connections to Amsterdam avenue, Washington Bridge and the speedway, all facilities for free movement of traffic to and from the new Hudson River Bridge.

We believe that these facilities should be provided in time to be available upon the completion of the bridge now under construction.

We are also of the opinion that additional facilities for the flow of traffic across the Harlem River must be provided at about the location of the end of this new traffic way in Highbridge Park. It is proposed to widen the existing 50-foot roadway of the Washington Bridge to 62 feet, which we consider should be accomplished coincident with the construction of the facilities outlined above. We are also of the opinion that an additional crossing of the Harlem River may be necessary in the future, as the traffic over the new Hudson River Bridge increases. The most feasible location of this additional bridge, we believe to be directly adjacent and south of the present Washington Bridge because of the physical character of the territory and the advantageous existing and proposed street plan at both ends of the present Washington Bridge. We are of the opinion that special study should be made of the design of the area where the roads from the Washington Bridge, Amsterdam avenue and the Speedway will converge at the east end of the proposed traffic way across Washington Heights, consideration being given at this time to a possible future bridge across the Harlem River.

Broadway Bridge.

It is proposed to double the width of the present 35-foot roadway across the Harlem River at Broadway, necessitating the construction of additional bridge capacity at this point. This facility is very desirable to eliminate a bottle neck in the present Broadway route from Manhattan to Yonkers which now connects with Riverside drive at Dyckman street and will connect with the Speedway at 10th avenue when the extension of 10th avenue is completed across Sherman Creek.

Extension of Harlem River Speedway.

It is proposed to extend 10th avenue southward across Sherman Creek to the Speedway, thereby creating a short connection between the Speedway and Broadway in the Dyckman street section just below the Harlem River. Fill is now being made in Sherman Creek for this extension, which will provide a shorter route to The Bronx, by-passing sections of Dyckman street and Broadway. This project merits early consideration along with the proposed additional width of roadway at the Broadway Bridge.

Connection Between West and South Streets at the Battery.

This project provides for a suitable connection along Battery Park between West street on the Hudson River and South street on the East River. It is not an urgent traffic relief measure at this time and should be carefully studied in connection with plans for the improvement of Battery Park. Ultimately it will be a desirable connection between the West Side and East Side marginal highways.

THE BRONX.

The various projects for the improvement of the arterial highway system of The Bronx are indicated on the map opposite this page and are discussed as follows:

Extension of Grand Boulevard and Concourse.

The Grand Boulevard and Concourse as now existing, extends from 161st street and Mott avenue to the Mosholu parkway above 209th street.

At the southern end traffic moves from the Concourse over the streets leading to the Macomb's Dam, 149th Street and 136th Street Bridges in order to reach Manhattan. At the northern end, traffic from the Concourse moves over the Mosholu parkway, or the drives in Van Cortlandt Park in order to reach the upper sections of The Bronx and points in Westchester County. There are no direct connections of large capacity with either the avenues of Manhattan or the parkway system of Westchester County.

Oversized Foldout

We are of the opinion that the direct extensions of the Concourse, both southerly and northerly, should be provided in order that the present Concourse can more adequately function as an artery for through traffic from Manhattan to Westchester County.

The southerly extension of the Concourse, because of the present amount of traffic flowing through this area to and from the Concourse, the existing development of this area and the location of the Harlem River in the area, is not only the more urgent extension to be provided, but presents the greatest difficulties.

It is proposed to extend the Concourse southerly by widening Mott avenue from East 161st to about East 153d street, providing a high level bridge across the Harlem River to connect with Mott avenue by an approach across Franz Sigel Park and with 7th avenue in Manhattan, along which it is suggested to build an elevated highway as far south as Central Park. It is also proposed to widen the roadway of Mott avenue from 153d street to 138th street.

Such a project as outlined above would not only provide a widened roadway along Mott avenue between the existing Harlem River bridges at 149th street and 138th street and the Concourse but would provide a direct unobstructed southerly extension of the Concourse across a high level bridge to Manhattan. Vehicular traffic using this high level bridge would not be periodically delayed by river traffic as is the case at present on the existing Harlem River low level drawbridges.

We believe that the suggested elevated highway along 7th avenue from this bridgehead to Central Park should not be built at this time, as in our opinion such a facility would not only have all the objections to any elevated structure being built in 7th avenue but would cause congestion along the drives of Central Park. We recommend, however, that consideration be given to providing an approach from this bridge to Lenox avenue as well as to 7th avenue. Lenox avenue, having an unusually broad roadway, now comparatively little used by through traffic, would be a desirable connection to this bridge. It would also be desirable to have the entrances to this bridge at points below the present 149th Street Bridge.

In the design of the high level connection from the Concourse to Manhattan, consideration should also be given to a connection at about 153d street in The Bronx to the possible future extension of Park avenue in Manhattan along Park avenue in The Bronx as a deck above the New York Central tracks.

It is proposed to extend the Concourse northerly through Van Cortlandt Park, generally along the route of the existing driveways to connect with the Saw Mill River parkway, with branches westward and eastward to be sections of the proposed future cross-Bronx highway, the westward extension to later continue on a viaduct across Broadway, along a widened 261st street to the proposed extension of Riverside drive in The Bronx, and the eastward extension to extend to Jerome avenue, to be continued later via 233d street, Van Cortlandt Park East, 240th street, Nereid avenue and Baychester avenue to the through traffic arteries to be provided in the eastern section of The Bronx. A branch of this extension, parallel and adjacent to Jerome avenue on its west side from 233d street to City line, may be provided.

It is proposed to provide two roadways, each 60 feet wide, along this extension of the Concourse, but as the route of the extension with its branches is almost entirely within Van Cortlandt Park we are of the opinion that such an extension should be provided at present to a point at the junction of the main extension and the west branch, the roadway from here to the Saw Mill River parkway to be the same width as the roadway along that parkway and the roadway of the branches to be about one-half the width of the proposed roadway of the main extension.

The facilities to be provided by the extension of the Concourse northerly would be a more suitable and adequate connection to points in Westchester County via the Saw Mill River parkway, not only from the Concourse but also in the future from Sedgwick avenue and from University avenue extended through Goulden avenue.

Extension of Bronx River Parkway at 233d Street.

The extension of the Bronx River parkway at 233d street provides a connection between the section of the parkway on the east side of the Bronx River below 233d street to the section of the parkway on the west side of the Bronx River above 233d street by building a bridge over the Bronx River and an underpass under the New York Central tracks and 233d street.

The bridge over the Bronx River is completed and we are of the opinion that the underpass should be provided to continue the connection between the two sections of the parkway and provide a much needed grade separation at 233d street along the route of the Bronx River parkway.

Extension of Bronx River Parkway Southerly to Bronx and Pelham Parkway.

The Bronx River parkway at present has its southern extremity at the Bronx Park just south of Gun Hill road, where a drive through the park connects with the parkway. It is proposed to extend this parkway southerly via Bronx boulevard and Bronx Park East to the Bronx and Pelham parkway.

The Bronx boulevard, bordering Bronx Park from the point of its connection with the Bronx River parkway at Duncomb avenue to Burke avenue, has a roadway 60 feet wide and has been recently paved. It is proposed to regrade and widen Bronx Park East from Burke avenue to the Bronx and Pelham parkway, making at least a roadway 60 feet wide, and we are of the opinion that this section should be widened and paved to complete the southerly extension of the Bronx River parkway to the Bronx and Pelham parkway.

The extension will directly connect the Bronx River parkway with the Bronx and Pelham parkway or Fordham road, and should greatly relieve the drives in the Bronx Park.

Improvement of Routes between Washington Bridge and the Proposed Triborough Bridge.

The improvement of certain routes from the Washington Bridge at Boscobel and University avenues to the proposed Triborough Bridge at Southern boulevard and Cypress avenue we believe should be provided upon completion of the Triborough Bridge.

In our opinion, the easiest, most direct route along existing streets between these two bridges, which we have termed Route 1, is along Boscobel avenue, River avenue, Exterior street and 135th street to Lincoln avenue, from thence over 133d, 134th, 135th, 136th, 137th or 138th streets to Cypress avenue.

Another route between these two bridges, which we have termed Route 2, is along Ogden or Nelson avenue to Exterior street, along Exterior street and 135th street to Lincoln avenue, thence to Cypress avenue along the same streets as outlined above.

Route No. 1.

In our opinion the improvements necessary to adapt these streets as the route between the bridges, outlined above, includes the widening of Boscobel avenue from the Washington Bridge to Jerome avenue and also the widening of Exterior street and 135th street from 149th street to Lincoln avenue. The roadways along these streets should be at least 60 feet wide and preferably wider. Boscobel avenue is at present a section of two cross-Bronx routes and is not only much used by traffic crossing the Washington Bridge bound to and from points east, but also bound to and from points south.

Because of the present use of Boscobel avenue as a traffic artery connecting with the east end of the Washington Bridge, the contemplated increase in traffic along this street when the Hudson River Bridge is completed and the existing activity in apartment house building in the neighborhood, we believe that Boscobel avenue should be widened as outlined above.

Route No. 2.

It is our opinion that before the completion of the proposed Triborough Bridge it would be desirable to widen the roadway of Ogden or Nelson avenue from the Washington Bridge to Jerome avenue and to widen Exterior street from Jerome avenue to 149th street, where it joins Route No. 1, so that the roadway of Exterior street would be at least 60 feet wide. The section of this route along Ogden or Nelson avenue is not so desirable as the section of Route No. 1 along Boscobel avenue and River street, as the latter has easier grades. However, that section of this route along Exterior street is preferable to the section of Route No. 1 along River street, because of few intersecting streets along Exterior street.

The separation of grades along these routes at such important intersections as 149th street, 138th street and 3d avenue would provide desirable additional facilities for the flow of traffic along these routes, between the bridges.

We also believe that Cypress avenue should be widened from the Southern boulevard to 138th street to act as a distributor of traffic to and from 133d, 134th, 135th, 136th, 137th and 138th streets, the same as Lincoln avenue at their western end, and to create a broad bridge plaza at the grade of the intersecting streets. There should, however, be provided a grade separation where the Southern boulevard crosses this proposed bridge plaza.

New Cross-Bronx Artery, Washington Bridge to Clason's Point.

It is proposed to create a new cross-Bronx artery from the east end of Washington Bridge to Clason's Point, partly by following the routes of existing streets and partly by extending this proposed artery across existing park lands. The route of this proposed artery is shown on the map on page 119.

The streets along the route of this proposed highway have roadways varying in width from 30 to 60 feet, the narrower width of roadways and streets being where the development is most concentrated. The existing bridge across the Bronx River, having a roadway 40 feet wide, is in good condition. Because the contours of the terrain along this route, grade separations could be provided by building viaducts across Jerome avenue and the Boston Post road and by tunnelling under the Grand Boulevard and Concourse and Claremont Park.

It would be desirable to provide a roadway 60 feet wide along the route of this proposed highway with grade separations at important street intersections. In this connection we believe that a thorough study should be made of not only the route of the proposed highway, but also its design, providing grade separations where considered necessary and desirable.

Such a highway would provide a most desirable cross-Bronx artery for through traffic extending directly from the Washington Bridge at its western end to the ferry at Clason's Point, with connections to the present and proposed principal north and south streets along the routes.

In our opinion, this highway as herewith described will be a necessary traffic facility to be provided in connection with the Hudson River Bridge now under construction, especially when Boscobel avenue, now a section of two cross-Bronx routes, becomes a section of a route between this bridge and the proposed Triborough Bridge.

Widening of Southern-Eastern Boulevard Route, Cypress Avenue to City Line.

It is proposed to widen the Southern and Eastern boulevards from the end of the proposed Triborough Bridge at Cypress avenue to the City line as shown on the map on page 119.

Considering the facilities to be provided by this proposed highway, its route through the territory and the present and possible future development along its route, we believe that provision should be made for a roadway or roadways totalling 120 feet wide along its route.

In our opinion, possibly the most feasible way to provide this width of roadway would be to double the present roadway widths by widening the Southern boulevard from Cypress avenue to 141st street and by widening Whitlock avenue from 163d street to the Eastern boulevard, to make the roadway of Whitlock avenue at least 60 feet wide from 141st street to 163d street and to make the Eastern boulevard from the Bronx River to City line similar in design and width to the existing Grand Boulevard and Concourse.

Such a scheme as outlined above would provide a concourse from the City line where it connects with the Boston Post road and the Hutchinson River parkway to the Bronx River, through a section of The Bronx either mostly at present undeveloped or along existing park land with adequate connecting roadways via Southern boulevard and Whitlock avenue through a developed section of The Bronx to the proposed Triborough Bridge.

We are of the opinion that a complete study of this project should be made, further consideration being given to the most desirable width of roadway to be provided, the design of the Concourse along Eastern boulevard, the necessary grade separations to be provided now or in the future along the route of this highway and the bridges across the New York Central tracks, the Bronx River, Westchester Creek and Eastchester Bay, which have roadways varying in width from 30 to 60 feet.

We also advise that the present park drive through Pelham Bay Park connecting the Eastern boulevard with the Pelham Shore road north of City line be improved as to alignment, grade and width, being made the same width as the proposed width of Pelham Shore road. We believe that this improvement should be made coincident with the improvement of the Pelham Shore road.

This highway when completed will not only be a direct route from the Triborough Bridge to points in Westchester County and New England, but will be a section of a marginal highway in The Bronx to extend from the Harlem River at Spuyten Duyvil along the Hudson River to 161st street, across 161st street and the northern section of The Bronx to the Eastern boulevard, thence along the Eastern and Southern Boulevard Route to the Triborough Bridge.

Improvement and Extension of University Avenue.

This project includes the separation of grades along University avenue at such important street intersections as Tremont avenue, East Burnside avenue, East Fordham road and East Kingsbridge road and the extension of University avenue across private property above East Kingsbridge road to Reservoir avenue and along the route of Reservoir and Goulden avenues to the proposed northerly extension of the Grand Boulevard and Concourse.

The project would provide a desirable north and south artery for through traffic of a width the same as University avenue connecting Washington Bridge with the proposed extension of the Grand Boulevard and Concourse, thence to the present and proposed parkways of Westchester County. We believe that this project should be provided as a route for through traffic, bound to and from the Hudson River Bridge now under construction.

Widening of Boston Post Road, Van Cortlandt Avenue with Roads Around Reservoir, and Gun Hill Road.

This project includes the widening of the Boston Post road, from The Bronx and Pelham parkway to City line, of Van Cortlandt avenue and the roads around Gun Hill Reservoir from the Grand Boulevard and Concourse to Gun Hill road and of Gun Hill road, from the proposed northerly extension of the Grand Boulevard and Concourse to the Boston Post road.

All of these widenings as outlined above would provide added facilities for the flow of traffic through this area of The Bronx, but we are of the opinion that with the exception of the Boston Post road, they should be deferred until after the completion of the projects heretofore discussed, at which time they may be found to be unnecessary. We, however, believe that a complete study should be made of these proposed Cross-Bronx widenings and compared to widenings along other possible routes and that the necessary land be acquired for the widening of the Boston Post road to at least 170 feet, to be of a similar design as the Grand Boulevard and Concourse. This proposed parkway along the route of the Boston Post road will provide a mid-Bronx north and south parkway about midway between the Concourse and the proposed parkway along the Eastern boulevard.

The other proposed widenings would provide more adequate connections between the Grand Boulevard and Concourse and either the Bronx River parkway or the Boston Post road.

Improvement of Webster Avenue, Gun Hill Road to 233d Street.

This project includes the widening of the roadway of Webster avenue from Gun Hill road to 233d street, together with the removal of the poles from the center of the roadway to the curb line, as already accomplished along Webster avenue above 233d street.

We believe that this improvement should be made, as it will not only greatly facilitate the movement of traffic between the Gun Hill road and the Bronx River parkway at 233d street, but will be an improvement to one of the most important north and south avenues in The Bronx.

Connection from Gun Hill Road to Bronx River Parkway.

It is proposed to make a connection between Gun Hill road and Bronx River parkway by building a viaduct north of Gun Hill road over the tracks of the New York Central Railroad. Such a connection would be desirable for traffic using Gun Hill road as a route between the Concourse and the Bronx River parkway.

We are of the opinion that a complete study be made of the proposed connection and that consideration be given to providing a grade separation at Webster avenue.

Extension of Riverside Drive and Improvement to 261st Street.

It is proposed to extend Riverside drive on Manhattan along the route of Palisade avenue in The Bronx to 261st street and to widen 261st street, extending it across Broadway to the proposed branch of the Grand Boulevard and Concourse in Van Cortlandt Park, as sections of a marginal highway for The Bronx.

Although this improvement will probably not be made until after the Hudson Memorial Bridge has been built over the Harlem River from Inwood to Riverdale, we believe that a study should be made of its route and design, so that the necessary property can be acquired ahead of more concentrated development along the route than existing at present. The proposed route of the extension of Riverside drive, at present through private country estates, presents an opportunity to extend Riverside Park between the proposed drive and the river.

This proposed highway along the route of Palisade avenue and 261st street will not only be a section of a future marginal highway in The Bronx, but will connect Riverside drive in Manhattan, with a proposed Riverside drive in Westchester County, of which studies are now being made by the Westchester County Park Commission.

It is our opinion that there should be a grade separation where the proposed extension of 261st street crosses Broadway to connect with the proposed branch of the Grand Boulevard and Concourse in Van Cortlandt Park.

Widening and Improvement of Existing Streets across the Northern Section of The Bronx.

It is proposed to widen 233d street from Jerome avenue to Van Cortlandt Park East, Van Cortlandt Park East from 233d to 240th street, 240th and 238th streets, from Van Cortlandt Park East to Baychester avenue, and Baychester avenue from 238th street to the Boston Post road and to erect a viaduct along the route of 238th street (Nereid avenue), across the Bronx River parkway.

This proposed highway will be a section of the future marginal highway in The Bronx, extending from the Harlem River at Spuyten Duyvil along the Hudson River to 161st street, and across the northern section of The Bronx to the Eastern boulevard, thence to the Triborough and Willis Avenue Bridges.

We are of the opinion that a study should be made of this project to determine the best route, the proper width of roadway to be provided and the location of grade separations. The proposed viaduct across the Bronx River Valley provides for a grade separation across the Bronx River parkway.

Widening of 233d Street and Baychester Avenue.

This project includes the widening of 233d street from Baychester avenue to the Boston Post road and of Baychester avenue, from the Boston Post road to Eastern boulevard, as sections or branches of the future marginal highway in The Bronx.

In connection with the marginal highway studies we believe that this section and branch of the highway should be considered, especially as to the width of roadway to be provided.

233d street has been recently opened from Baychester avenue to the Boston Post road and is now being graded and paved as a street 100 feet wide with roadway 60 feet wide. Baychester avenue is laid out as a street of equal width to 233d street.

Widening of Sedgwick Avenue.

This project includes the widening of Sedgwick avenue to provide a street 100 feet wide from Jerome avenue at McCombs Dam Bridge to the proposed northerly extension of the Concourse at Mosholu parkway.

Sedgwick avenue, as may be seen on the map on page 119, is the first continuous north and south street east of the Harlem River. Its route is generally along the side hill and underpasses High Bridge and Washington Bridge. There are few intersecting cross streets along most of its length because of the steep slopes above and below it.

As an artery for through traffic to be provided in the future, between Jerome avenue at McCombs Dam Bridge and the northerly extension of the Grand Boulevard and Concourse at Mosholu parkway, it follows a most desirable route. It connects with Exterior street at its southern end and should in the future become a most important artery for through traffic using the proposed Triborough Bridge bound to and from points in the eastern section of Westchester County.

This project will probably not be urgent for some time but we believe that the necessary properties for the widening of Sedgwick avenue should be acquired as soon as possible in view of the present development of properties taking place along certain sections of this route and also to be sure to preserve for the future a route so desirable for the flow of through traffic.

Improvement of Cross-Bronx Route.

It is proposed to improve a route across The Bronx from the Grand Boulevard and Concourse to the Southern-Eastern boulevard route via 161st street from Sheridan to Elton avenue, Elton avenue from 161st to 163d street and 163d street from Elton avenue to Whitlock avenue.

The present roadway along this route is about 60 feet wide and has a double surface car line along its centre. The poles for overhead trolley wires are along the curb, except for about a half mile along 163d street from Elton to Stebbins avenue, where they are in the centre of the roadway. There are several dangerous street intersections at the 3d avenue and Westchester avenue crossings due to steep grades at the approach to the intersections and elevated structures on these avenues. A right angle turn at the foot of a steep grade just west of the Westchester avenue crossing, and steep grades along 163d street, east and west of the Jackson and Linton avenue crossing are also objectionable features. The elimination of the street car lines and of the elevated columns at the 3d avenue and Westchester avenue crossings would greatly facilitate the flow of traffic along this route.

We suggest that a complete study be made for the improvement of the route, consideration being given to the following items:

A roadway along the route, at least 60 feet wide, unobstructed by centre poles and elevated columns and where possible by surface car tracks.

Grade separations at the Westchester and 3d avenue crossings and also at the Jackson and Linton avenue crossings.

Curves flattened at 163d street and Elton avenue and at 163d street and Westchester avenue.

Because its location not only provides access to important districts, but also intersects important north and south highways such as Jerome avenue, the Grand Boulevard and Concourse, the proposed highway along Park avenue, 3d avenue, Prospect avenue, Westchester avenue and the Southern boulevard and connects with the McComb Dam Bridge across the Harlem River, we advise that an early study of this route be made.

Improvement of Park Avenue.

The improvement of Park avenue in The Bronx, from the Harlem River to Fordham road or above, by decking over the New York Central tracks along this route, combined with the proposed improvement of Park avenue above 96th street in Manhattan and the proposed combined railroad and highway bridge across the Harlem River would extend Park avenue as now existing below 96th street on Manhattan to Fordham road or above in The Bronx.

The proposed highway should connect with the southerly extension of the Grand Boulevard and Concourse at about 152d street and be in the nature of an express highway with no cross street intersections from about 125th street on Manhattan to above 138th street in The Bronx.

From above 138th street to Fordham road, the tracks of the New York Central Railroad are in a cut varying in width from 55 to 75 feet in the middle of Park avenue and above Fordham road about at natural grade along the edge of the Bronx Park.

A deck built above these tracks at the grade of the existing lateral roadways along Park avenue south of Fordham road would provide a total width of roadway varying from 80 to 135 feet including the lateral roadways. This roadway would intersect most of the present and proposed important cross-Bronx routes at grade and, therefore, provide direct access to the developed area of The Bronx which this route practically bisects. A deck built as an elevated highway above these tracks and above the grade of the existing lateral roadways along Park avenue would provide grade separations at all of the cross-Bronx streets. It would be necessary to provide ramp connections at the important cross-Bronx routes.

We are of the opinion that a complete study should be made of this project and we believe that not only this proposed deck should be built at the grade of the lateral roadways and crosstown streets, but that consideration should be given to extending the highway above Fordham road to Gun Hill road. This would not only result in an improvement to the properties bordering it from above 138th street to Fordham road, but would create an express highway above Fordham road connecting with the Bronx River parkway at Gun Hill road and via Gun Hill road with the proposed northerly extension of the Grand Boulevard and Concourse and with the Boston Post road. The extension, properly executed, would greatly improve the appearance of the route of the New York Central tracks along the edge of the Bronx Park. Furthermore, Fordham road, now one of the heaviest traffic routes across The Bronx, should not be further burdened by becoming the terminus of such a highway.

Tremont Avenue Bridge.

Tremont avenue in The Bronx at present dead ends at Sedgwick avenue high above the Harlem River. The roadway of Tremont avenue, from University to Sedgwick avenue has recently been widened to 44 feet and follows a steep grade down to Sedgwick avenue.

Burnside avenue, another cross-Bronx route connecting at its eastern end with Tremont avenue just west of Webster avenue, also at present practically dead ends at Sedgwick avenue a block north of Tremont avenue, but has a narrow side hill roadway connection to a short section of an exterior street along the Harlem River. Burnside avenue also follows a grade down to Sedgwick avenue.

We are informed that it is proposed to build a low level bridge across the Harlem River to connect Tremont avenue in The Bronx with the Speedway and Dyckman street.

We suggest that a thorough study be made of this project and that consideration be given to the possibility of building a high level bridge from a point at about Sedgwick avenue between Tremont and Burnside avenues in The Bronx to Fort George and Amsterdam avenues at the northern end of Washington Heights on Manhattan. Such a bridge would provide a direct highway connection between Tremont, Burnside and Sedgwick avenues in The Bronx with Amsterdam, Fort George and St. Nicholas avenues on Washington Heights in Manhattan, not subject to interference by river traffic as would be the case in a low-level drawbridge, and would fit in with facilities to be provided in other projects, herewith discussed.

Brooklyn-Queens.

The various projects for the improvement of the highway system in Brooklyn and Queens are indicated on the map opposite this page and are discussed as follows:

Atlantic Avenue Improvement.

Atlantic avenue extends from Flatbush avenue in Brooklyn to the Jamaica section of Queens, a distance of approximately ten miles. Although the avenue has a uniform width of 120 feet, the roadway is of varying width due to the location, within the avenue line, of the tracks of the Long Island Railroad, which in some places are on an elevated structure and in others on the surface. The project has to do with improvements in the avenue to be made in connection with the depression of the elevated and surface tracks below the street level between Nostrand avenue in Brooklyn and Lefferts avenue in Queens, a distance of approximately eight miles. Specifically the improvements consist of roadway widening, elimination of grade crossing and a connection leading from Lefferts avenue to 95th avenue.

The removal of the obstructions, particularly the surface tracks, will not only increase the available roadway width, thereby providing additional highway capacity for east-west traffic, but will materially facilitate the passage of traffic crossing the highway.

We believe certain grade separations should be effected along Atlantic avenue. An overpass for the intersecting highway in each instance, will probably be the most practical solution, due to the location of the then depressed Long Island Railroad tracks. These proposed grade separations along Atlantic avenue are as follows:

1. Proposed north-south highway at Oxford street (provided for in Brooklyn Chamber of Commerce Plan).
2. Eastern parkway (part of circumferential highway).
3. East New York avenue.
4. Conduit boulevard and Force Tube avenue.
5. Rockaway boulevard.
6. Woodhaven boulevard.

Connecting curves to provide for right and left-hand turns into or out of Atlantic avenue will be required at the intersections number 4 to 6, when Atlantic avenue is opened as a through east and west vehicular highway of largely increased capacity. Detailed studies will be required for each intersection to determine the locations of these curves to best serve the traffic at these particular points.

From a traffic standpoint, this project is a well conceived traffic relief measure and its early consummation is very desirable.

Atlantic Avenue Extension and Connections East of Morris Park Station.

As Atlantic avenue will become a principal east and west highway through the Boroughs of Brooklyn and Queens after the removal of the Long Island tracks, it will be necessary to provide means whereby the traffic may first, avoid the congestion now existing in the Jamaica District and, secondly, be allowed to flow out on to the principal highways into Queens and Nassau County which form a natural outlet for the Atlantic avenue traffic.

This project is divided into four principal parts as follows:

Construction of a Diagonal Street from Morris Park Station to 101st Avenue.

As Atlantic avenue will have its terminus as a through thoroughfare at approximately Morris Park Station, a diagonal street having a width of at least 120 feet should be cut through from the end of Atlantic avenue to approximately the intersection of 132d street with 101st avenue. This street would be used for two-way traffic as far as Chichester avenue; and for east bound traffic beyond that point to 101st avenue. 101st avenue is an improved street 44 feet wide curb to curb, but not fully paved. It should be paved curb to curb, when it would then become suitable for carrying all the east bound traffic from Atlantic avenue to Liberty avenue.

Construction of a Diagonal Street Between Chichester and Liberty Avenues.

This street should be at least 80 feet wide with a roadway width of 50 feet. It would provide a connection for westbound traffic between Liberty avenue and Chichester

Oversized Foldout

avenue, which upon completion of the diagonal street and the depression of the Long Island tracks beneath Atlantic avenue, would then become a one-way street for westbound traffic feeding into Atlantic avenue.

This street together with the one described above is recommended to be constructed on a diagonal basis so as to afford easy directional flow of traffic between Atlantic avenue and the other highways with which this main artery connects.

Construction and Improvement of Liberty Avenue, 109th Street, Hollis Avenue and Hempstead Turnpike.

The improvement of Liberty avenue between Sutphin boulevard and Merrick road is practically completed. Some little fill has yet to be placed. Upon the consolidation of all the fill, pavement 60 feet wide will be placed upon this section.

Liberty avenue, 109th street and Hollis avenue between Merrick boulevard and Hempstead turnpike are mapped as 80-foot streets. Title proceedings are under way to acquire Liberty avenue between Merrick boulevard and 109th street. 109th street for a short distance is at present an 80-foot wide street and is not paved to its full width. In order to make this capacity fully effective, this pavement should be extended to the curbs. Hollis avenue is mapped to a width of 80 feet but has not been built. Title should be acquired and a 50-foot wide curb to curb street built.

This route will provide a connection from the end of Atlantic avenue to the Hempstead-Farmingdale turnpike in Nassau County. A small portion of this turnpike lies, however, in Queens, namely, between its intersection with Hollis avenue and the Nassau County line. It should be paved for a width of 60 feet.

Improvement of Westchester and Foch Boulevards.

In another section of this report, dealing with the widening of Merrick boulevard, adequate connection will be provided through the widening of this boulevard between Liberty avenue and Westchester boulevard.

All necessary land has been acquired for the construction of Westchester and Foch boulevards between Merrick boulevard and the Nassau County line. We are advised that it is the intention of the Borough authorities to construct a highway having a roadway width of at least 44 feet and possibly 50 feet. Through Merrick boulevard this new highway will provide a connection between Atlantic avenue and the Southern State Parkway which we were advised would be opened on July 1, 1929, as far as Hempstead Reservoir. The Southern State Parkway has a 40-foot concrete paved strip and the connection thereto from Queensboro should have an effective traffic capacity not less than this 40-foot highway.

The above improvements are necessary to make the Atlantic avenue improvements fully effective from the standpoint of through traffic and their execution should be brought about concurrently.

Improvements to Northern Boulevard.

Northern boulevard is at present one of the important arterial highways between Northern Long Island and Manhattan and upon completion of the Triborough Bridge will assume a still greater importance as a through highway. At the present time there are four locations where there are considerable barriers to traffic traversing the route because of reductions in width, grades, location of street car tracks, poor condition of paving, etc., which should be improved as follows:

Ditmars Avenue to Flushing River.

The width of the present street is 100 feet while the effective paved width is only 25 feet. Acquisition is under way to make this a 150-foot wide street with a 60-foot roadway for the length of the section which is approximately 5,300 feet. The land can probably be acquired at this time at a lower figure than could be done subsequently, as the highway now traverses territory for the most part not now built up.

Street arrangements similar to that employed on the Northern boulevard to the west of this section would seem desirable, although it may prove advisable to separate the street car tracks from the rest of the highway devoted to vehicular use, still maintaining a 60-foot width for the latter purpose. This seems desirable as within a few years Astoria avenue will be pouring into this section of the Northern boulevard a large amount of traffic from the now proposed Triborough Bridge.

Construction of New High Level Bridge Over Flushing River.

The present low level double leaf bascule bridge carrying four lanes of traffic, including two surface car lines, is inadequate to handle rush hour traffic. Interruptions resulting from river traffic further reduce its effective capacity.

GENERAL VIEW OF QUEENS

The installation of a six-lane vehicular high level bridge with its easterly approach extending over Lawrence street and the single track surface line of the Long Island Railroad would, in conjunction with the proposed widening of the highways at each end of this bridge, go a long way towards eliminating the present objectionable congestion. The surface car tracks, it was stated, would be placed in a tube under the Flushing River specially provided for them. In this connection if the two-way railway tube necessitates a cross over of the surface tracks, this should be done under or off of the vehicular roadway in order not to interrupt the vehicular traffic flow.

This project although not now advanced beyond the planning stage would in our opinion provide immediate traffic relief as well as additional capacity for the Triborough Bridge traffic when that project is completed for the reason that it would be six lanes wide instead of four; the street car tracks would be removed from bridge deck; the structure would be a high level instead of low level bridge and would provide a grade separation over Lawrence street and the Long Island Railroad.

Widening Between Flushing River and Main Street.

The section between the easterly bank of the Flushing River and Main street, Flushing, is too narrow and causes much congestion. The present width is 80 feet with 51-foot roadway width. The street continues westerly at this width to Prince street where it narrows down to 70-foot total and 42-foot roadway width. This latter width continues to Lawrence street which is just east of the bridge over the Flushing River. The present bridge will accommodate four lanes of traffic (two in each direction) including two street car tracks.

Main street, Flushing, a 100-foot street, 65-foot roadway width, dead ends at right angles at Northern boulevard, which continues easterly beyond this junction at a roadway width of 53 feet.

It is proposed to widen the section of Northern boulevard between Lawrence and Main streets to 150 feet.

The section being discussed is a bottleneck to traffic for two reasons: First, the traffic approaching from the west is free moving and although the roadway width of Northern boulevard is approximately undiminished after crossing the Flushing River, there are three cross streets and a grade crossing of the Long Island Railroad in this short section which decrease the speed of the moving vehicles; secondly, as this short length of Northern boulevard is a retail business section, there is a solid line of parked cars on each side of the street which practically reduces the available width to two lanes of moving traffic, which for the most part operate in the street car tracks.

Lawrence street also feeds a certain amount of traffic into Northern boulevard, which further accentuates the "bottleneck" effect produced in this section.

A new bridge is proposed at a high level spanning Lawrence street and the Long Island Railroad tracks, as well as the Flushing River, but no plans have been prepared and probably nothing will be done until the street approaches on both ends are widened. The present bridge will accommodate four lanes of moving traffic, including two street car tracks.

Widening at Douglaston.

A section of the boulevard about one mile long at Douglaston extending from 220th street to Douglaston boulevard, due to its narrowness (20-foot wide pavement), grades and bad pavement is a serious obstacle to the free passage of traffic. The resultant congestion occurs principally on Sundays and holidays, when traffic between New York and Long Island is heaviest.

It is proposed to construct a fixed span bridge over the Alley Pond Creek to replace the present two-lane swing drawbridge now seldom, if ever, operated for the benefit of river traffic. This new bridge would, of course, be at a considerably greater elevation above mean high water than the present one and would have a deck width at least equivalent to the width of the connecting highway on each side of it. A width of 80 feet for the deck of this bridge has been suggested, although the roadway width of the Northern boulevard for the greater portion of its length is only 60 feet.

It may be desirable to construct this proposed bridge at a width of 80 feet to take care of the possible future widening of the Northern boulevard beyond the 60-foot roadway width now considered as ultimate. We understand that $200,000 has been appropriated by the Board of Estimate and Apportionment for the construction of the bridge.

Improvements to Nassau Boulevard.

Nassau boulevard is a project designed to create an arterial highway connecting Brooklyn with Queens and points on the northern shore of Long Island. Its route begins at Myrtle avenue and Harmon street in Brooklyn and extends along Harmon street to Metropolitan avenue; thence along Elliot avenue (proposed) to Queens boulevard; thence along Nassau boulevard (proposed) to Strongs Causeway; thence along Nassau boulevard to the Nassau County line, where it will connect with the proposed Northern State Parkway leading to the north shore of Long Island. In order to create this highway certain improvements must be made, as follows:

Widening Harmon Street from Myrtle Avenue to Metropolitan Avenue.

Harmon street between the above limits has a 30-foot roadway. The Borough Planning Commission of Queens has proposed widening the street from 60 to 80 feet, thereby permitting a roadway width of 44 feet. With such a street width it would be possible to obtain a 50-foot roadway. However, this hardly seems necessary, as Myrtle avenue, the Brooklyn end of this improvement and the principal feeder street thereto, has a roadway width of only 40 feet.

This improvement is not only highly desirable, but in our opinion very necessary. In conjunction with the improved Elliot street and Nassau boulevard, it will provide an additional route for traffic around the congested area of Jamaica. Intersecting both Myrtle and Metropolitan avenues as it does, Harmon street will remove a certain amount of through traffic from those streets which otherwise would find its way out to Long Island over the now congested Jamaica and Hillside avenues.

Construction of Elliot Avenue from Metropolitan Avenue to Queens Boulevard.

Elliot avenue is a proposed highway to connect Harmon street on the south with Nassau boulevard on the north. A right-of-way 80 feet wide has been acquired between Metropolitan avenue and Queens boulevard, upon which it is proposed to build a 44-foot roadway.

Inasmuch as this section, in conjunction with Nassau boulevard, will provide traffic relief for not only Myrtle avenue, but Metropolitan avenue as well, we are of the opinion that Elliot avenue within the limits as above indicated should be constructed with a roadway width of approximately 60 feet. Sufficient right-of-way to make this section a 100-foot street could now probably be acquired without excessive costs as it traverses a relatively undeveloped area. This link, in conjunction with the other portions of Nassau boulevard, when completed, will also serve to minimize the congestion along Hillside and Jamaica avenues.

Construction from Queens Boulevard to Strongs Causeway.

This section of the boulevard is to be constructed across the meadows at a width of 160 feet. We understand that title is not yet vested but that such is being urged by the Borough President's office in order that spoil from subway construction may be utilized in securing the necessary fill.

The ultimate pavement arrangement as proposed for the Boulevard from Queens boulevard to Nassau County line consists of one 60-foot wide paved strip for through traffic with a 25-foot service roadway on each side of the main section. This type of roadway arrangement will, of course, apply to the section here under consideration.

A bridge will be needed in this section of the route to span the Flushing River. We are advised that the construction of the bridge will be carried on concurrently with that of the highway, and that it will be a high level double leaf bascule draw type.

Construction of Viaduct Over Alley Pond Creek.

The construction of a viaduct over Alley Pond Creek will eliminate the bad congestion occurring at this location during Sunday and holiday travel caused by the existing bad grades, dangerous curves and the narrow roadway at this location. The location of this bottleneck section is well out in the northeastern end of Queens, and although at a considerable distance from Manhattan carries a large amount of traffic at certain times. As it is only two lanes wide in a route having a six-lane width each side of it, it appears necessary and desirable that this project be carried concurrently with the other boulevard improvements in order to get the maximum use of an otherwise satisfactory highway.

Improvement of Stewart Railroad Right-of-Way.

There is an abandoned railroad right-of-way (known as Stewarts) extending from Main street in Queens to Hillside and Braddock avenues in Queens which it is proposed to convert into an arterial highway later to become a part of a connection between the Triborough Bridge and central Long Island. From the standpoint of present traffic conditions this project can be considered in two sections as follows:

Nassau Boulevard to Hillside Avenue, Queens.

This section of the project is needed for immediate relief from the congestion existing along Jamaica and Hillside avenues in Queens caused by traffic between eastern Long Island and Queens and Manhattan. The relief afforded the Jamaica district by this construction is dependent upon the completion of the Nassau boulevard-Eliot street improvement and the work in connection with the two projects should preferably be carried out concurrently.

Main Street to Nassau Boulevard.

This section of the project will become desirable upon the completion of the Triborough Bridge and its construction is not urgent at this time.

Widening of Woodhaven Boulevard.

Woodhaven boulevard forms a link in a natural feeder system to the Rockaway Peninsula and extends from Queens boulevard on the north to Liberty avenue on the south, where it connects with the Cross Bay boulevard.

The Woodhaven boulevard is the most convenient highway to the popular resort districts in the Rockaways for the majority of the population in Manhattan and Queens and is heavily used, particularly on Sundays and holidays. The widening of the section from Queens boulevard to Liberty and Rockaway boulevards will create an approximately 150-foot highway from one end to the other and will, when completed, provide accommodation for a minimum of six lanes of moving traffic.

Including Queens boulevard it will cross the following existing or proposed principal highways:

Proposed Borden avenue extension; Metropolitan avenue; Myrtle avenue; Jamaica avenue; Atlantic avenue; Liberty avenue and Rockaway boulevard; Linden avenue; Conduit boulevard.

The Board of Estimate and Apportionment has authorized title proceedings to widen Woodhaven boulevard from Queens boulevard to Forest Park (Myrtle avenue) to a width of 150 feet. At present this highway is only wide enough for two lanes of traffic, one in each direction, and one slow moving truck causes a disproportionate congestion, particularly during morning and evening peaks and on holidays.

From Forest Park (Myrtle avenue) to Liberty avenue and Rockaway boulevard, the total street width is only 50 feet and the property owners along this section, which is slightly in excess of a mile in length, have persistently opposed the widening for many years. Its necessity has been recognized by both the Borough administration, the Queensboro Planning Commission and the Queens Chamber of Commerce as a very desirable improvement in this highway.

From Liberty avenue to the Rockaway Peninsula the highway is completed and will accommodate six lanes of traffic to the southerly end of Big Marsh Island. From this point to its intersection with Beach Channel drive, a distance of about three-quarters of a mile, the highway is only one-half width or suitable for three lanes of traffic.

A double-leaf high level bascule bridge having a width equivalent to the highway on each side of it spans Beach Channel.

We understand that both the highway and the bridge have been designed for ultimately accommodating six lanes of traffic and that this improvement will eventually be carried out, although no proceedings are under way or are planned at the present time.

Improvement and Extension of 137th Street, Queens.

This project is designed to provide a by-pass around two badly congested intersections of Queens boulevard with Hillside and Jamaica avenues in Queens. The improvement consists of two parts as follows:

The construction of an extension to 137th street 100 feet wide between Queens boulevard and 87th avenue, a distance of approximately 1,700 feet.

The widening of 137th street to 100 feet between 87th avenue and Jamaica avenue, a distance of approximately 1,300 feet.

This improvement, in conjunction with that proposed for Van Wyck boulevard, will enable traffic moving between Queens boulevards and points south of Atlantic avenue to avoid the congestion in the Jamaica area caused by a large amount of local traffic and also permit the through traffic to make use of an existing underpass beneath the tracks of the Long Island Railroad at Van Wyck avenue.

Widening of Van Wyck Avenue.

Van Wyck avenue, in conjunction with the extension and improvement of 137th street, will form a connection from Queens boulevard on the north to Linden and

Conduit boulevards on the south, thereby enabling the traffic from Queens boulevard to reach points along the southern shore of Long Island via the Southern State parkway, Merrick road and Conduit boulevard, respectively, without traversing the congested streets of Jamaica. Van Wyck avenue will also provide a traffic connection between Queens boulevard and points along the Hempstead-Farmingdale turnpike in Long Island via Liberty avenue, 109th avenue and Hollis avenue, when the projects covering the latter route are completed.

The present width of Van Wyck avenue is sufficient to accommodate only two lanes of moving traffic and the Borough Planning Commission of Queens has recommended that the street width from 137th street to Conduit boulevard should be increased to 100 feet, which would provide a 60-foot roadway and would be adequate to accommodate the expectable vehicular traffic over this route. This improvement will involve the widening of an underpass beneath the tracks of the Long Island Railroad in Jamaica.

Construction of Plaza at Van Wyck Avenue and 101st Avenue.

The intersection of Van Wyck avenue and 101st avenue will be a crossing and turning point for traffic between Queens boulevard, Atlantic avenue and points in central and southern Long Island, and we believe that the expectable volume of traffic will necessitate the construction of special facilities at this intersection to minimize interference between the several traffic streams. While a grade separation may eventually be required, a plaza would appear to be adequate for a number of years and would provide space for later construction of a grade separation.

This improvement is necessary to make fully effective the proposed improvements to 101st avenue, 137th street and Van Wyck avenue, and should be made concurrently with the widening of 101st avenue.

Widening of 101st Avenue.

This project covers the widening of 101st avenue to 100 feet from Sutphin boulevard to the point of intersection with the proposed 100-foot diagonal street from Atlantic avenue as previously described, to conform with the width of this diagonal street and with the existing width of Liberty avenue at the Sutphin boulevard end of 101st avenue. This work should be completed coincidently with the completion of the Atlantic avenue improvements.

Paving Liberty Avenue between Sutphin and Merrick Boulevards.

Liberty avenue will form a portion of the easterly end of the Atlantic avenue thoroughfare for traffic between downtown Brooklyn and points in Long Island via the 109th street and Hollis avenue route. The street within the limits above mentioned is completed and when the fill is properly consolidated the roadway pavement should be placed.

Merrick Road Widening.

Merrick road from Liberty avenue to the Nassau County line is paved for a width of only 21 feet. We understand that the right-of-way is 100 feet wide, but has been encroached upon by certain buildings. An additional 20-foot width of pavement is contemplated to provide a paved highway capable of carrying four moving lanes of traffic. We believe that this improvement is desirable to take care of the constantly increasing Sunday and holiday traffic over this highway.

Construction of New High Level Bridge over English Kills at Grand and Metropolitan Avenues.

Grand and Metropolitan avenues, two important Brooklyn thoroughfares have their point of intersection at the English Kills, a branch of the Newtown Creek, and cross this stream by means of a low level swing drawbridge having a 19-foot roadway common to both streets. The roadway of the bridge is only two lanes wide and includes a double line of car tracks. This arrangement constitutes an obstruction for traffic using both Grand and Metropolitan avenues and the congestion at this point is increased when the bridge is opened to allow the passage of river boats.

We are advised by the Department of Plant and Structures that $650,000 has been appropriated to replace the present bridge with a double leaf bascule type bridge with six traffic lanes, but built at the same elevation as the present structure. The construction of a high level bridge would be more desirable, but the elevation of the land and the character of the property in the area contiguous to the bridge approaches is such as to practically preclude the possibility of constructing such a bridge without involving rather heavy property damages.

Construction of Circumferential Highway Through Brooklyn and Queens.

The Brooklyn-Queens circumferential highway project is designed to provide the following:

    1. An additional route for interborough traffic between Brooklyn and Queens.
    2. An intercepting highway to relieve the north and south streets in the congested area of Brooklyn and Queens of through east and west traffic transfering from one east and west highway to another.
    3. A by-pass around Manhattan for through traffic between points north and south of New York City, via the proposed Triborough Bridge and Narrows Tunnel.

Beginning in Queens at the intersection of Potter avenue and Astoria avenue, the proposed route of this highway follows the right-of-way of the New York Connecting Railroad to the intersection of Chauncey street and Central avenue in Brooklyn, and thence to the Eastern parkway, Howard avenue, Kings highway, Stillwell avenue and 75th street, Brooklyn, from which street there are several alternate routes to the proposed Narrows Tunnel. The route for the section of this highway between Central avenue and Chauncey street to the Eastern parkway has not yet been determined, and is a matter for further study by the Borough officials. The section of the proposed route between Astoria avenue and Queens boulevard is known as the Triborough boulevard project for which plans have been prepared providing for a right-of-way width of 130 feet. No plans have been prepared for the section between Queens boulevard and the connection to be established with the Eastern parkway.

Supplementary to the above route, it is proposed to utilize a route beginning at Kings highway and Linden boulevard and following Linden boulevard, Caton avenue and Fort Hamilton parkway to 75th street. In connection with this supplemental route, it will be necessary to widen and improve Caton avenue between Bedford avenue and Gravesend avenue.

The section of this project to be known as the Triborough boulevard should be completed concurrently with the completion of the proposed Triborough Bridge to assist in distributing and collecting the Triborough Bridge traffic to and from points east of the proposed circumferential route in Brooklyn and Queens. The widening and improvement of Caton avenue may be deferred until such time as the supplemental circumferential route is required by the increased volume of traffic.

Widening of Astoria and Ditmars Avenues.

This project is designed primarily to provide, in conjunction with Northern boulevard and other existing highways, a route for traffic between the proposed Triborough Bridge and points in northern Long Island, and also to serve as a distributing and collecting highway for certain other Triborough Bridge traffic.

It is proposed to increase the width of Astoria avenue from Van Alst street to Ditmars avenue, and Ditmars avenue to its intersection with Northern boulevard, to 130-foot right-of-way, with two 40-foot roadways separated by a 20-foot dead strip. A portion of Astoria avenue is now occupied by surface car tracks and consideration should be given to the removal of these tracks from the roadway.

The foregoing improvement should be completed not later than the time when the Triborough Bridge is opened to traffic, as Astoria avenue will be the principal approach to the bridge in the Borough of Queens.

Proposed Route from Astoria Avenue to Nassau Boulevard.

This project is designed to provide, in connection with the proposed highway along the abandoned right-of-way of the Stewart Railroad from Nassau boulevard to Hillside and Braddock avenues, as previously described, a diagonal highway in Queens for the distribution and collection of Triborough Bridge traffic using highways other than the Northern boulevard to and from points in northern Queens and Long Island. The project consists of the following:

    1. Widening of 108th street from Astoria avenue to 51st avenue, and 51st avenue from 108th street to 117th street; and extension of 51st street from 117th street across the Flushing River to the abandoned right-of-way of the Stewart Railroad.

    2. Construction of a new highway from 51st street extension, along Stewart Railroad right-of-way to Nassau boulevard.

The proposed width of the new highway to be constructed along the abandoned right-of-way of the Stewart Railroad is 100 feet, with a 60-foot roadway. No definite plans have been developed for the widening of 108th street and 51st avenue and the extension of 51st avenue into Flushing, but we believe that the width of these highways should be made not less than the width of the section on the railroad right-of-way.

The highways included under this project will form an important connecting link between the proposed Triborough Bridge and numerous highways of northern Queens and Long Island, and should be completed by the time the Triborough Bridge is opened to traffic.

Construction of Express Highway from Proposed Upper Deck of Queensboro Bridge.

It is proposed to construct an express highway extending from the Queens end of the proposed upper deck of the Queensboro Bridge, immediately east of Van Alst avenue, on an elevated structure, south to Harris avenue and thence east over Harris avenue and private right-of-way to Thompson avenue at the point where that avenue becomes a viaduct over the Long Island Railroad yards. After crossing over the railroad yards on the existing viaduct or a new viaduct, the proposed express highway will descend approximately to the railroad yard level and extend along the southerly line of the railroad right-of-way to an undetermined location in Woodside.

According to present plans, this highway and the upper deck of the Queensboro Bridge will be used for eastbound traffic only, and will by-pass such traffic around the congested area at the eastern approach to the present, or lower, deck of the bridge. The proposed highway will accommodate a large portion of the bridge traffic now using Northern boulevard and Skillman avenue, and will reduce the congestion on these two streets.

This particular project is intimately related to the project for the construction of the upper deck of the bridge, and the two projects should be completed simultaneously.

Borden and Caldwell Avenue Improvements.

This project is designed to provide a feeder highway connection with the Queens end of the proposed 38th Street Tunnel, and consists of the following:

    1. Widening of Borden avenue from the tunnel entrance to Maurice street.

    2. Extension of Borden avenue from Maurice street eastward to Caldwell avenue.

    3. Widening of Caldwell avenue from Borden avenue extension to Dry Harbor road.

    4. Extension of Caldwell avenue from Dry Harbor road to Woodhaven boulevard.

It is proposed that this highway shall have a continuous roadway width of 60 feet, with the maximum possible street widths up to 100 feet.

A double line of car tracks occupies the centre of Borden avenue, with the exception of a short section between Bradley and Greenpoint avenues. We are of the opinion that consideration should be given to the removal of these tracks and the substitution of bus service when the street improvements are made, in order to eliminate obstruction to motor vehicular traffic caused by street railway operations.

This project is necessary for the full utilization of the 38th Street Tunnel facilities and should be completed coincidently with the completion of the tunnel construction.

Replacement of Present Retractile Drawbridge at Borden Avenue Over the Dutch Kills.

This project is in line of the Borden avenue feeder to the 38th Street Tunnel. The present bridge has an available roadway width of only 33 feet and would be entirely inadequate to handle the traffic from the proposed tunnel if the tunnel is terminated to the west of the present bridge. If, however, the tunnel mouth is located to the east of this bridge, there appears to be no necessity for replacing the present structure, as it would not be called upon to handle any of the through tunnel traffic.

Widening of 9th Street from Hamilton Avenue to Smith Street.

9th street in the Borough of Brooklyn will form an important feeder distribution route in connection with the Brooklyn-Manhattan Tunnel. The City is widening this street to a roadway width of 77½ feet between Prospect Park West and Smith street in connection with rapid transit subway construction, and it will be necessary to widen the section from Smith street to Hamilton avenue in order to provide a route of uniformly adequate width. This latter improvement should be completed before the time when the Brooklyn-Manhattan Tunnel is opened to traffic.

Construction of Two New Bridges Over the Gowanus Canal at Hamilton Avenue and 9th Street.

The present Hamilton Avenue and 9th Street Bridges over the Gowanus Canal are wide enough for only four lanes of traffic, two of which are occupied by street car tracks.

We are of the opinion that these bridges will become obstructions to traffic when Hamilton avenue and 9th street are used as feeders for the Brooklyn-Manhattan Tunnel, particularly as the roadway width is only 35 feet and allows but little clearance for vehicular traffic on each side of the street car tracks. The Department of Plant and Structures has been allotted funds to the extent of $30,000 for the preparation of plans and making borings for a new bridge at Hamilton avenue capable of accommodating six lanes of moving traffic. No plans for the replacement of the 9th Street Bridge were prepared or contemplated at the time of our investigation.

Miscellaneous Projects for Ultimate Development.

In addition to the foregoing projects, there are numerous projects which are not required as traffic relief measures for the immediate future, but which are proposed as a further development of the arterial highway system in the Boroughs of Brooklyn and Queens. The following is a list of such projects, numbered in accordance with the key numbers on the map on page 129, showing major existing and proposed arterial highways, bridges and tunnels in the two Boroughs.

Key Number.	Description of Project.
30	Construction of section of Linden boulevard from Rockaway parkway to Merrick and Westchester boulevards, to provide a main highway connection between the southern part of Brooklyn and the highways extending into southeastern Queens and southern Long Island.
31	Construction of Interborough parkway from Bushwick avenue in Brooklyn through Highland Park, Cypress Hills Cemetery and Forest Park to Metropolitan avenue and Union turnpike; widening of Union turnpike from Metropolitan avenue to Grand Central parkway, and extension of Union turnpike from Homelawn avenue to the Nassau County line. This project is designed to provide an additional route for east and west interborough traffic and to relieve congestion on Hillside and Jamaica avenues.
32	Construction of Grand Central parkway from Union turnpike to Nassau County line as an additional east and west park thoroughfare.
33	Extension of Hillside avenue from Braddock avenue to Nassau County line, parallel to Jamaica avenue and Jamaica turnpike, to supplement the latter route for east and west traffic.
34	Completion of unconstructed sections of Beach Channel drive along the north shore of Rockaway Peninsula and construction of North Shore drive from eastern terminus of Beach Channel drive to the Nassau County line, to increase the highway facilities along Rockaway Peninsula.
35	Construction of Sea Girt avenue on Rockaway peninsula from Rockaway boulevard to Nassau County line, to provide a shore connection to Atlantic Beach and Long Beach.
36	Construction and improvement of a route through Queens from Whitestone via 149th street, Parsons boulevard, Kissena Park, 164th street, 163d street, New York boulevard, Farmers boulevard and a viaduct over Jamaica Bay to a terminus at Beach 43d street and Amstel boulevard on Rockaway Peninsula, as an additional north and south arterial highway.
37	Improvement and construction of Cross Island boulevard from Whitestone through Queens to Hungry Harbor road at the Nassau County line, for the same purpose as project 36 above.
38	Construction and improvement of a north and south arterial route from Northern boulevard to Rockaway boulevard through the eastern part of Queens, for the same purpose as project 36 above.
39	Improvement and construction of Lawrence boulevard from Main street, Flushing, to College Point in Queens, to improve the highway facilities between these two points.
40	Extension of Main street, Flushing, from Kissena boulevard to Grand Central parkway, as an additional route between Flushing and Jamaica.
41	Widening of Betts avenue from Queens boulevard to Maspeth avenue, to provide an improved direct route between Maspeth and Woodside.
42	Improvement and extension of Junction boulevard from Astoria avenue to Queens boulevard, as an additional improved connection between those two highways.
43	Widening of Jamaica avenue from Grand street, Jamaica, to Nassau County line, to increase the vehicular capacity of this highway.

Key Number.	Description of Project.
44	Construction of Bayview avenue from Highland avenue to West 37th street in Coney Island, to connect Surf avenue with West 37th street.
45	Improvement and construction of Maspeth avenue, Vandervoort avenue and Old Wood Point road in the Greenpoint section of Brooklyn, to provide improved highway connections with points in Brooklyn and Queens.
46	Widening of Flushing avenue in Queens from Brooklyn Borough line to Grand avenue, as an additional improved route between Brooklyn and the Elmhurst section of Queens.
47	Removal of street car tracks on Myrtle avenue from Fulton street, Brooklyn, to Jamaica avenue, Queens, to increase the vehicular capacity of this highway.
48	Removal of elevated railway structure on Fulton street, Brooklyn, from the East River Ferry to Broadway, to improve Fulton street.
49	Removal of elevated railway structure on Flatbush avenue, Brooklyn, from Fulton street to 5th avenue, to eliminate the structure columns located in the roadway.
50	Improvement and construction of Rockaway parkway from a point near Linden boulevard to a marginal street along Jamaica Bay, to connect with Seaview avenue and serve as a feeder to the Canarsie area.
51	Improvement of Remsen avenue from East New York avenue to Seaview avenue in Queens, for the same purpose as project 50 above.
52	Construction of Avenue K, Flatlands avenue and Fairfield avenue from Flatbush avenue to Cross Bay boulevard in Brooklyn and Queens, as an additional connection between the last named highways.
53	Construction of Seaview avenue and Avenue U from Flatbush avenue to Fresh Creek Basin in Brooklyn, as a local highway connection.
54	Construction of a highway along the shore of Gravesend Bay in Brooklyn from 4th avenue to Coney Island Creek, as a parkway development and as an additional connection between Coney Island and the proposed Narrows Tunnel.
55	Improvement and construction of a route in Brooklyn from Fort Hamilton Park to Neptune avenue, via Cropsey and Harway avenues, West 18th street and West 17th street, including a new bridge across Coney Island Creek at Harway avenue, to provide an additional route to Coney Island.
56	Improvement and construction of Neptune Canal and Guider avenues in the Coney Island district from West 37th street to Emmons avenue, to provide an east and west connection across the southern section of Brooklyn.
57	Widening of Shell road from 86th street to Canal avenue, as an additional feeder to Coney Island.
58	Construction of Emmons avenue from the end of Guider avenue to Gerritsen avenue in Marine Park, as a continuation of project 56, to form a shore boulevard along Rockaway Inlet.
59	Widening of roadway on Stillwell avenue from 86th street to Surf avenue in Brooklyn, to improve this highway approach to Coney Island.
60	Construction of bridge across Newtown Creek on the line of Maspeth avenue, to serve as an additional connection between Brooklyn and Queens.
61	Widening of deck of present bridge across Beach Channel on Cross Bay boulevard route to Rockaway Peninsula.
62	Construction of a new bridge of eight lanes capacity over Sheepshead Bay at Ocean avenue, Brooklyn, to improve this approach to Coney Island.
63	Construction of a new bridge of eight lanes capacity over Kent Basin at Washington avenue in Brooklyn, to make the bridge width commensurate with the width of the highway.
64	Replacement of present bridge over Gowanus Canal at Carroll avenue with a new bridge of greater width.
65	Construction of a vehicular tunnel under Rockaway Inlet from Flatbush avenue, Brooklyn, to Rockaway Peninsula, where a ferry line is now in operation.

The preliminary engineering and legal work in connection with these projects is in various stages of completion. Obviously the dates of construction are uncertain, being dependent upon the rate of development in the territory involved and other factors of an intangible nature.

RICHMOND.

At the present time the highway traffic problems of the Borough of Richmond are largely local in character, which is the result of the isolation of the island and the sparsely settled nature of most of the area. The recent completion of two mainland bridge connections with New Jersey, a similar connection under construction and the proposed vehicular tunnel connection with Brooklyn will undoubtedly stimulate the development of the island and bring about the necessity for additional and improved highway facilities particularly arterial routes connecting with their terminals.

The map on page 143 shows the present development of the highway of the island together with certain projects as proposed by the borough officials and by ourselves, which are briefly discussed as follows:

The principal existing highways traversing Staten Island are shown in black. It should be noted, however, that while these highways comprise the present arterial system they are in most instances less than 80 feet wide. Hylan boulevard, Washington avenue from Plaza of Goethals Bridge to Willowbrook road, a section of Bay street from Hannah street to the Manhattan Ferry House and Richmond terrace from this point to Hamilton avenue were the only existing highways having a width of 100 feet at the time of our field investigation.

The proposed highways shown in red indicate projects which will necessitate the location and construction of new highways and the highways shown in red and black indicate proposed projects involving the widening of existing or dedicated highways. These various projects are numbered consecutively from 1 to 26 and may be grouped as follows:

1. Open, grade and pave Lorraine avenue (Page street) from Hylan boulevard to plaza of Outerbridge crossing.
2. Open, grade and pave Pleasant Plains avenue from Amboy road to the plaza of Outerbridge crossing.
3. Open, grade and pave Allentown lane (Ramona boulevard) from Arthur Kill road to Richmond avenue near Fresh Kills Bridge.
4. Widen Richmond avenue to 80 feet from Hyan boulevard to Arthur Kill road.
5. Widen Richmond avenue to 100 and 110 feet from Arthur Kill road to bounding street of Willowbrook Park near Rockland avenue. A new bridge across Richmond Creek is involved.
6. Widen Sand lane to 70 and 80 feet.
7. Widen Richmond terrace to 68 feet from Nicholas street to Stuyvesant place.
8. Widen Bay street from Hannah street to Simonson avenue.
9. Open a new highway to be known as West Shore boulevard, 200 feet wide, from plaza of Kill Van Kull Bridge to plaza of Outerbridge crossing and connect with Washington avenue near South avenue.
10. Widen Morning Star road from plaza of Kill Van Kull Bridge to Washington avenue.
11. Open streets bounding proposed Willowbrook Park and widen to 100 feet with connection to Victory boulevard at Bulls Head.
12. Widen the following streets to 100-foot highways: Xenia street, Quintard street, Tacony street, Main avenue, Baltic avenue, Targee street and Clove road.
13. Widen Victory boulevard to 100 feet for its entire length.
14. Widen Manor road to 100 feet from Victory boulevard to Rockland avenue.
15. Widen Rockland avenue to 100 feet from Forest Hill road to Richmond road.
16. Widen Richmond road and Arthur Kill road from Amboy road to proposed West Shore boulevard.
17. Open new 100-foot boulevard from Poillon avenue to Pleasant Plains avenue.
18. Extend Seaside boulevard from its present terminus at South Beach to Midland avenue.
19. Construct a new 100-foot highway from Vedder avenue to Rockland avenue intersecting with Richmond avenue.
20. Widen Fingerboard road from Bay street to Richmond road.
21. Widen Hooker place and Prospect street between Morning Star road and Trantor place.
22. Open Pennsylvania avenue from its intersection with Hylan boulevard to DeKalb street; widen DeKalb street to Clove road and widen Clove road from

DeKalb street to Forest avenue; widen Forest avenue from Clove road to Willowbrook road.

23. Widen Tompkins avenue from Fingerboard road to Broad street, and Broad street from Tompkins avenue to Bay street.

24. Open and widen Sears avenue (Bloomfield road) from plaza of Goethal's Bridge to Chelsea avenue; widen Chelsea avenue and Travis avenue from Richmond avenue to Forest Hill road. Widen Crawford avenue from Richmond road to Altoona avenue, and Altoona avenue to Amboy road; widen Tysen's lane from Amboy road to Hylan boulevard.

25. Extend Seaside boulevard to Alter avenue; widen Alter avenue from Seaside boulevard to Scotland avenue; widen Scotland avenue from Alter avenue to Seaview avenue.

26. Widen Bay street from Simonson avenue to Fingerboard road.

At the time of our field investigation, projects Nos. 1 to 5, inclusive, were either under construction or contracted for.

The completion of projects Nos. 1 and 2 will afford better highway facilities for traffic moving over outerbridge crossing; project No. 1 will provide a direct route over a 100-foot highway between the bridge plaza and Hylan boulevard, which is the principal highway serving the east shore of the island, and project No. 2 will provide a direct route to Amboy road, which parallels Hylan boulevard about half a mile to the west.

The five major projects, Nos. 3, 7, 9, 13 and 16, which may be considered as main arterial highways are described more in detail as follows:

Project No. 3 provides for the construction of a new highway to be known as Ramona boulevard, which will extend from the intersection of Allentown lane and the proposed West Shore boulevard to Richmond avenue at its intersection with Arthur Kill road, and was under construction at the time of our field investigation. The widening of Richmond avenue comprising projects Nos. 4 and 5, also under construction, provide an arterial highway, connecting with Ramona boulevard, from Hylan boulevard to Richmond Hill road. To complete this highway and afford a means of through traffic to the Kill Van Kull Bridge, project No. 19, comprising a new highway from Vedder avenue to Rockland avenue, intersecting with Richmond avenue, has been proposed by the officials of the Borough of Richmond. To provide for cross traffic between this highway and the east shore and to provide a connecting link with the Goethal's Bridge we have suggested project No. 24, which will connect with projects Nos. 14 and 15, thereby completing a cross highway with a feeder route and connecting with the north and south arterial highway.

Project No. 7, providing for the widening of Richmond terrace from Nicholas street to Stuyvesant place, will provide an improved highway to serve the industrial district along the west shore and an additional feeder highway to the Kill Van Kull Bridge.

Project No. 9, to construct a new 200-foot boulevard connecting the three bridges along the west shore will provide a direct route for interstate traffic passing over these bridges.

Project No. 13, to widen Victory boulevard to 100 feet for its entire length provides a diagonal feeder intersecting the principal arterial highway along the west side of the island.

Project No. 16, to widen Richmond road and Arthur Kill road from Amboy road to the proposed West Shore boulevard, provides an additional diagonal highway intersecting the main arterial highways at the southern portion of the island.

In order to provide additional highway capacity to serve the terminal of the proposed tunnel to be constructed at the Narrows between Staten Island and Brooklyn and to provide a direct route connecting the tunnel with the Kill Van Kull and the Goethal's Bridge, which will permit traffic to flow between these points without passing through the business area, we have suggested projects Nos. 20, 21, 22, 23 and 26.

Project No. 25, to extend Seaside boulevard to Alter avenue and widen Alter avenue from Seaside boulevard to Scotland avenue, and Scotland avenue from Alter avenue to Seaview avenue, is offered as a modification of project No. 18, which provides for extending Seaside boulevard from its present terminus at South Beach to Midland avenue, in order to take advantage of the existing highways rather than construct a new highway that would necessitate an expensive bridge structure.

The remainder of the projects are more in the nature of local improvements, which are desirable to facilitate traffic desiring to reach the main arterial highways; and comprise projects Nos. 6, 10, 11, 12, 17 and 18. Project No. 11, included in the above

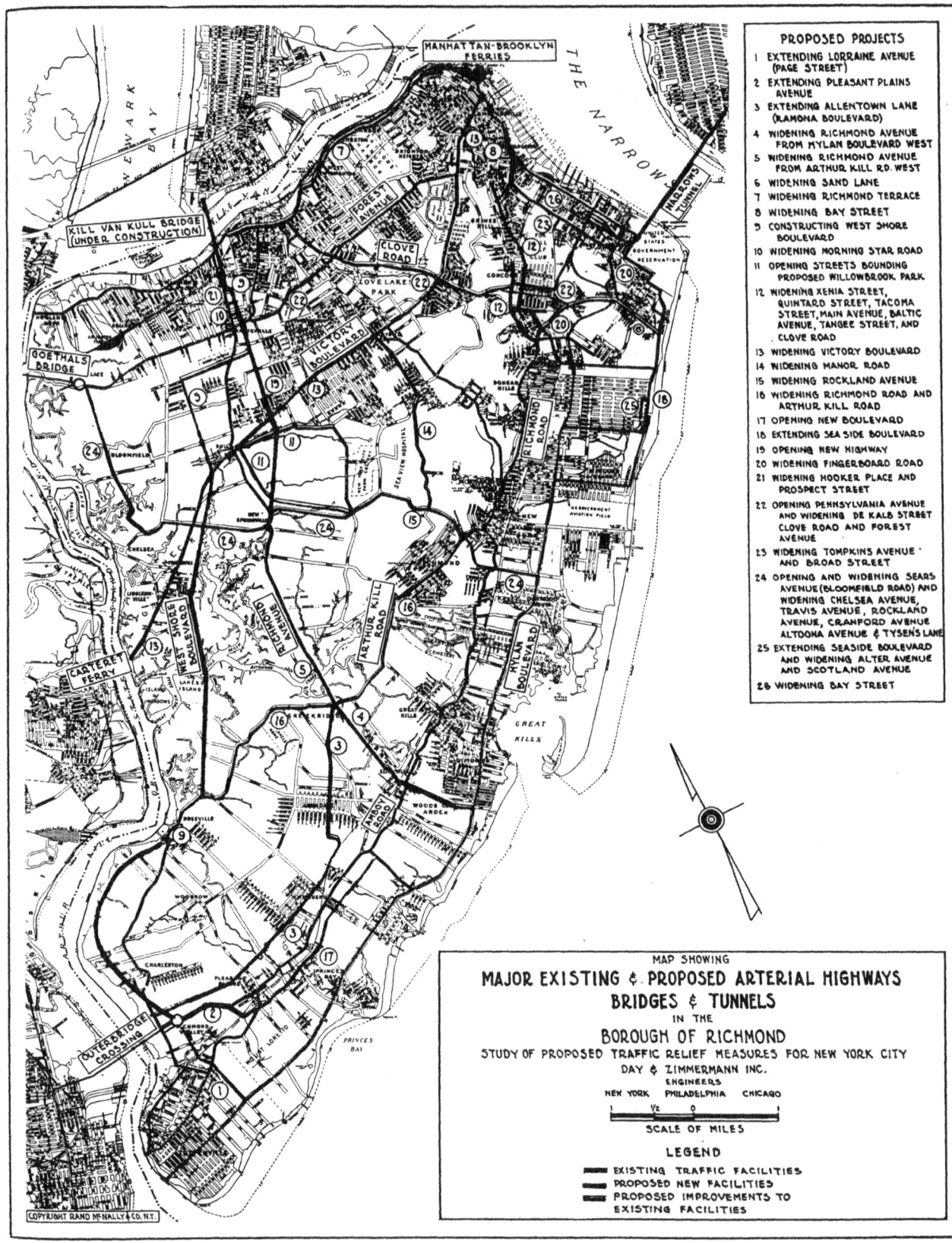

group provides for opening the streets bounding the proposed Willowbrook Park to a width of 100 feet. In this connection it is noted that the proposed highway on the southwest side of the park parallels an existing highway and a portion of project No. 24, which appears to accomplish the same results as the proposed highway.

MISCELLANEOUS BRIDGE PROJECTS.

In addition to the major bridge and tunnel projects presented in earlier sections, there are several suggested vehicular connections across the East River which are briefly set forth as follows:

Ferry Point-Whitestone Connection.

The section of the East River separating Queens from The Bronx extends for practically seven miles from the site of the Triborough Bridge to Long Island Sound. The only vehicular connection now available is the ferry connecting Clason Point in The Bronx with College Point in Queens. The traffic over this ferry has been growing rapidly and there is considerable demand for additional facilities, particularly in the summer months, which has resulted in proposals to construct either a bridge or a tunnel across the East River in this vicinity or between Whitestone and Ferry Point. The City Committee on Plan and Survey in its report recommended that this traffic demand should be met by a new ferry connection between Ferry Point in The Bronx and Whitestone in Queens.

The provision of added ferry service will relieve the situation materially, and further relief will be afforded by the Triborough Bridge. The situation will ultimately require the construction of a bridge or tunnel, and in our judgment warrants the undertaking of preliminary surveys and plans.

86th Street Bridge.

In the report of the City Committee on Plan and Survey it was recommended that a bridge be built between 86th street, Manhattan, and Astoria and it was also suggested that a spur from the Triborough Bridge to about 96th street would postpone the need for the proposed bridge at 86th street.

The proposed site offers favorable conditions from the viewpoint of construction and design, particularly as spans would be shortened by the availability of the northern end of Welfare Island for pier locations. On the Manhattan side the bridge terminal would be about one and one-quarter miles above the Queensboro Bridge and slightly less than two miles below the 125th street spur of the Triborough Bridge, and the approach would begin at about 2d avenue. The suggested location of a spur from the Triborough Bridge terminating at 96th street would result in a more even distribution of bridgeheads in this section of Manhattan under existing conditions, but would make it more difficult to obtain advantageous spacings should further additional connections be required to meet future traffic needs. In our judgment, consideration should be given in future planning to the possibilities of improved distribution of interborough traffic offered by a spur from the Triborough Bridge to about 106th street and a bridge in the vicinity of 79th street.

On the Queens side of the crossing, the approach could be located in Grand avenue, which would place the terminal about one and one-half miles north of the Queensboro Bridge and only about one-half mile below the Triborough Bridge terminal at Hoyt avenue. Astoria avenue and the Northern boulevard would be the main connections with the highway system along the north shore of Long Island for both the Triborough and the 86th Street Bridges, and it would appear desirable from the viewpoint of traffic that any additional crossing in this section of the river should have its Queens terminal farther south, as for example at Broadway or Graham avenue. In such event the terminals in this section of Queens would be spaced about one mile apart.

The proposed construction of a bridge across the East River in the vicinity of 86th street is intended to afford relief in sections of Queens and Manhattan where traffic conditions are expected to be materially improved upon the completion of the Triborough Bridge and the north-south highway and in our judgment further consideration of this project may well be deferred until the results of the new facilities enumerated have been established by actual experience.

SECTION V

DETAILS OF STREET TRAFFIC IN MANHATTAN

Traffic counts are made by the Police Department at locations where traffic conditions necessitate studies in order to provide relief by regulation. At such points counts are made of the traffic in each direction, by hourly periods, from 7 a. m. to 7 p. m. on week days, with occasional counts made during the evening hours or on Sundays. No periodic counts are made by which seasonal variation or growth in traffic can be definitely determined.

AVAILABLE DATA.

The bulk of the data available covers locations in the congested mid-Manhattan section with more scattered data covering other sections of Manhattan and The Bronx, Queens and Brooklyn. No counts are available for Richmond. We have studied the counts for some 150 locations, particularly those in the mid-Manhattan section where the greatest flows are encountered and for which more complete data are available, and in addition a sufficient number of counts to indicate the general characteristics of traffic in other sections of Manhattan such as along Canal street and to the south, in the vicinity of 110th and 125th streets and in the bridge approach areas of Brooklyn and Queens, in order to determine the relative volume of traffic at the various locations, the relation of directional flows, the proportions of passenger and commercial vehicles and the relation of average hourly to maximum hourly flows.

There are no figures available for the total traffic on all of the streets at any one time. However, by combining intersection counts taken at various times during the same period of the year figures can be developed indicating the approximate traffic flows in various sections of the City.

TRAFFIC FLOWS.

Mid-Manhattan.

The traffic flows in each direction for the principal intersections in mid-Manhattan are shown on the diagram on page 26. It will be seen from this diagram that in all cases the flows are greater on the individual avenues than on the crosstown streets. An average for all intersections indicates that the avenue flows are about two and one-half times as large as the flows in the crosstown streets. This ratio varies materially as will be seen from an examination of the diagram and of the tabulation below. There is also shown on the diagram a preponderance of commercial vehicles on the avenues at the outer edges of the district and a larger proportion of commercial vehicles on the avenues than on the individual crosstown streets.

Ratio of North and South to East and West Traffic.

Street.	Total Traffic.	Commercial Vehicles.
23d street	2.9 to 1	2.4 to 1
34th street	3.1 to 1	2.7 to 1
42d street	2.9 to 1	2.9 to 1
57th street	1.6 to 1	1.4 to 1
Average all intersections	2.5 to 1	2.3 to 1

Avenue Traffic, Mid-Manhattan.

The diagram on page 146 shows the distribution of the combined northbound and southbound vehicular traffic on individual avenues at their intersections with the principal crosstown streets in mid-Manhattan. The diagram also shows by the heavier shading the proportion of commercial vehicles in each case.

It will be noted that, in general, the larger flows are on the centrally located avenues which are in the heart of the retail district and are also used as thoroughfares for through traffic. 1st avenue, 7th avenue and 10th avenue are also used as through thoroughfares. Park avenue has the heaviest traffic volumes at 34th and 42d streets, amounting to about 2,600 and 2,800 vehicles per average hour, respectively, at these intersections. The proportion of commercial vehicles to the total avenue traffic is greater in the southern section of the district, as seen in the following tabulation:

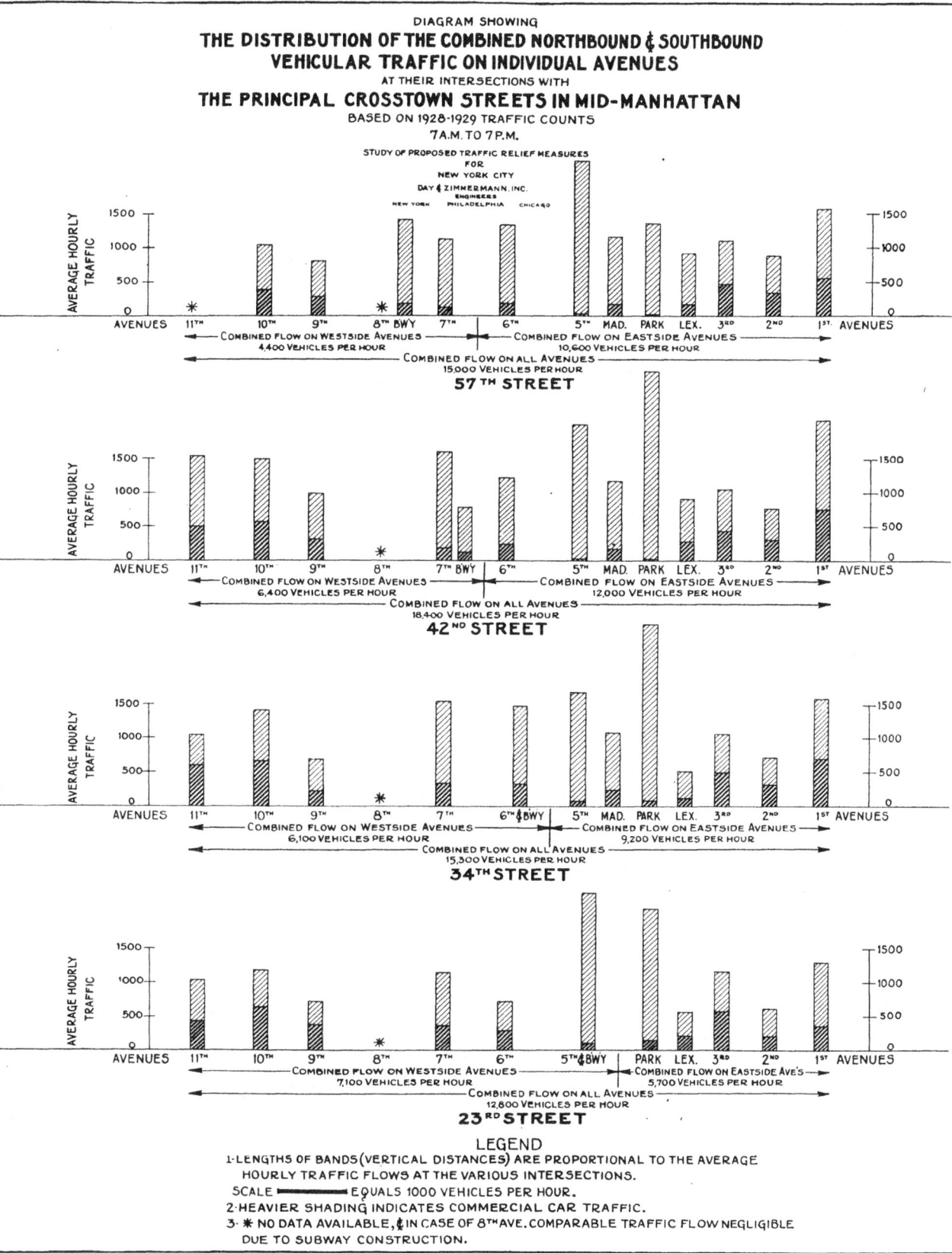

Percentage of Commercial Vehicles to Total Traffic on the North and South Avenues in Mid-Manhattan at Intersections with the Principal Crosstown Streets.

Crosstown Streets Intersected.	Percentage Commercial Vehicles.
23d street	29.7
34th street	25.2
42d street	21.6
57th street	19.7
Average	23.8

Effective Traffic Lanes.

A study has been made of the number of lanes available for moving traffic on each of the avenues in the midtown section. It is assumed that traffic could not move effectively in the lanes adjacent to the curbs due to standing vehicles whether parked or stopped for unloading or loading, and that street car tracks would be available for moving lanes of traffic. After deducting the parking lanes, the remaining width of roadway is divided into lanes approximately nine or ten feet in width. In some instances this may allow for an odd number of lanes, which is impractical, and for this reason the next smaller number of even lanes is established as the number of effective lanes, thus making these lanes wider on some avenues than on others. For instance, 5th avenue with a 55-foot roadway is considered as having four effective lanes and 11th avenue with a 60-foot roadway is also considered as having four effective lanes. Lexington avenue is considered to have four effective lanes, which are comparatively narrow due to the roadway being only 51 feet wide.

On the above basis the number of effective lanes is assumed to be four for all the avenues excepting Park avenue and 8th avenue, the latter having six and Park avenue six below and eight above Grand Central. All of the avenues combined at 42d street, omitting 8th avenue, have 54 effective lanes, carrying 18,400 vehicles in an average hour between 7 a. m. and 7 p. m., or an average of approximately 340 vehicles per lane. Park avenue has the greatest average hourly flow of approximately 520 vehicles per lane for six effective lanes, four of which are on the viaduct and two on the street proper. It is interesting to note that during peak hours approximately 2,100 passenger cars pass through two comparatively narrow lanes on the viaduct or at the rate of 1,050 vehicles per lane per hour under normal traffic conditions, with traffic light control allowing a ratio of two to one for avenue and crosstown traffic.

Crosstown Traffic, Mid-Manhattan.

On page 148 is a diagram showing the distribution of the eastbound and westbound vehicular traffic at 5th avenue on crosstown streets from 30th street to 59th street, inclusive. The lengths of bands are proportional to the average hourly traffic flows on the various streets, the heavier shaded portions indicating the relative volumes of commercial traffic. The district covered by this diagram extends for 30 blocks or approximately a mile and a half north and south and involves a combined average hourly flow of approximately 13,300 vehicles in both directions during the period from 7 a. m. to 7 p. m.

It will be noted that there are wide variations in the flow on the various streets ranging from approximately 270 to 480 vehicles per average hour in one direction. The average for all the streets is approximately 390 vehicles per hour and in general the smaller volumes are in the southern portions of the district. It would be difficult to assign definite reasons for the relative flows on the various streets, but in general they are influenced by locations of industries, railroad terminals, large hotels, and congestion resulting from trucking and parking, as well as the barrier to crosstown traffic formed by Central Park just north of the district.

Further examination of the diagram will show that the traffic volumes in the district as a whole are substantially equal in each direction. The proportions of commercial car traffic vary considerably for the individual streets, ranging from 11 per cent. to 31 per cent., with an average of 20 per cent. for the group as a whole. The group of ten streets from 30th street to 39th street, inclusive, has an average of approximately 26 per cent. commercial cars and both the group from 40th street to 47th street, inclusive, and the group from 48th street to 59th street, inclusive, have an average of about 18 per cent. commercial cars.

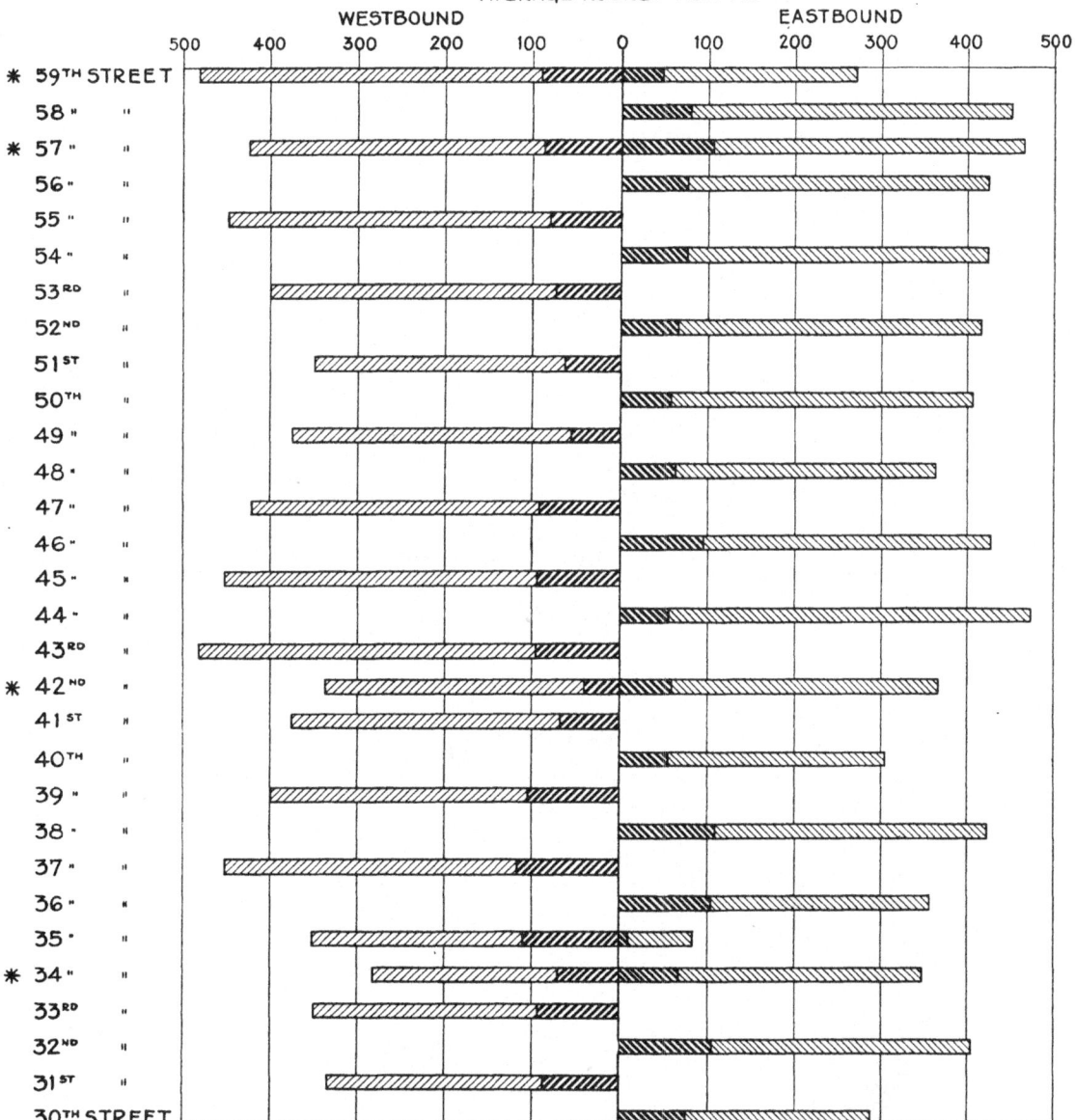

The crosstown streets generally have sufficient width for four lanes of traffic, two of which are occupied by standing cars, either parked or loading and unloading, leaving two lanes for moving vehicles which incidentally are not always available for free movements. For all the streets from 30th street to 59th street, inclusive, the average flow at 5th avenue is approximately 200 vehicles per effective lane. This is comparable to the average flow per effective lane on all of the north and south avenues of approximately 340 vehicles at 42d street and 290 at 57th street.

Canal Street Traffic Flows.

Canal street has heavier traffic flows than any other crosstown street with volumes varying at different locations. The heaviest flows occur east of Broadway where the average hourly traffic from 7 a. m. to 7 p. m. in both directions amounts to approximately 1,500 vehicles, of which number approximately two-thirds is comprised of through traffic using the East River bridges or the Holland Tunnel.

The proportion of commercial vehicles to the total traffic varies widely, the average being 51 per cent. and about 72 per cent. at Washington street and 47 per cent. at Lafayette street. The average proportion of commercial vehicles in all directions combined at all intersections observed is 46 per cent.

From a study of hourly fluctuations of Canal street, traffic at Lafayette street, it was developed that the traffic is not continuous throughout the day, marked peaks occurring in each direction during both morning and afternoon. The maximum hourly traffic for both directions combined amounts to approximately 1,650 in the morning and 1,800 in the afternoon. The flow of traffic in Lafayette street is the greatest flow crossing Canal street, amounting to approximately 1,750 vehicles during the morning rush and with an hourly average after that until late afternoon of 1,400 vehicles. In view of the above it is evident that the relatively heavy traffic flows on Canal street interfere seriously with the free movement of north and south traffic, forming what might be termed as a barrier or dam.

Fluctuations in Traffic Flows.

Studies of hourly fluctuations in traffic flows have been made for several locations. Examinations of those for 1st, Park, 5th and 10th avenues at 34th street all show afternoon peak loads; but in general the results of the examination of data for other locations indicate that the range in volumes is small between 8 a. m. and 6 p. m. and much less than the fluctuations on the East River bridges. This is explainable by the fact that there is such a considerable volume of traffic moving at all hours locally both for business and personal uses that the passenger vehicles carrying persons to and from their work do not cause a very marked peak. It is interesting to note that the variations in traffic on 1st avenue approximate in a general way those found on the East River bridges, which is probably due mostly to a large portion of 1st avenue traffic using the Queensboro Bridge. The hourly fluctuations on 10th avenue are the least for the avenues studied.

Studies of the hourly variations on 34th, 37th and 38th streets at 5th avenue indicate very uniform flows in vehicles per hour during the period from 8 a. m. to 6 p. m. This appears to be a general characteristic of crosstown traffic as indicated by inspection of counts at a number of other locations on crosstown streets. A study of the situation at 57th street, however, shows quite different characteristics which more nearly approximate the variations shown by the East River bridges.

Commercial traffic on both the avenues and crosstown streets does not have as wide fluctuations as the passenger car traffic, being rather uniform during the day, similar to the commercial traffic on the East River bridges.

The relation of average hourly traffic to maximum hourly traffic varies considerably for different locations and directions, but in general the average hours appear to be approximately two-thirds of the maximum hours.

It has been noted that on the avenues the maximum hours in each direction do not occur simultaneously, the southbound peaks occurring in the morning and the northbound peaks in the afternoon

COMMERCIAL VEHICLES

Studies of specific districts in Manhattan indicate varying proportions of commercial and passenger cars. The greatest proportion of commercial cars is found in the Canal street district where traffic counts show an average of 46 per cent. in all directions combined at the intersections observed, with an average of 51 per cent. for the traffic on Canal street and a maximum proportion of 72 per cent. at one intersection. In the district along and east of the Bowery, counts at 20 intersections indicate that one-third of the total traffic in all directions is commercial.

The ratio of commercial cars to the total vehicles gradually reduces to the north, as will be seen in the following tabulation which shows the percentage ratio of commercial vehicles to the total traffic in all directions at the intersections of the principal crosstown streets with all of the north and south avenues combined:

Crosstown Street.	Per Cent. Ratio of Commercial Vehicles to Total Traffic.
14th Street	34
23d Street	30
34th Street	25
42d Street	22
57th Street	20

Farther to the north, at 125th street, the traffic counts available indicate that approximately 25 per cent. of the total traffic is commercial.

These proportions of commercial vehicles are comparable to those found on the East River bridges. For the four bridges combined, commercial cars are 29 per cent. of the total during the 12-hour period between 7 a. m. and 7 p. m., which is the same period during which the street traffic counts were made; and for a 24-hour period the proportion of commercial vehicles is 24 per cent. A comparable figure for the Holland Tunnel traffic is 28 per cent. Records of ferry traffic do not show the classification of vehicular traffic. However, data obtained in connection with our interborugh origin and destination studies show that traffic for a weekday from 7 a. m. to 7 p. m. in February, 1929, on the Staten Island Municipal Ferries was 54 per cent. commercial vehicles.

The above stated proportions of commercial vehicles to the total traffic may be briefly summarized as follows:

District.	Proportion of Commercial Vehicles to Total Traffic.
Canal Street	46 per cent.
Lower East Side	33 per cent.
14th Street	34 per cent.
Mid-Manhattan	24 per cent.
125th Street	25 per cent.
East River Bridges	29 per cent.
Holland Tunnel (24-hour period)	28 per cent.
Staten Island Ferry	54 per cent.

As previously stated, there are no figures available for the total traffic on all the streets at any one time. However, the foregoing figures indicate that commercial vehicles comprise substantially one-fourth of the total traffic.

Origin and destination studies of both avenue and crosstown street traffic developed interesting features of commercial vehicle movements. It was found from a study of the distance traveled by commercial vehicles that the movement of this class of traffic on the avenues as a whole is quite similar to the movements of passenger vehicles; and that on the crosstown streets a greater proportion of commercial vehicles show "long haul" crosstown movements than is the case with passenger car traffic.

SECTION VI

DETAILS OF BRIDGE, TUNNEL AND FERRY TRAFFIC

The centering of business activity on the Island of Manhattan and the limited number of bridges and tunnels across the rivers surrounding it, results in a concentration of traffic over such facilities and in the areas adjoining their terminals. The magnitude of these traffic flows and of their effect upon traffic conditions in Manhattan, together with the large costs involved in providing additional bridges or tunnels, emphasizes the importance of developing fully the characteristics of bridge, tunnel and ferry vehicular traffic in New York City.

The distribution of the traffic between the various facilities and sections of the City, its rate of growth, and other general characteristics such as the distribution between passenger cars and commercial vehicles, the variations in flow as to direction and during different hours in the day, the relation of maximum flows to average flows, and seasonal variations, etc., have a direct application in the analysis of present traffic conditions and of relief measures under consideration, as well as providing data of value in the design of new facilities and the estimation of their probable use.

AVAILABLE DATA.

The diagrams, tabulations and statements presented to show the characteristics of the traffic in question are based upon records placed at our disposal by City officials and others concerned. The extent and nature of the data available and the sources of the information are summarized in the following paragraphs:

East River Bridges.

The results of annual traffic counts for recent years on each of the East River bridges were furnished by the Department of Plant and Structures. The counts for each bridge were made on a weekday in the latter part of October, and in the judgment of the officials, represents an average of the traffic prevailing throughout the year. The results are presented for 24 hours by half-hour periods, classifiied as to passenger, commercial and horse-drawn vehicles, etc., in comprehensive detail. This information was supplemented by the results of counts made at various times by the Police Department, but no consecutive daily or monthly data is available.

Harlem River Bridges.

The Department of Plant and Structures furnished the results of annual counts for each of the Harlem River bridges. These counts were also made during the latter part of October, as representing a normal weekday, but details of hourly flow and classification were not available.

Municipal Ferries.

Complete data for the monthly and the yearly vehicular traffic in 1927 and 1928 for each ferry, but not classified as to type of vehicle, was assembled by the Department of Plant and Structures. Typical weekday, Sunday and holiday flows were selected by the officials, and certain classified hourly data was furnished in connection with the origin and destination counts made at our request in February, 1929.

East River Private Ferry.

A ferry is operated across the East River by the East 34th Street Vehicular Ferry Company, a private corporation, and information concerning average daily traffic volumes and other data was furnished by its officials.

Holland Tunnel.

Daily and monthly records by classes of vehicles and typical hour by hour flow charts for both weekdays and Sundays were made available by the tunnel officials. This data was presented in comprehensive form for the entire period since the opening of the tunnel on November 12, 1927, and constitutes a valuable index of daily traffic fluctuations.

Hudson River Ferries.

The ferries crossing the Hudson River from New Jersey to Manhattan are all operated by private corporations. General data concerning the vehicular traffic over them was made available to us by courtesy of the Port of New York Authority.

Staten Island-New Jersey Bridges and Ferries.

Data concerning vehicular traffic over the various bridges and ferries connecting Staten Island with New Jersey was also made available to us by the Port of New York Authority.

The studies and tables presented are in large part based on data obtained from the sources indicated and while no departures have been made from the records as received, the figures have in many instances been rounded out for ease in presentation.

TRAFFIC VOLUMES IN 1928.

The distribution and relative volumes of week-day traffic, typical of 1928 data, entering and leaving Manhattan by means of the facilities indicated is shown in the diagram at page 7309.

The total week-day traffic, estimated at 449,800 vehicles, is distributed geographically approximately as follows:

Between Manhattan and	Week-day Traffic.	Per Cent. of Total.
Brooklyn-Queens	199,200	44.3%
Bronx	189,600	42.2%
New Jersey	58,100	12.9%
Staten Island	2,900	.6%
Total	449,800	100.0%

The preponderance of interborough traffic and particularly of East River bridge traffic is strikingly shown by the diagram and the above tabulation.

An enumeration of the various interborough and Hudson River vehicular crossing facilities and the traffic flows over them will serve to develop more fully their relative importance.

East River Bridges.

The volume of traffic over the four East River bridges, as counted on Thursday, October 25, 1928, is shown in the following table:

East River Bridges.	Week-day Traffic.	Per Cent. of Total.
Queensboro	71,600	37%
Manhattan	59,500	31%
Williamsburg	41,200	21%
Brooklyn	22,200	11%
Total	194,500	100%

The counts were made from midnight to midnight and show that approximately 68 per cent. of the traffic flowed during the "daytime" hours between 7 a. m. and 7 p. m.

Harlem River Bridges.

The volume of week-day traffic over the eight Harlem River bridges as counted during October, 1928, is shown in the following table:

Harlem River Bridges.	Week-day Traffic.	Per Cent. of Total.
Willis Avenue	31,900	17%
3d Avenue	23,400	12%
Madison Avenue	25,200	13%
145th Street	17,800	10%
Macomb's Dam	36,500	19%
Washington	25,000	13%
University Heights	12,100	6%
Ship Canal	17,700	10%
Total	189,600	100%

East River Municipal Ferries.

In addition to the four bridges, the City operates six ferry routes across the East River between Manhattan and Brooklyn-Queens. The daily volume of vehicular traffic over these ferries is small in proportion to the traffic over the bridges, and is largely made up of heavy commercial and horsedrawn vehicles which find the terminals convenient.

The number of vehicles transported by each ferry during 1928 and a typical October week-day count are shown in the following table:

East River Municipal Ferries.	1928 Vehicular Traffic.	Typical Week-day Traffic.
Astoria	388,900	1,600
Greenpoint	153,800	500
Grand Street	60,000	250
Atlantic Avenue	45,100	170
Hamilton Avenue	95,700	320
39th Street	123,200	460
Total	866,700	3,300

Clason's Point Ferry.

The City also operates an important ferry between Clason's Point in The Bronx, and College Point in Queens, providing, at present, the only existing direct route for vehicular travel between these two Boroughs. The total number of vehicles transported in 1928 amounted to 832,000 and the typical October week-day traffic was 2,300.

East River Private Ferry.

A private corporation, the East 34th Street Vehicular Ferry Company, operates a ferry route across the East River between Manhattan and Brooklyn. This line operates on weekdays only, between 6 a. m. and 12 p. m., and the average daily traffic amounts to 1,400 vehicles.

Staten Island Municipal Ferries.

The City operates two ferry routes from St. George, at the northern end of Staten Island, one to the Battery and one to 39th street, Brooklyn. The Staten Island-Battery ferry carried 1,072,000 vehicles in 1928 and the typical October weekday traffic amounted to 2,900. The Staten Island-Brooklyn ferry carried 325,100 vehicles in 1928 and the typical October weekday traffic amounted to 890.

These two ferries, together with a privately owned ferry operating between Staten Island and Brooklyn, which is said to carry about the same volume of traffic as the Municipal ferry, afford the only present facilities for vehicular travel between Staten Island and the other Boroughs.

Hudson River Ferries.

The total volume of vehicular traffic in 1928 carried by the Hudson River Ferries, all of which are operated by private corporations, amounted to 12,005,000 vehicles. Of this number 10,100,000 utilized terminals north of Canal street and 1,905,000 utilized terminals south of this point. No data being available concerning daily traffic, it was necessary to estimate a typical weekday volume comparable with the October counts of bridge traffic, which on the basis of factors derived from a study of seasonal fluctuations for the Municipal ferries approximates 35,000 vehicles per day.

Holland Tunnel.

The Holland Vehicular Tunnel, connecting New Jersey and New York, with its Eastern portal at Canal street, was opened for public use on November 12, 1927. The total volume of traffic during the year 1928 amounted to 8,745,000 vehicles and complete records are available of daily traffic. The average weekday traffic in October 1928, comparable with the bridge counts, amounted to 23,100 vehicles. It is to be noted, however, that Sunday and Holiday traffic through the tunnel is greatly in excess of the weekday traffic, a typical Sunday count of the same month being 46,200 or double that of the average weekday.

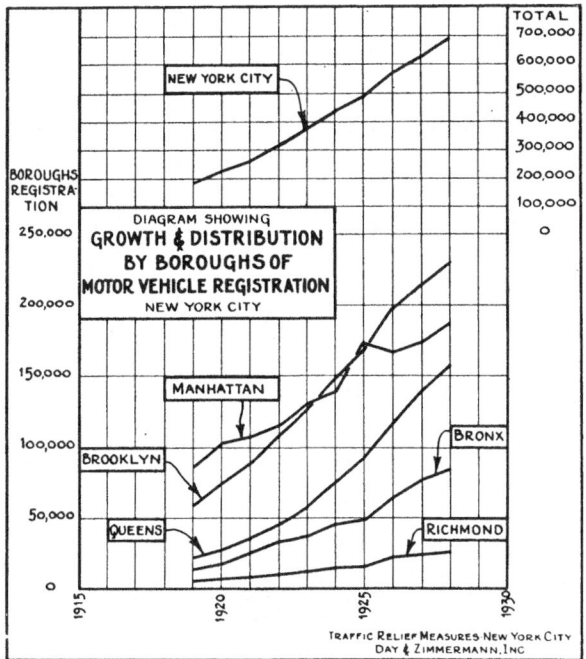

Figure 1

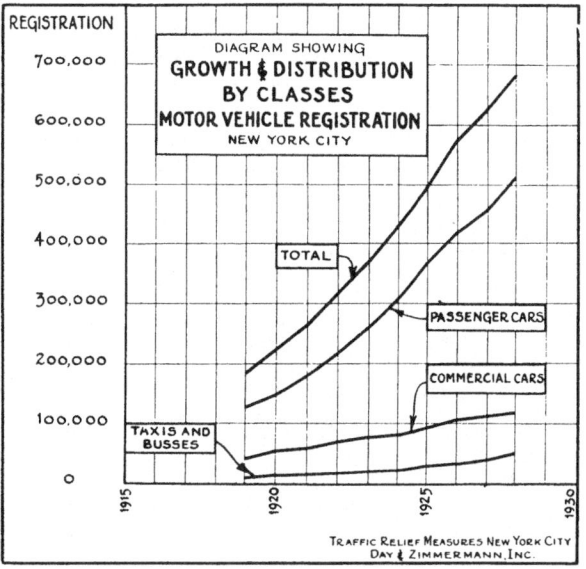

Figure 2

Staten Island-New Jersey Bridges and Ferries.

The volume of weekday and Sunday traffic selected as typical for the month of October, 1928, over the vehicular facilities connecting Staten Island and New Jersey, is shown in the following table:

Bridges and Ferries.	Weekday Traffic.	Sunday Traffic.
Outerbridge Crossing	960	4,700
Goethals Bridge	930	3,700
Perth Amboy Ferry	450	1,000
Elizabeth Ferry	630	600
Bergen Point Ferry	1,390	2,600
Carteret Ferry	220	400
Total	4,580	13,000

Certain of the above facilities, like the Holland Tunnel, and some of the municipal ferries, show a very large Sunday traffic in comparison with the weekday volume.

MOTOR VEHICLE REGISTRATION.

The swift and widespread growth in the use of motor vehicles has been self-evident during the past decade. The development of low priced passenger automobiles, the public demand for taxi and bus service, the general increase in standards of living and many other factors have all contributed to a remarkable increase in motor vehicle registration and an unforeseen necessity for highway facilities. A study of the relations between registration, population and traffic provides a measure of trends not available elsewhere.

The results of an extended analysis and detailed study of the relations between motor vehicle registration, population and traffic, together with estimates for the future, are set forth in the "Report of the Regional Plan of New York and its Environs on Highway Traffic" and have been freely drawn upon by us for this investigation, and supplemented by further analysis in the light of more recent data and developments.

Registration in 1928.

As reported by the State Department of Taxation and Finance, the total 1928 registration of motor vehicles in New York City amounted to 681,614, including 7,073 motorcycles and 3,742 dealer and trailer licenses. The distribution by major classifications among the five boroughs is shown in the following table:

1928 Motor Vehicle Registration.

Borough.	Passenger.	Commercial.	Taxi and Bus.	Total.
Manhattan	120,946	45,398	17,601	183,945
Brooklyn	178,186	37,500	11,340	227,026
Queens	132,479	18,289	4,486	155,254
Bronx	62,406	9,997	7,281	79,684
Richmond	20,553	3,820	517	24,890
Total	514,570	115,004	41,225	670,799
Per Cent. of Total	77%	17%	6%	100%

The combined registration of Brooklyn and Queens amounts to 57 per cent. of the total for New York City.

The total 1928 registration in New York State amounted to 1,714,242 or substantially 7 per cent. of the 24,750,000 registered vehicles reported for the United States by the National Automobile Chamber of Commerce.

Growth in Registration.

The total 1928 registration in New York City of 681,614 may be compared with 38,894 in 1912 and 187,258 in 1919.

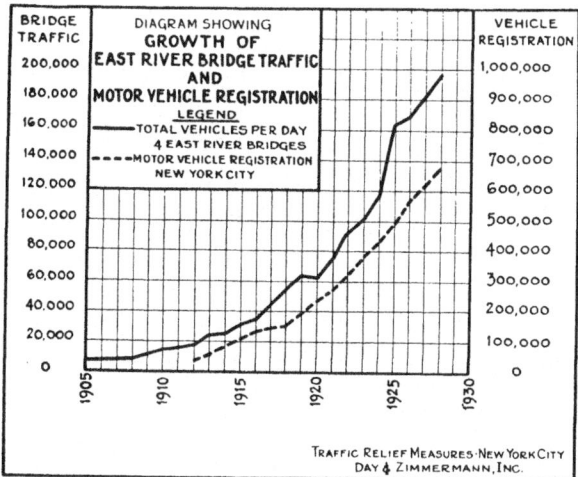

Figure 1

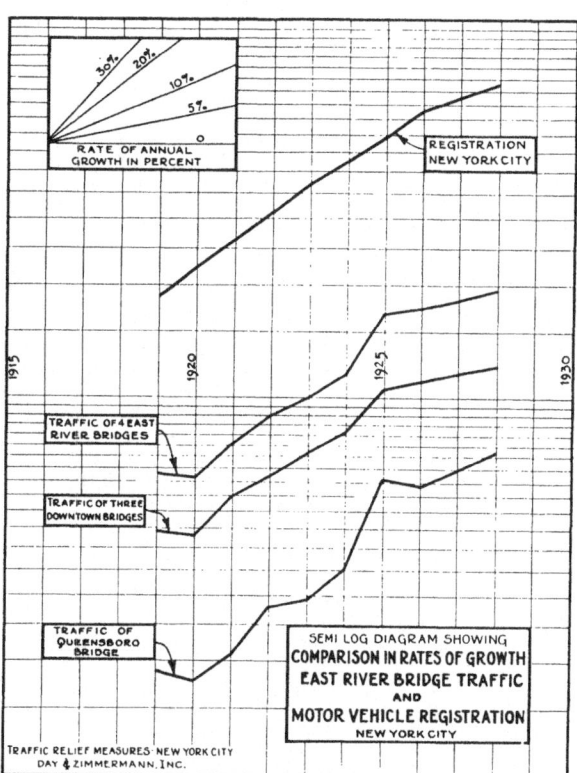

Figure 2

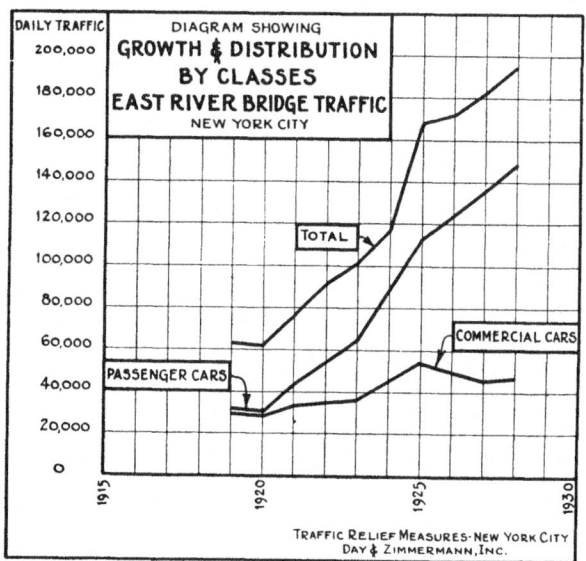

Figure 3

Notwithstanding the large number of motor vehicles placed in service within a comparatively short span of years, an important characteristic of registration figures is found in the general falling off in rate of growth. Total registration in the United States has increased during recent years at constantly lessening rates; as reported by Babson the annual percentage increases have been approximately 23 per cent., 17 per cent., 14 per cent., 10 per cent. and 5 per cent., which trend may be indicative, if not of a saturation point, at least of an approach to a constant relation between population and registration.

An investigation of registration figures for New York State, New York City and environs, and New York City, shows that the general trends are similar, and that the declining rate of growth exhibited by the country as a whole is also evidenced in the Metropolitan District.

The growth of registration for New York City in recent years is shown on page 154 in Figures 1 and 2 by Boroughs and by major classifications, respectively. The rates of growth exhibited by the above curves were also studied by plotting the data on logarithmic charts in order to develop any tendencies which might be of particular interest from the standpoint of estimating future traffic.

It is evident from the above charts that passenger cars are increasing at a faster rate than commercial cars, and that registration of all classes of vehicles in the Borough of Queens is growing at a faster rate than in the other Boroughs.

Estimates of Future Registration.

It is interesting to note that registration figures for 1927 and 1928 emphasize the tendencies reported by the Regional Plan Committee in 1926 on the basis of data then available and that the decline in rate of growth has continued to such an extent that the estimates of future registration may be subject to a further downward revision. The trend as indicated by the figures to 1928 would seem to place the estimated registration in 1935 of motor vehicles in New York City at approximately 1,075,000.

GROWTH IN TRAFFIC.

East River Bridges.

The general growth of week-day vehicular traffic over the four East River bridges, during past years, in comparison with motor vehicle registration in New York City, is shown on page 156 by Figure 1. Traffic over the bridges has increased more than three times in the past eight years.

The rates of growth of traffic over the Queensboro Bridge and over the three downtown bridges is compared with total traffic and registration in the semi-logarithmic diagram, Figure 2, shown on page 156. With this type of plotting volume relations are distorted, the important factor being the slope of the curve which indicates rate of growth regardless of volume. A general similarity between the growth characteristics of registration and traffic is evident, and a slightly higher rate of growth is indicated for the Queensboro Bridge than for the downtown bridges.

Growth in traffic over the East River bridges by classes of vehicles is shown on page 156 by Figure 3, which shows that passenger car traffic has grown at a much faster rate than commercial car traffic.

The close relation between bridge traffic and registration may be demonstrated by the proportion of 0.29 weekday crossings per registered vehicle in 1921 compared with 0.29 in 1928.

Harlem River Bridges.

Annual counts of weekday traffic in October over each of the Harlem River bridges were available for the years 1920 to 1928, inclusive, and indicate a wide variance in rates of growth for the individual bridges. The growth in traffic, however, over the combined eight bridges has practically paralleled the growth in East River bridge traffic, as shown by the diagram on page 158.

A study of the growth in traffic on the individual bridges indicates that traffic over the Willis Avenue, 3d Avenue and Macomb's Dam Bridges is increasing rapidly while that on the Madison Avenue, 145th Street and University Heights Bridges has shown little increase in recent years.

Municipal Ferries.

The total volume of vehicles carried by the ten municipal ferries in 1928 amounted to 3,330,000 or a 9 per cent. increase over the 1927 volume of 3,050,000. This increase may be compared with increases of 7 per cent. for East River bridge traffic and 17 per cent. for Harlem River bridge traffic over the same period, as shown by October weekday counts.

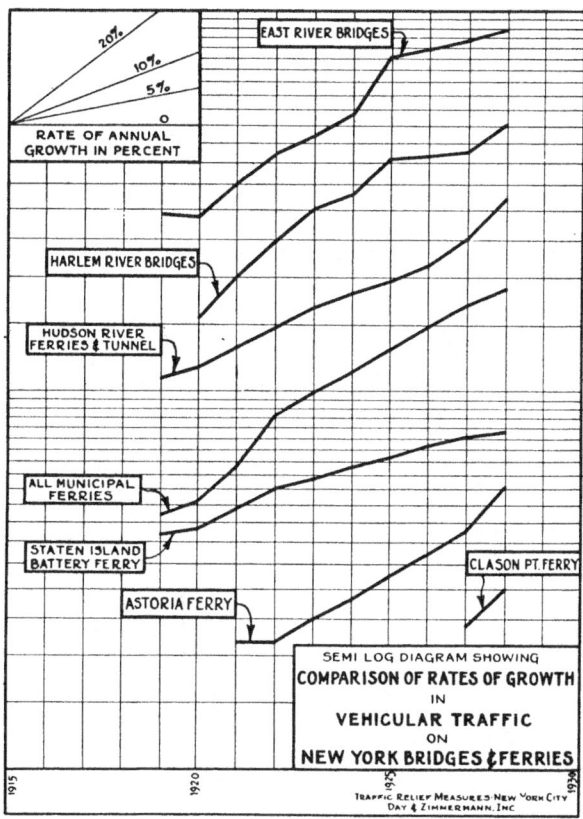

Hudson River Ferries and Tunnel.

The total volume of vehicular traffic over the Hudson River by years from 1923 to 1928, inclusive, is shown in the following table, together with the annual percentage increase and the division of traffic between the ferries and the Holland Vehicular Tunnel:

Hudson River Vehicular Traffic.

Year.	Volume of Traffic.	Per Cent. Annual Increase.	Division of Traffic.	
			Ferries.	Tunnel.
1923	10,700,000	......	10,700,000	....
1924	11,706,000	9.3%	11,706,000	....
1925	12,589,000	7.5%	12,589,000	....
1926	13,736,000	9.1%	13,736,000	....
1927	16,085,000	17.1%	15,099,000	986,000
1928	20,735,000	28.9%	11,990,000	8,745,000

It appears from the above table that the opening of the Holland Tunnel on November 12, 1927, was followed by a large increase in vehicular traffic. The tunnel officials estimate that approximately 45 per cent. of the tunnel traffic during 1928 was new traffic which would not have crossed the river except for the improved traffic facilities provided by the tunnel, and that the remaining 55 per cent. was diverted from the ferries.

The short time during which the Holland Tunnel has been in operation limits the comparison of its growth in traffic with that of other facilities. The records show that traffic in December, 1928, was 35 per cent. greater than in December, 1927, and that March, 1929, traffic was 37 per cent. in excess of that in March, 1928.

Comparison of Rates of Growth.

A general comparison of the trends of growth in the traffic using the facilities discussed in the preceding pages may be obtained from semi-logarithmic diagram shown on page 158 in which the slope of the individual curves indicates the rate of growth regardless of volume.

A specific comparison of the individual trends for eight, five, three and one year periods prior to 1928 is shown for certain facilities in the following table:

Average Annual Percentage Increases Over Periods of Years.

Vehicular Facilities.	Eight Years, 1920-1928.	Five Years, 1923-1928.	Three Years, 1925-1928.	One Year, 1927-1928.
East River bridges	16%	15%	6%	7%
Queensboro Bridge	20%	21%	6%	11%
Harlem River bridges	16%	11%	8%	17%
Municipal ferries	18%	14%	13%	9%
Staten Island Ferry	8%	6%	5%	3%
Hudson River ferries and tunnel	14%	15%	20%	29%

Traffic over the Hudson River is alone in showing a consistent increase in the rate of growth. The other facilities show a decreasing trend in rate of growth for five and three-year periods compared with the eight-year period. The increase of last year, 1928, over 1927 shows a higher rate than some of the average rates for longer periods, but the indications of one year are of limited significance in measuring trends.

ANALYSIS OF EAST RIVER BRIDGE TRAFFIC.

The traffic counts on the East River bridges have been made in October of each year, it being the judgment of the officials in charge that the flows at that time of the year represented average week-day traffic volumes and characteristics. Studies of seasonal data available for the municipal ferries, Holland Tunnel and such other data as exists serve to substantiate this judgment, although no day by day traffic counts have been made for the bridges.

Day and Night Traffic.

The 1928 count, a summary of which appears in a preceding page, was made on Thursday, October 25, and under apparently normal weather and traffic conditions. The following table sets forth the number of vehicles counted for each bridge during the 12-hour periods representing daytime and nighttime flows:

Traffic on October 25, 1928.

East River Bridges.	Day, 7 A. M. to 7 P. M.	Night, 7 P. M. to 7 A. M.	Total, 24 Hours.
Queensboro	48,270	23,330	71,600
Manhattan	41,220	18,280	59,500
Williamsburg	27,430	13,770	41,200
Brooklyn	15,400	6,800	22,200
Total	132,320	62,180	194,500
Per Cent. of Total	68%	32%	100%

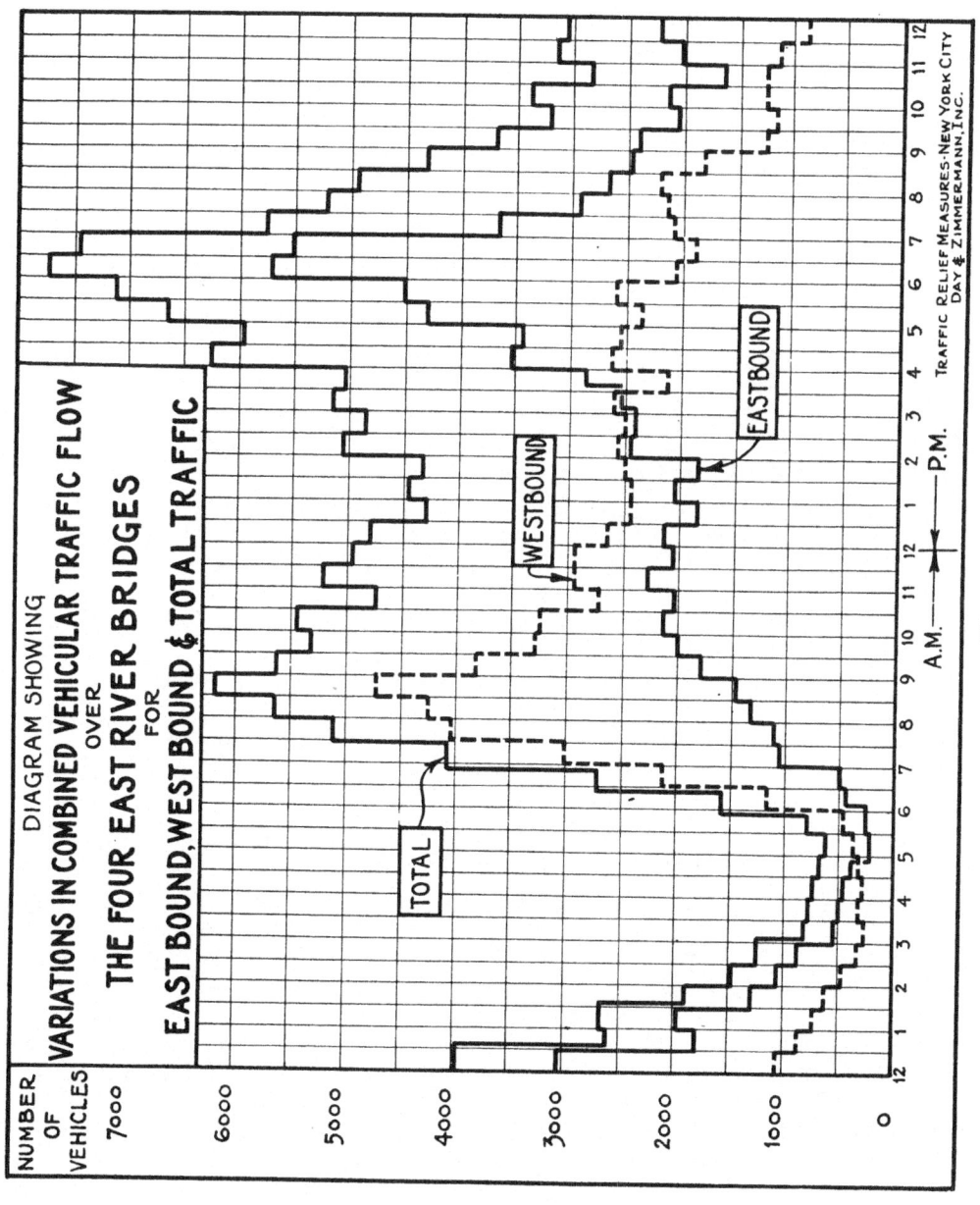

Figure 1

Passenger and Commercial Car Traffic.

The volume of day traffic amounts to 68% of the total for all classes of vehicles combined, but this percentage varies between passenger and commercial car traffic as follows:

Four East River Bridges.

Class of Vehicles.	Day, 7 A. M. to 7 P. M.	Night, 7 P. M. to 7 A. M.	Total, 24 Hours.	Per Cent. of Total.
Passenger cars	93,860	53,830	147,690	76%
Commercial cars	38,460	8,350	46,810	24%
Total	132,320	62,180	194,500	100%
Per Cent. of Total	68%	32%	100%	

The classification of vehicles made during the counts include about one per cent. horse-drawn, which, for ease of presentation, have been included with commercial cars. The table shows that 24 per cent. of all traffic over the four bridges is commercial. Queensboro Bridge, which carries 37 per cent. of the total traffic, shows a similar ratio for commercial vehicles. Passenger car traffic in the daytime is 1.8 times that at night whereas commercial car traffic is 4.6 times that at night. However, it is to be noted that almost one-fifth of the total interborough trucking movements on this day occured between 7 p. m. and 7 a. m.

Hourly Flow of Week-day Traffic.

The variations in the flow of traffic throughout the day are shown on pages 160 and 162 by load curves plotted from the half hourly counts made by the Department of Plant and Structures.

The total flow of week-day traffic over the four East River bridges is unbalanced directionally, as illustrated by Figure 1 (page 160), westbound flow predominating from 5 a. m. to 3 p. m. and eastbound flow predominating from 3 p. m. to 5 a. m. This characteristic, common to all interborough traffic, is caused during rush hours by commuting traffic. The westbound traffic peak between 7.30 and 9.30 a. m. is duplicated by an eastbound peak between 5 and 7 p. m. The evening peak, however, is sharper and greater than the morning peak and is further accompanied by a sustained flow of westbound vehicles, consisting of dinner and theatre traffic entering Manhattan. This combination causes the peak flow of traffic in both directions to occur between 6 and 7 p. m. and on this day the maximum hourly traffic in both directions amounted to 15,222 vehicular crossings.

The commercial car traffic over the bridges is quite uniform throughout the day. This characteristic is illustrated by Figure 2 (page 162), showing commercial and passenger car traffic over the Queensboro Bridge, and typical of the other bridges as well. The heavy peaks in total traffic are clearly created by the passenger car traffic, much of which is obviously commuting in nature.

Accumulation of Vehicles in Manhattan.

In order to arrive at an indication of the daily load imposed upon the streets of Manhattan by traffic over the East River bridges, the excess of westbound over eastbound vehicles crossing the bridges, or vice versa, was determined for each half-hour period using the data shown by Figure 1 at page 160.

The flow of traffic was predominantly westward from 5 a. m. to 3 p.m., thereafter turning eastward, and by 7 p. m. about two-thirds of the maximum accumulation had left Manhattan. Based on this study, the maximum accumulation in Manhattan of vehicles using the East River bridges was substantially 30,000 vehicles, or about 15 per cent. of the total traffic in the 24 hours.

Relative Utilization of Bridges.

The relative utilization of the various bridges may be derived from the relation between the total traffic flows and the number of vehicular lanes, as shown in the following table:

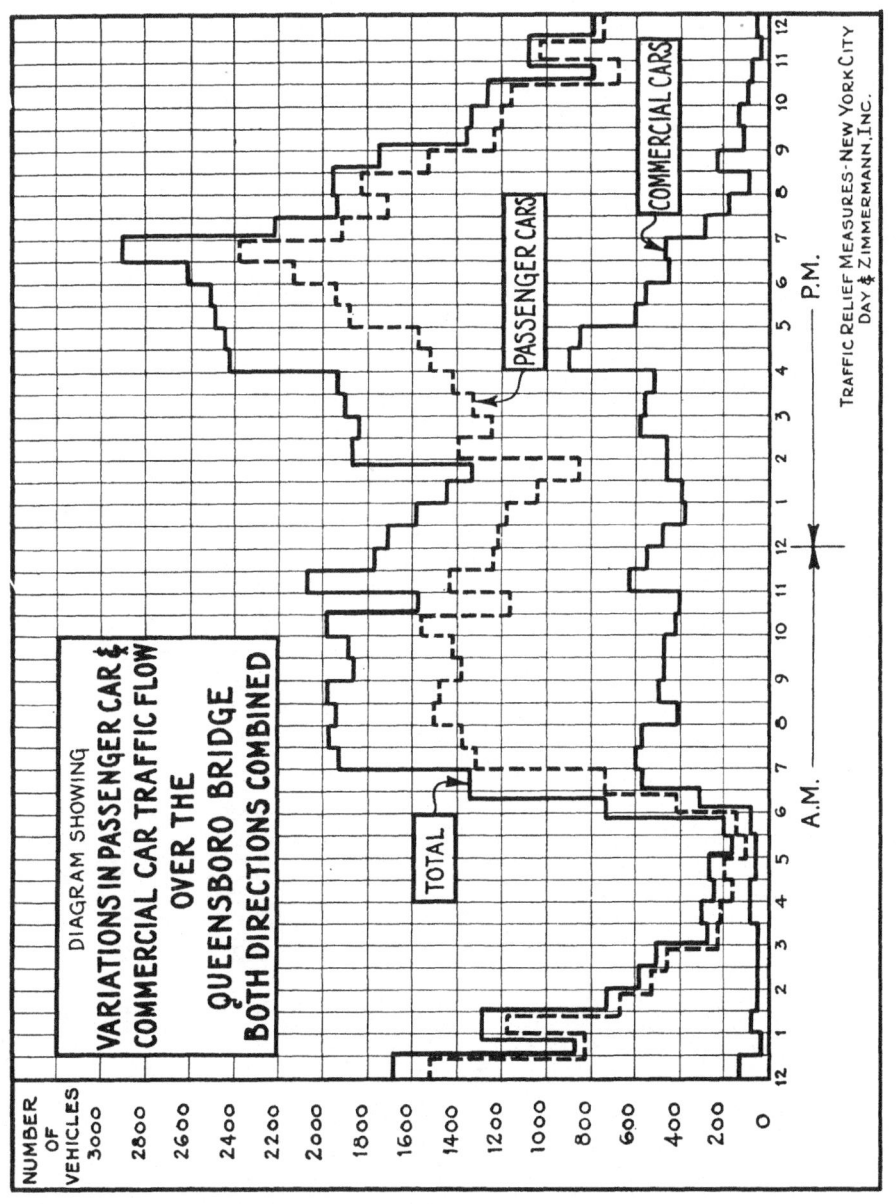

Figure 2

East River Bridges.	Traffic on October 25, 1928.	Number of Lanes.	Average Flow Per Lane.
Queensboro	71,600	6	11,900
Manhattan	59,500	6	9,900
Williamsburg	41,200	4	10,300
Brooklyn	22,200	4	5,600
Total	194,500	20	9,700

It appears from the above table that the average flow per lane on the Brooklyn Bridge is approximately one-half of that obtaining on the other bridges, which may be partly accounted for by the presence of street cars and horse-drawn traffic on both roadways and the greater congestion in the bridge head areas.

Maximum Traffic Flows.

The flow in vehicles per lane during rush hours on October 25, 1928, was as follows:

East River Bridges.	Number of Lanes in One Direction.	Maximum Hourly Flow, One Direction, Vehicles.	
		Per Bridge.	Per Lane.
Queensboro	3	3,800	1,270
Manhattan:			
Upper Deck	2	2,600	1,300
Lower Deck	2	1,600	800
Combined	4	3,900	970
Williamsburg	2	2,000	1,000
Brooklyn	2	1,800	900
Average, All Bridges	11	11,250	1,030

The above figures for maximum traffic flows per lane are somewhat larger than the similar data derived from the 1927 count. Lack of available information as to the traffic conditions existing when the specific flows occurred render it difficult to determine the extent to which they represent capacities insuring satisfactory traffic conditions. However, our general advice and the results of our observations indicate that they occurred during rush-hour periods when congestion existed on the bridges and approaches.

ANALYSIS OF HOLLAND TUNNEL TRAFFIC.

Traffic in 1928.

The total number of vehicles crossing the Hudson River in 1928 by means of the Holland Vehicular Tunnel amounted to 8,745,000. The distribution of this traffic between weekdays and Sundays and holidays was as follows:

	Number of Days.		Volume of Traffic.	
	Amount.	Per Cent.	Amount.	Per Cent.
Weekdays	303	83%	6,462,000	74%
Sundays and Holidays	63	17%	2,283,000	26%
Total	366	100%	8,745,000	100%

The average traffic on Sundays and holidays throughout the year amounted to 36,300 vehicles or 1.7 times the average weekday traffic of 21,300 vehicles. The above mentioned averages for the year 1928 are less than those now obtaining, due to the high rate of growth in tunnel traffic.

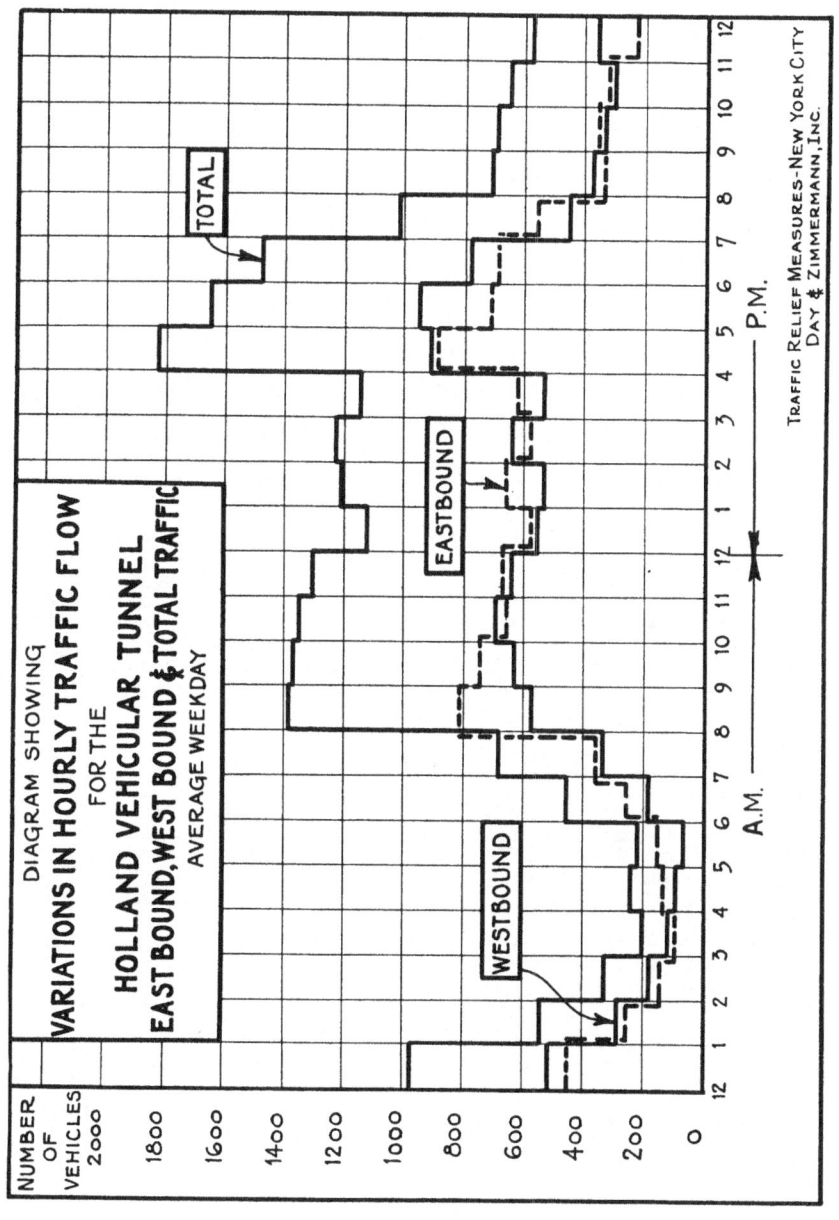

Figure 1

Relation of Daily to Annual Traffic.

The average weekday traffic through the tunnel during October, 1928, amounted to 23,100 vehicles, slightly less than the average for all days of the year.

In estimating yearly traffic, on the basis of known or estimated typical daily flows, it is customary to apply to such figures a factor recognizing seasonal variation, the order of magnitude being about 340. In preceding pages, reference has been made to the use of traffic counts in the latter part of October as typical of average weekday conditions in the vicinity of New York.

Using the average weekday traffic passing through the tunnel during October, 1928, and the total 1928 traffic, would result in a factor of substantially 380. This relatively high factor results from the very heavy Sunday and holiday flows characteristic of Holland Tunnel traffic. Furthermore, the extremely rapid growth in traffic experienced during the first 15 months of operation would indicate that unless this growth should continue, the factor as thus derived is probably somewhat too low. This situation, and the extent to which Holland Tunnel traffic may be taken as characteristic of traffic over other or proposed facilities, must be recognized in using it for estimating yearly traffic.

Passenger and Commercial Car Traffic.

The proportions of passenger and commercial cars to total traffic during the year 1928, were as follows:

Per Cent. of Total Traffic.

	Week Days.	Sundays and Holidays.	All Days of the Year.
Passenger Cars	72%	96%	78%
Commercial Cars	28%	4%	22%
Total	100%	100%	100%

The proportion of commercial cars to total traffic on week days for the Holland Tunnel, viz., 28 per cent., compares with the similar relation of 24 per cent. found on the October weekday count for the East River bridges. There has been a gradual increase in the proportion of commercial car traffic through the tunnel and the officials expect this trend to continue.

Hourly Flow of Traffic.

The hourly fluctuations in traffic through the tunnel are shown on pages 164 and 166 by Figures 1 and 2, typical load curves for weekday and Sunday traffic. Comparison with the similar curves shown for the East River bridges indicates that there is not the pronounced difference between eastbound and westbound weekday traffic through the tunnel that is found over the bridges, the directional flows through the tunnel being more equally distributed throughout the day.

Analysis of Daily Traffic.

An analysis of the daily traffic flows shown on the typical load curves provides certain characteristics which are set forth in the following table:

Characteristics of Traffic Flow Through the Holland Tunnel.

	Weekdays.	Sundays.
Total 24-hour traffic	22,250	46,255
Total 12-hour traffic (7 a. m. to 7 p. m.)	15,710	27,425
Per cent. of 24-hour	71%	59%
Average Hourly Traffic in Both Directions—		
24-hour	928	1,926
12-hour	1,310	2,285
Maximum hourly flow in both directions	1,820	3,300
Ratios, Maximum Hour in Both Directions—		
To average 24-hour	1.96	1.72
To average 12-hour	1.39	1.44
Maximum hourly flow in one direction	950	1,980
Ratio, maximum hourly traffic, both directions to one direction	1.92	1.67

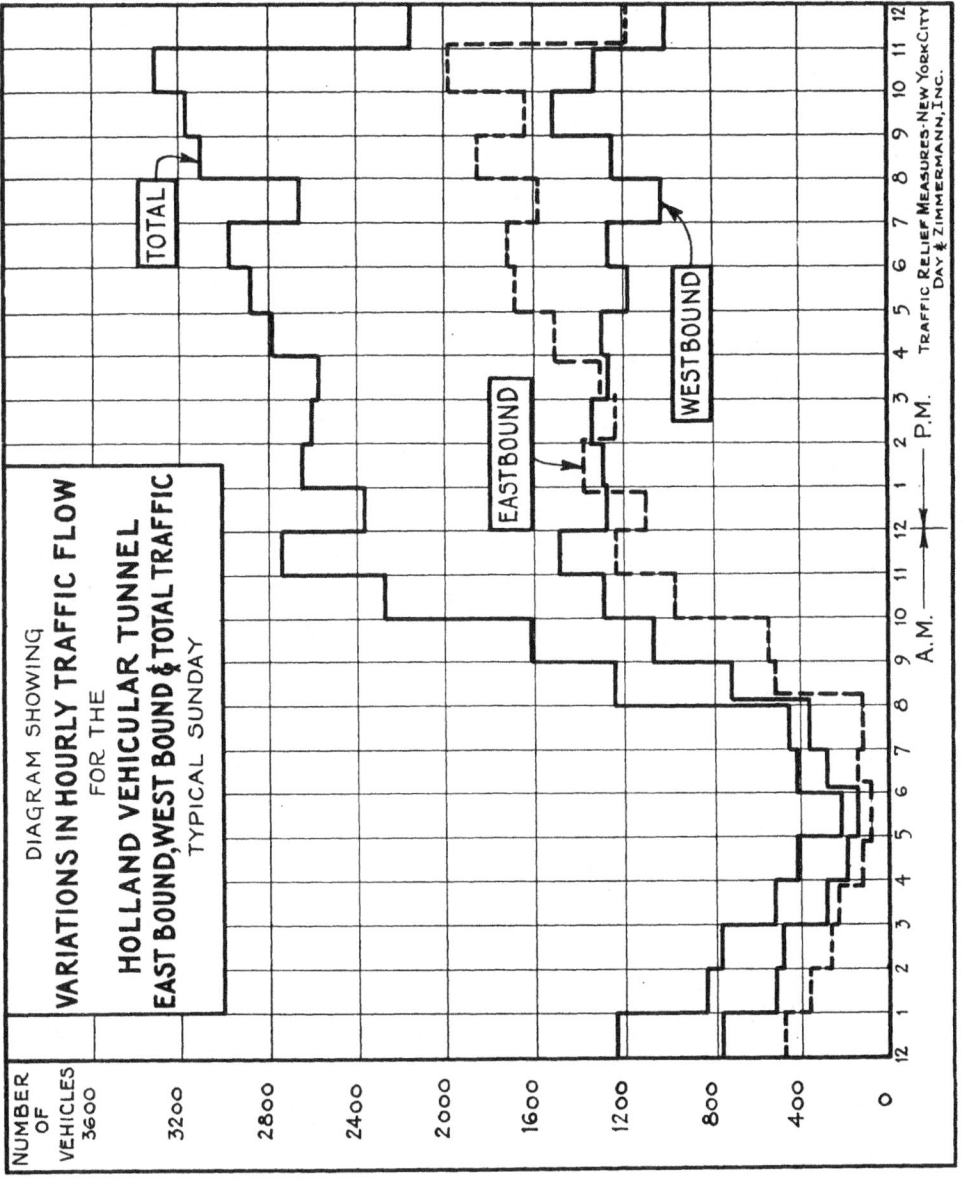

Figure 2

The rated capacity of each tube, as stated by the tunnel authorities, is 1,900 vehicles per hour with mixed traffic and 2,540 for all passenger cars. It appears from the above table and diagrams that the maximum hourly traffic in one direction on Sundays is about 80 per cent. of the rated tube capacity, whereas weekday traffic peaks are approximately 50 per cent. of the rated capacity.

ANALYSIS OF MUNICIPAL FERRY TRAFFIC.

Although vehicular traffic over the ten Municipal ferries is relatively small when compared with the traffic over the East River bridges, its variation from month to month, as shown by the operating records, furnishes the only definite index of seasonal fluctuations in interborough vehicular traffic.

Monthly Flow of Traffic.

The diagram on page 168 shows for the past two years the variation of daily vehicular traffic by months, both for weekdays and for Sundays and holidays. The total volume of ferry traffic in 1928 was 3,330,000 vehicles, and represents a nine per cent. increase over that in 1927.

The characteristics of seasonal fluctuations are similar for both years. January contained the lowest volume and July the peak volume of traffic, and May and October were close to the average for all days of the year.

Sunday and holiday traffic in the summer is shown to be very much larger than weekday traffic, although the difference is not so marked for the ten ferries combined as it would be for certain of the ferries favorably located for participation in Sunday traffic. Three of the ferries are not operated on Sundays and their inclusion tends to reduce the divergence.

Traffic over the Staten Island-Battery Ferry, which carried 33 per cent. of the total ferry traffic in 1928, exhibits the same general seasonal characteristics as shown in the diagram for all Municipal ferries combined. The same characteristics are shown by the traffic over the Clason's Point Ferry, important as the only direct vehicular connection between Queens and The Bronx. Both ferries carry very heavy Sunday and holiday traffic during the summer months.

Passenger Cars and Commercial Car Traffic.

Available records of ferry traffic do not show the classification of vehicular traffic. Data obtained in connection with our interborough origin and destination studies show that traffic for certain weekdays in February, 1929, on the Staten Island Municipal Ferries was comprised of 46 per cent. passenger automobiles, 52 per cent. trucks and two per cent. horse-drawn vehicles.

Relation of Daily to Annual Traffic.

The relation between the typical October weekday traffic and the total annual traffic, for all Municipal ferries and also for the Staten Island-Battery Ferry, is shown in the following table:

Relation of Annual Traffic to Typical October Weekday Traffic.

	1927.	1928.
All Municipal Ferries	346	345
Staten Island-Battery Ferry	372	367

The above ratio is comparable with 380 as developed for the Holland Tunnel traffic in 1928.

GENERAL SUMMARY.

In summarizing the data and factors heretofore presented, certain general conclusions may be developed from the study of interborough vehicular traffic, which become useful in studying the various measures proposed for traffic relief, and in estimating future traffic requirements.

The tremendous growth which has taken place in interborough vehicular traffic is evidenced by the fact that traffic over the East River bridges was about 13 times greater in 1928 than it was in 1910. The average annual percentage increase during the period 1925-1928, inclusive, has been six per cent. Three major factors influencing growth in traffic are, growth in population, relation of motor vehicle registration to population, and utilization of vehicles or relation between traffic and registration.

It has been shown elsewhere that motor vehicle registration has evidenced in recent years a decline in rate of growth. For New York City as a whole, this tendency is

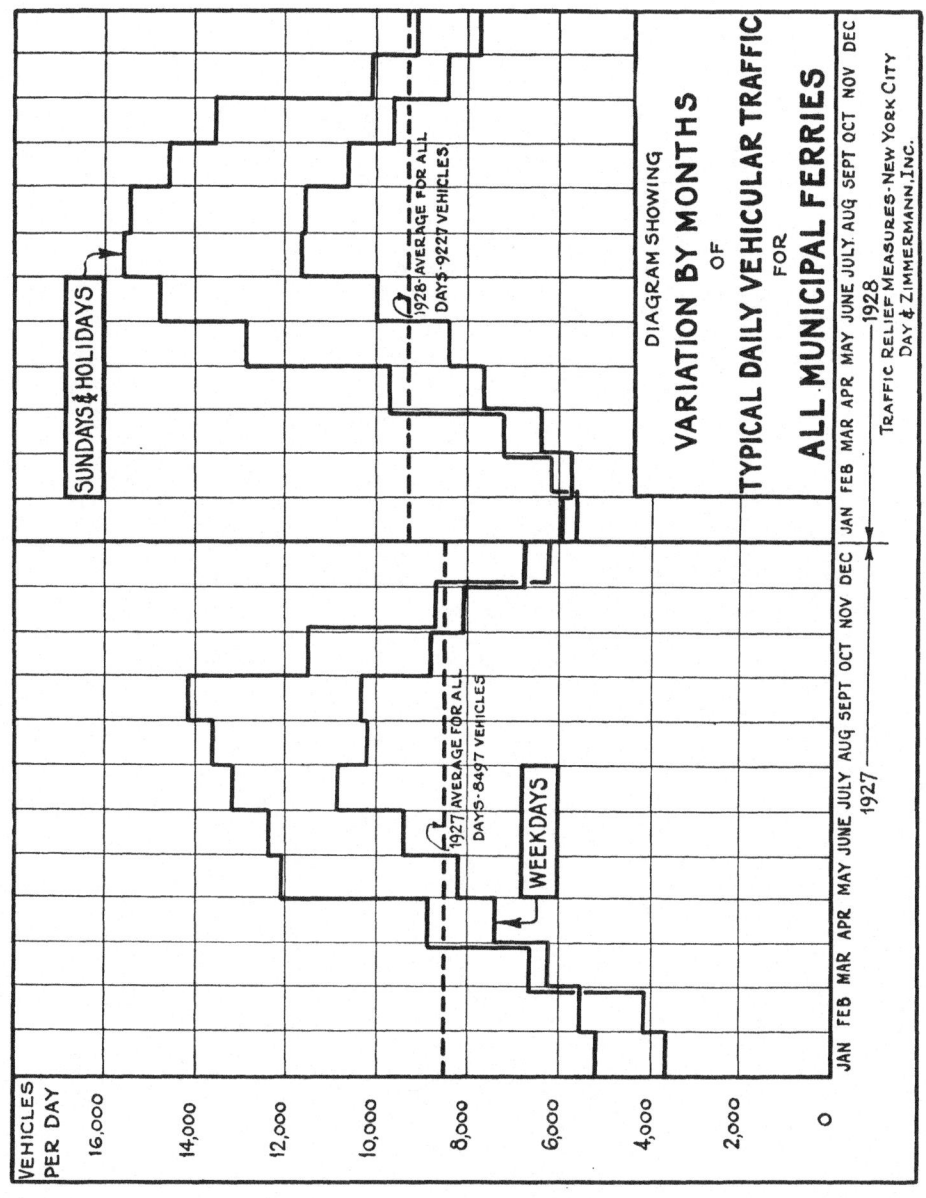

very apparent; but to a smaller degree in the Borough of Queens than in the other boroughs. The past rate of growth in the registration of passenger vehicles has greatly exceeded that of commercial vehicles.

The relation between the number of motor vehicles registered in New York City and vehicular traffic over the East River bridges has remained fairly constant for the past ten years, although the number of crossings per registered passenger vehicle has increased and per registered commercial vehicle has decreased. The rate of growth in East River bridge traffic for the past three years has been considerably less than the average rate established prior to 1925, and it is generally believed that congestion on the bridges and approaches is responsible to a large degree for the decline.

In considering the effect of new facilities upon existing conditions, the results of the Holland Tunnel for its first year of operation are of particular interest. Total traffic for the year 1928 amounted to 8,745,000, and the tunnel officials estimate that only 55 per cent. of the vehicles were diverted from the ferries, the remaining 45 per cent. being new traffic which would not have crossed the river except for the improved facilities provided by the tunnel. It is general experience that the provision of new facilities and routes is accompanied by a considerable volume of induced traffic.

A continuation of the past trend of registration provides an estimate of 1,075,000 motor vehicles registered in New York City at the end of 1935, or an increase of 58 per cent. over 1928, for the seven-year period. The ratio of East River Bridge crossings to registration in New York City has remained fairly constant at about one weekday crossing per three registered vehicles for the past ten years. Assuming a continuation of this ratio results in an estimate of approximately 310,000 weekday crossings in 1935, or an increase of 58 per cent. over the 1928 traffic. The trend of increase in bridge traffic during the past three years indicates a smaller figure in the order of 280,000 weekday crossings in 1935, or an increase of only 44 per cent. over 1928.

On the other hand, the provision of new facilities may reasonably be expected to stimulate a resumption of the growth trend established prior to 1925, as well as to induce a certain amount of traffic which otherwise would not have moved. From this viewpoint a much larger estimate for future East River traffic would be in order.

All interborough vehicular facilities have participated in the growth in traffic volume apparent during the past ten years and no evidence is available which would indicate any factor, other than highway limitations, operating to halt the public demands for interborough vehicular facilities, while on the other hand, several conditions are clearly apparent, such as the limitations of the transit system, the declining first cost of passenger automobiles, and the public desire for this type of transportation, which are tending to increase the general utilization of motor vehicles for commuting and business purposes.

Certain characteristics of weekday traffic over the facilities enumerated are summarized in the following table with a view towards presenting the main points of similarity or difference:

Characteristics of Weekday Traffic.

	East River Bridges.	Holland Tunnel.	Staten Island Ferry.
Total 24-hour traffic	194,500	22,250	3,400
Total day traffic (7 a. m. to 7 p. m.)	131,900	15,710	2,200
Per cent. of 24 hours	68%	71%	65%
Average hourly traffic in both directions—			
24 hours	8,100	928	142
12 hours	11,000	1,310	183
Maximum hourly traffic in both directions	15,222	1,820	217
Per cent. of 24-hour traffic	8%	8%	6%
Maximum hourly traffic in one direction	11,250	950	121
Ratios, maximum hourly traffic in both directions—			
To average traffic, 24 hours	1.9	2.0	1.5
To average traffic, 12 hours	1.4	1.4	1.2
To maximum flow, one direction	1.4	1.9	1.8

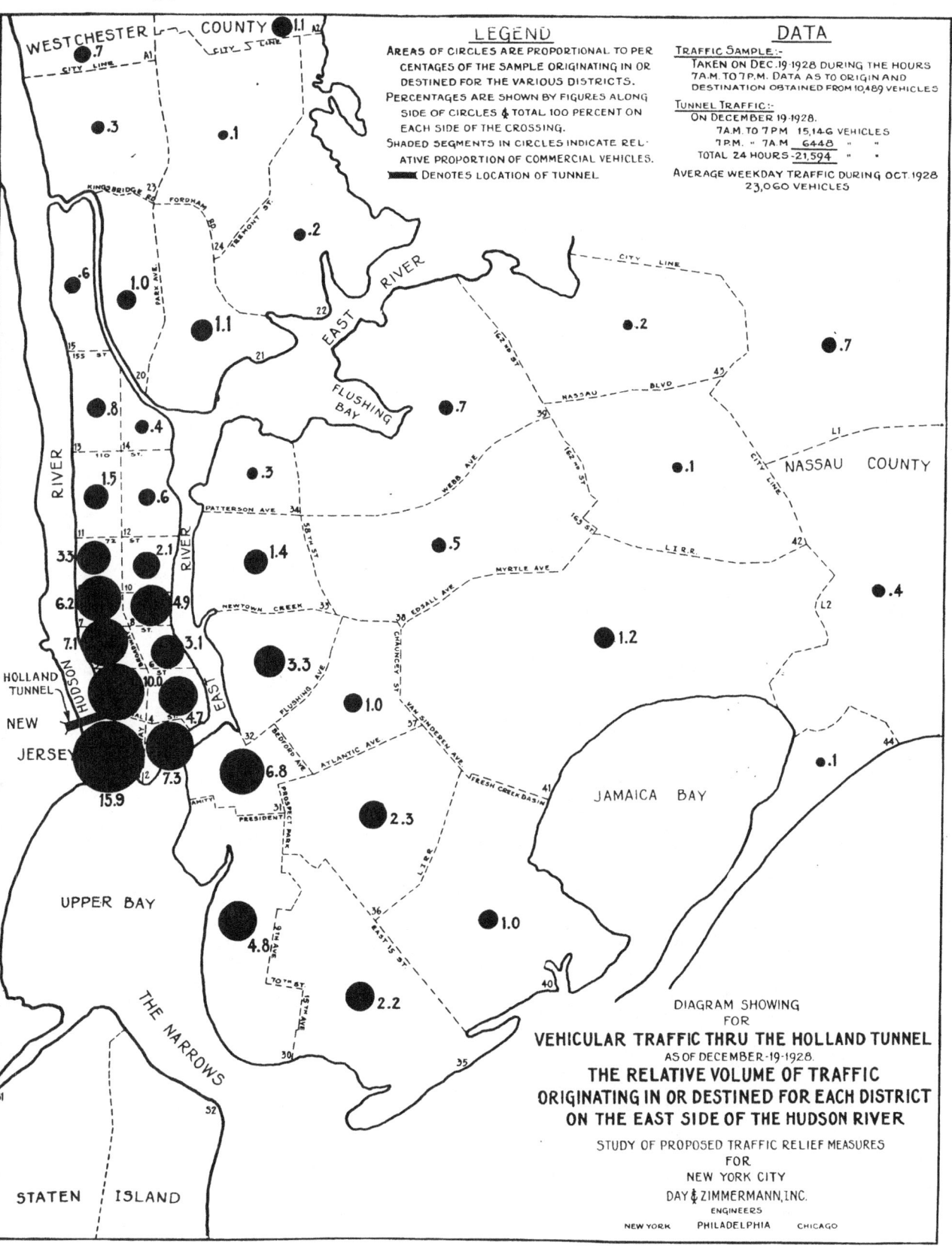

SECTION VII

DETAILS OF ORIGIN AND DESTINATION STUDIES

PURPOSE AND SCOPE

Much helpful data was found available in the records of the Police Department and in those of the Department of Plant and Structures, particularly as to the volume of traffic over bridges or at street intersections in various portions of the City, but there was a scarcity of specific data as to where the traffic in question came from, where it was going to, and by what routes it was moving. Information of the latter kind is essential to the analysis of present conditions, including the causes of congestion and the degree of relief which would be afforded by the various facilities proposed as traffic relief measures.

The magnitude of the problems of securing and of applying data of this nature in a traffic situation as large and as complicated as that in New York becomes evident when it is realized that the combined traffic flow over the East River bridges reached a maximum of approximately 15,000 vehicles per hour and that over the north and south avenues in mid-Manhattan approximately 27,000 vehicles per hour in the latter part of 1928.

With the assistance of the Police Department, counts to secure such origin, destination and routing data were planned and executed covering traffic flowing through the Holland Tunnel, over the East River bridges, along the north and south avenues, and along the east and west streets of mid-Manhattan. It required the services of approximately 100 traffic officers to collect the desired data on each of these counts. Similar data was obtained by the Department of Plant and Structures from traffic on the various municipal ferries and some general data obtained in 1928 on the 125th Street Ferry over the Hudson River was made available to us by the courtesy of the Port Authority of New York.

For purposes of classification, the City and adjoining territory was divided into a number of districts, the boundaries of which reflect a consideration of the general nature of the district, the street plan, the natural routes for traffic to follow, and the existing and proposed interborough bridges, tunnels and highways. Classification further involved the perparation of numerous tables and diagrams from which could be determined the general characteristics of the traffic, including the class of vehicle, the districts from which or to which the traffic was moving, the major arteries traversed, and the nature and extent of the burden it imposed upon the highways.

REPRESENTATIVENESS OF SAMPLES.

It is obvious that due to the areas involved and the number of vehicles moving, data could not be secured simultaneously for all of the flows mentioned, nor could it be secured from all of the traffic involved in any particular case without prohibitive disturbance and inconvenience to the public and without unwarranted cost for observers.

It was therefore necessary to devise methods which would yield samples of a size, taken during hours, and in a manner such that their indications would be fairly representative of the characteristics of the total traffic involved. Analysis of the individual samples obtained in the light of data covering the traffic from which they were taken, and comparison of the indications as to flow and routing at specific points as obtained from the bridge counts, the tunnel counts, and the street counts, respectively, resulted in a concordance that indicated that the samples obtained were quite representative of the traffic from which they were taken.

All of these counts and practically all of the traffic data available relate to weekday traffic. The Sunday and holiday traffic, particularly in the summer months, would undoubtedly show quite different results, but this does not diminish the applicability of the data secured for the present purposes.

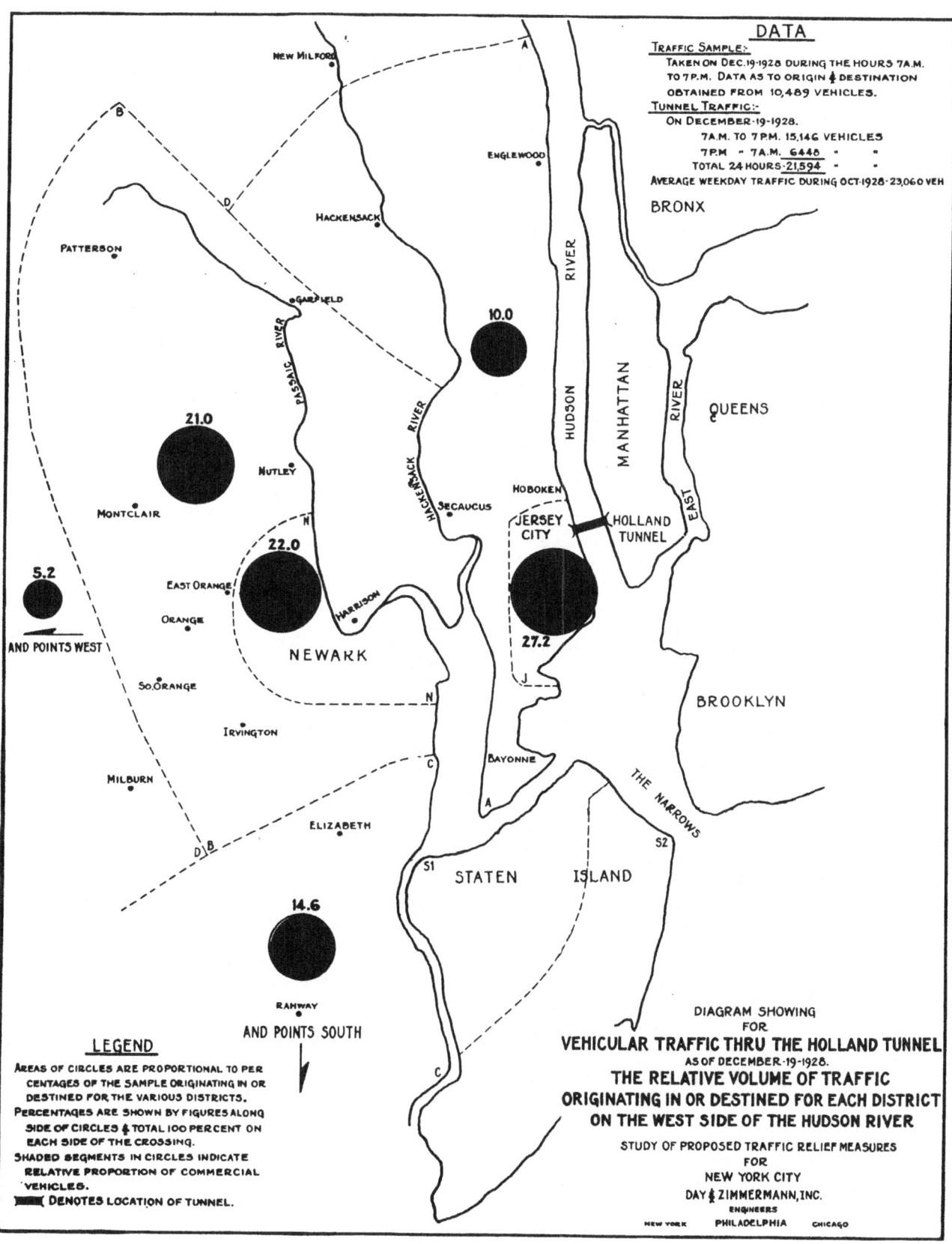

HOLLAND TUNNEL TRAFFIC.

Counts of this nature were made of the Holland Tunnel traffic on December 19, 1928, and data as to origin, destination and routing was obtained by direct inquiry from 80 per cent. of the westbound and 60 per cent. of the eastbound traffic flowing between the hours of 7 a. m. and 7 p. m. The total number of vehicles in the sample thus obtained was 10,489.

Analysis of Sample.

The characteristics of the traffic flows on this day were compared with those shown in corresponding hours of typical days by the records of the Tunnel Commission. The comparison covered the total traffic flow, the variation in flow by hours, the relation between eastbound and westbound flows, and the distribution between passenger cars and commercial vehicles.

The indications of the entire sample as to origins, destinations and routing were compared with the indications of a morning, mid-day and afternoon hour, and with the indications of the three hours combined. The analysis indicated that the sample was a very representative one of weekday traffic, and that using the data for the three hours referred to gave substantially the same result as was obtained by using the entire sample. This conclusion was the basis for the decision that on the bridges, avenues and streets representative results could be secured by taking samples during certain hours of the day and combining their indications.

Results of Count.

The relative volume of Holland Tunnel traffic originating in or destined for each district in New York is shown diagrammatically on page 170. The area of the circle in a given district is proportional to the percentage relation the number of vehicles going to or coming from that district bears to the number of vehicles in the entire sample. The percentage is also shown by the figures alongside of the respective circles. The shaded areas show the proportion of commercial vehicles in each group.

While the diagram shows the distribution of the traffic sample, it may also be taken as representative of the distribution of the total weekday traffic, which during the 12 hours in question averaged about 1,300 and reached a maximum of about 1,800 vehicles per hour.

Referring to the diagram the notable indications are that approximately 24 per cent. of the traffic moves across lower Manhattan streets on its way to or from Brooklyn and Queens, the larger portion using the Manhattan Bridge. About 68 per cent. of the traffic originates in or is destined for Manhattan points, largely west side districts below 47th street.

Study of the data obtained as to the routes followed by this traffic shows that about two-thirds of it flows up the west side avenues and that of this portion approximately one-half uses Varick street and 7th avenue. Approximately one-quarter of the total tunnel traffic, and very largely made up of commercial cars, moves across town via Canal street and forms a very considerable portion of the traffic flow in that street. Reduction of this crosstown flow by provision of other routes which would not bring it into conflict with north and south traffic would be an evident advantage.

Referring to the diagram on page 172, which shows the relative volume of the traffic originating in or destined for districts on the west side of the Hudson, it is interesting to note that about one-half of the traffic comes from or goes to Jersey City, Newark and their respective environs, and that only about one-sixth of the tunnel traffic comes from Elizabeth, Rahway and more southern points.

The distribution indicated on the two diagrams just referred to is for the daytime 12 hours on a winter weekday and is not typical of Sunday and holiday tunnel traffic, which is about double the volume of weekday traffic, is almost entirely passenger car traffic and includes a much larger proportion of traffic moving to and from more distant points.

EAST RIVER BRIDGE TRAFFIC.

Collection and Analysis of Data.

The practical impossibility of collecting data by direct inquiry from all traffic flowing over the bridges, or of ever stopping a very considerable portion of the traffic for such purpose, has already been referred to and led to the adoption of the following method: Traffic officers stationed at the approaches distributed to all traffic flowing over the bridges during a morning, a mid-day and an evening hour, questionnaires in the form of return post cards. An appeal for co-operation on the cards was supplemented verbally by the officers and by suitable publicity in the newspapers.

Some 31,700 cards were handed out during the three hours in question, but of these only about 15 per cent. were returned, resulting in a traffic sample covering 4,733 vehicles. This sample is substantially 15 per cent. of the traffic flowing during the particular hours in which it was collected, and 3.6 per cent. of that flowing during the hours from 7 a. m. to 7 p. m.

The data contained on the cards was tabulated to develop the relative volumes of traffic originating in or destined for each district on either side of the crossing, the relative volumes of traffic moving between any one district and each of the districts on the other side of the crossing, and the major routes used by the larger portion of the traffic, particularly through the congested areas. In the following paragraphs and accompanying diagrams an effort has been made to portray the salient characteristics developed as a result of these studies.

Comparison of Traffic Flows.

In order to aid in the interpretation of the diagrams the vehicular traffic flows over the four East River bridges as determined in October, 1928, are repeated in the following tabulation, which is for 24-hour vehicular traffic:

Bridge.	Vehicles Per Day.
Queensboro	72,000
Williamsburg	41,000
Manhattan	60,000
Brooklyn	22,000
Total	195,000

The comparable weekday flow through the Holland Tunnel is 23,100 vehicles per 24 hours. The total flow on all the north and south avenues at 42d street is substantially 221,000 vehicles per 12 hours, or assuming the same relationship between 24-hour and 12-hour flows as developed for the bridges, about 325,000 vehicles per 24 hours.

Presentation of Results.

The following tabulation shows the origin and destination of the 4,733 vehicle movements making up the sample and the bridges over which they moved. The numbers along the top of the table refer to the districts in Queens and Brooklyn, and those along the left hand column to the Manhattan-Bronx districts. The location of the districts is indicated by outline and numbers on the accompanying diagrams. The following example will illustrate the nature of the information contained in the table:

> District 6, which includes the east side of Manhattan between 14th street and 32d street, was the point of origin or destination for 338 vehicle movements across the East River bridges. 40 of these movements were between District 6 in Manhattan and District 36 in Brooklyn and of these movements 27 were over the Manhattan Bridge.

The information in this table is also the basis for diagrams showing for the various bridges the relative volumes of traffic originating in or destined for each district. In comparing these diagrams it must be kept in mind that the areas of the circles are proportional to a percentage of the particular traffic sample, and that circles of equal areas on the various diagrams do not represent equal traffic volumes.

An extensive series of tabulations and diagrams were prepared, based on the same data, and giving among other things the percentage of the total sample of East River bridge traffic moving between a particular district on one side of the crossing and any or all of the districts on the other side. These tabulations and diagrams, too numerous to include in full in this report, together with the routing data, were of particular use in analyzing the present flow of traffic between certain districts over the existing routes and in estimating the volume of traffic which could more advantageously use such new routes as would be made available by the various bridges, tunnels and highways under consideration as traffic relief measures.

Oversized Foldout

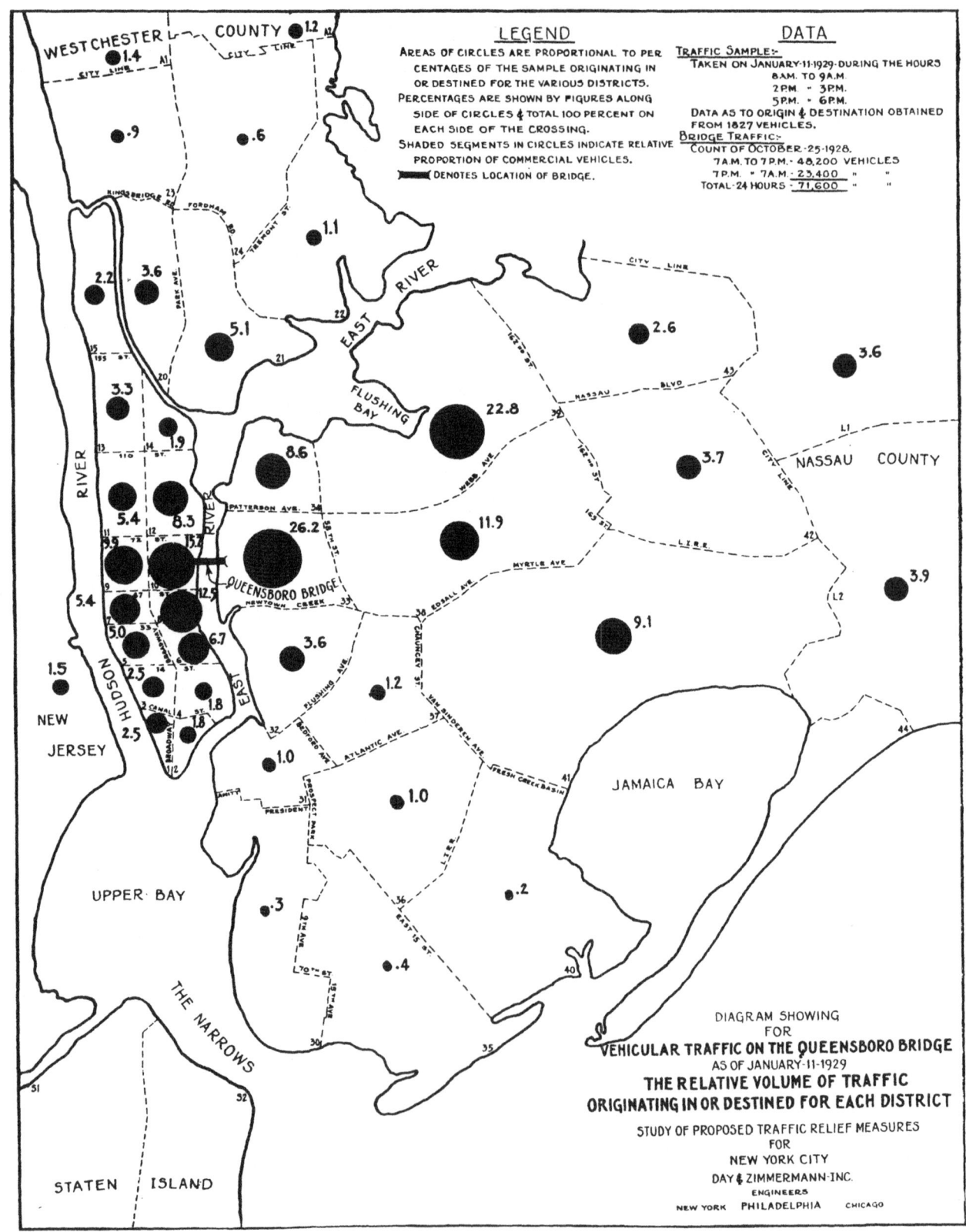

Queensboro Bridge Traffic.

The diagram on page 178 shows that on the east side of the crossing the bulk of the traffic originates in or is destined for Queens, only a very small portion flowing to or from Brooklyn. The districts immediately adjacent to the bridge and the Flushing district account for approximately 26 per cent. and 23 per cent., respectively, of the total sample.

The diagram also shows that on the west side of the crossing the larger portion of the traffic moves to or from districts in mid-Manhattan, and that considerable portions move north of 72d street and south of 33d street. Approximately 21 per cent. moves to or from districts in Manhattan north of 110th street or in The Bronx and about 10 per cent. to or from districts south of 14th street or in New Jersey.

Routing studies indicate that, of the traffic moving north of 72d street, the greater portion now uses east side avenues, being evenly distributed on 1st to 5th avenues, inclusive. Most of the traffic moving south of the bridge uses 1st avenue and Park avenue, and approximately one-third of all the traffic moves to or from the west side on 30th to 59th streets, inclusive.

The commercial car traffic is about 23 per cent. of the total vehicular traffic. The diagram shows that on the east side of the crossing there is a greater concentration of commercial traffic in the districts adjoining the East River, whereas on the Manhattan side of the crossing there is no marked concentration of this type of traffic, except perhaps in the west side district between 33d and 47th streets.

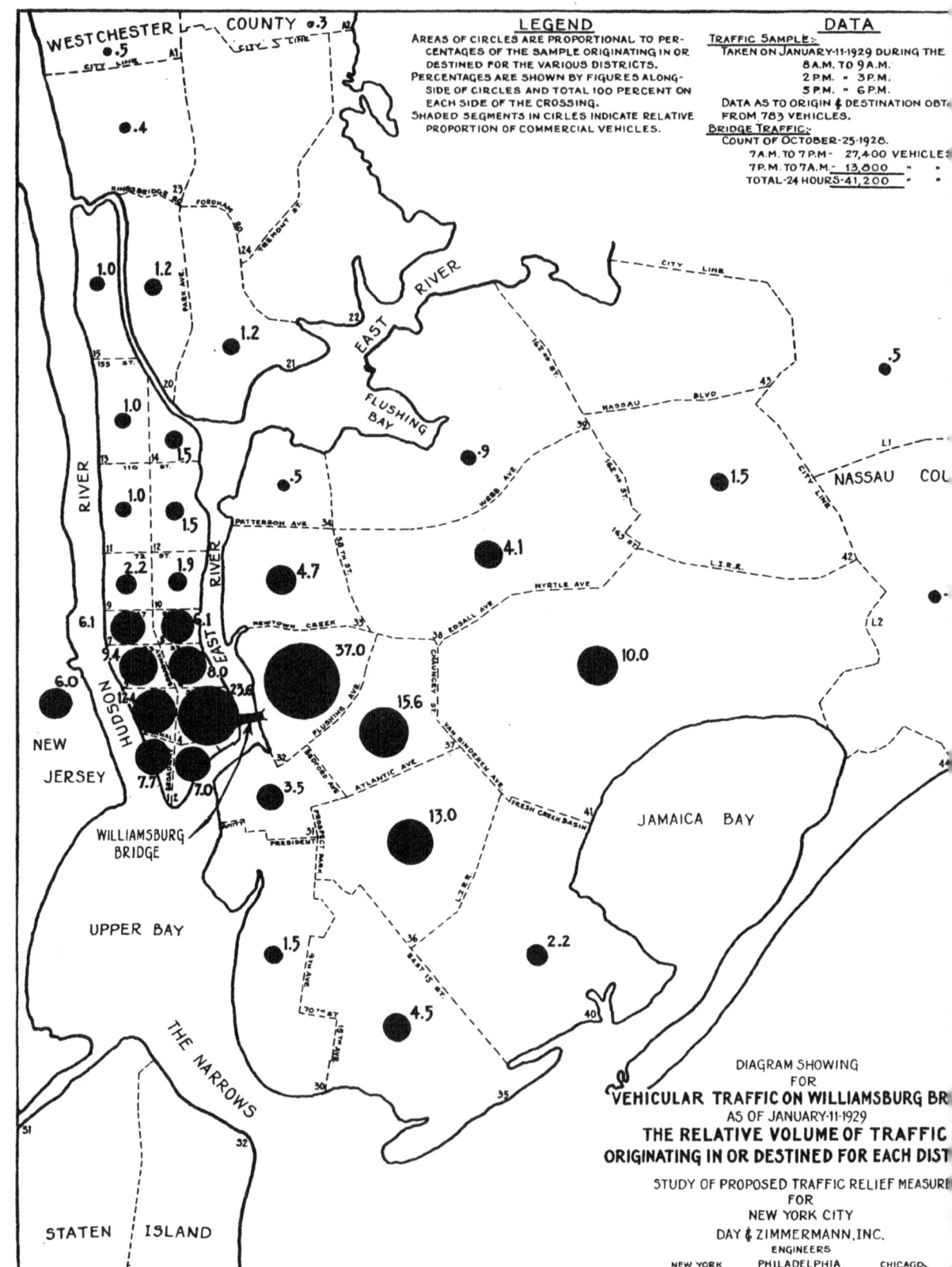

Williamsburg Bridge Traffic.

The diagram on page 180 shows that on the east side of the crossing the bulk of this traffic originates in or is destined for Brooklyn, only a small portion moving north of Newtown Creek. The district immediately adjacent to the bridge accounts for 37 per cent. of the total traffic. On the west side of the crossing about 57 per cent. of all the traffic moves to or from points in Manhattan below 14th street or in New Jersey. The districts between 14th and 72d streets account for approximately 34 per cent. of the traffic, the remaining portion moving north of 72d street.

Routing studies indicate that approximately one-half of the traffic uses either 1st avenue, 3d avenue or Lafayette street, the heaviest movement occurring on 1st avenue. About one-fourth of the total traffic moves on miscellaneous streets below Canal street, and the remaining portion uses west side avenues above Canal street, with the heaviest movements on 7th avenue and West street.

The commercial car traffic is about 30 per cent. of the total vehicular traffic. The diagram shows that on the east side of the crossing there is a greater concentration of this type of traffic in the districts nearer the East River and Upper Bay, and on the Manhattan side a similar concentration is found in the west side districts below 33d street and in the New Jersey district.

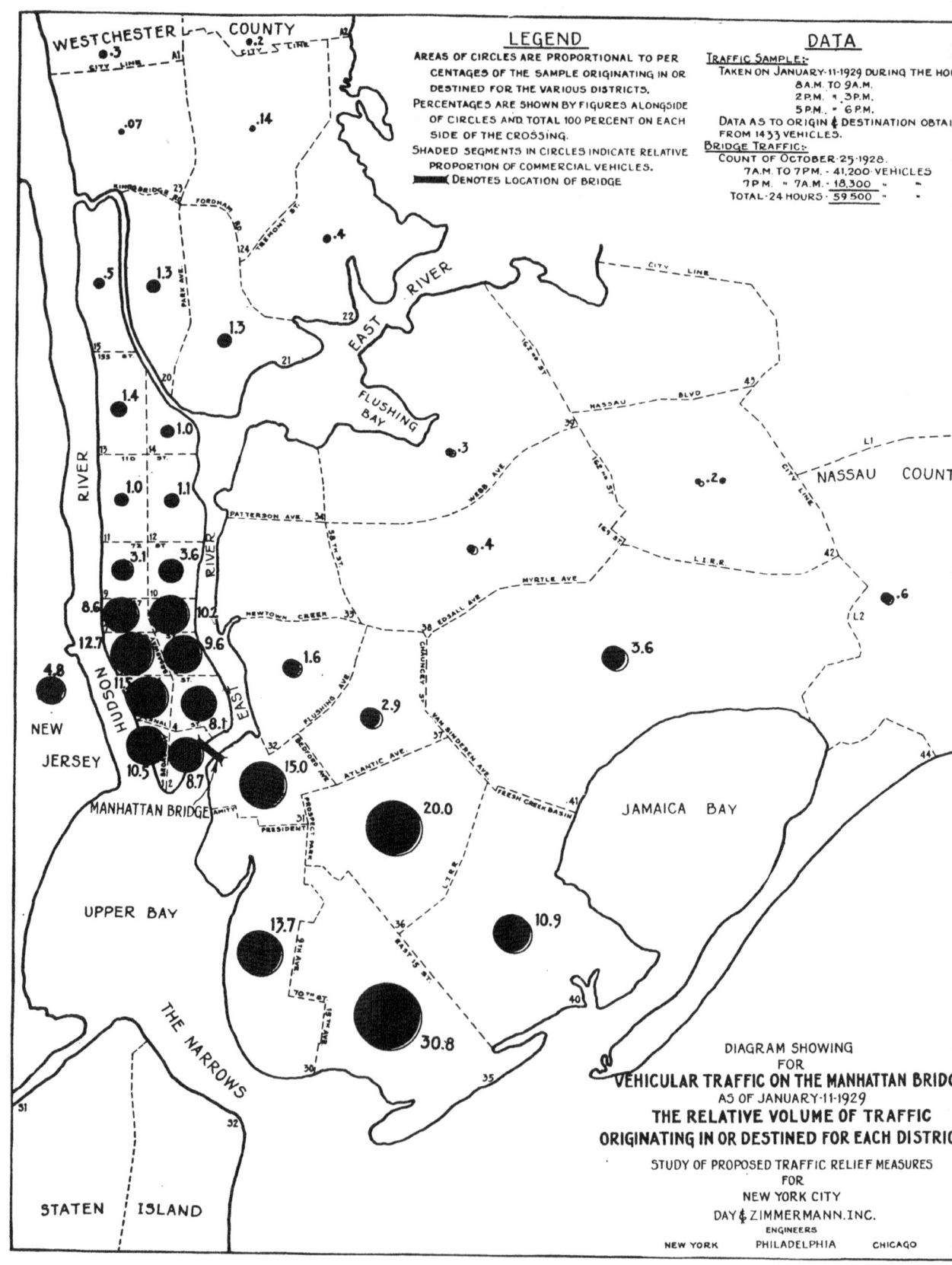

Manhattan Bridge Traffic.

The diagram on page 182 shows that on the east side of this crossing approximately 90 per cent. of the traffic moves to or from points south of the bridge. The district below the Prospect Park area accounts for about 31 per cent. of the total traffic. On the Manhattan side of the crossing approximately 85 per cent. of all the traffic originates in or is destined for districts in Manhattan below 47th street or in New Jersey, with about 50 per cent. of the total traffic moving to or from the west side of Manhattan below 47th street.

Routing studies indicate that about two-thirds of the traffic uses east side avenues, the heaviest movement occurring on Lafayette and 4th avenues. Substantially all of the remaining traffic moves directly across town, mostly on Canal street, using 7th avenue or West street to or from points to the north or south.

The commercial car traffic is about 28 per cent. of the total vehicular traffic on this bridge. On the Brooklyn side of the crossing a greater concentration of this type of traffic is found in the districts adjoining the East River and Upper Bay. On the west side of the crossing there is no marked concentration, except perhaps in the districts below 14th street in Manhattan and in New Jersey.

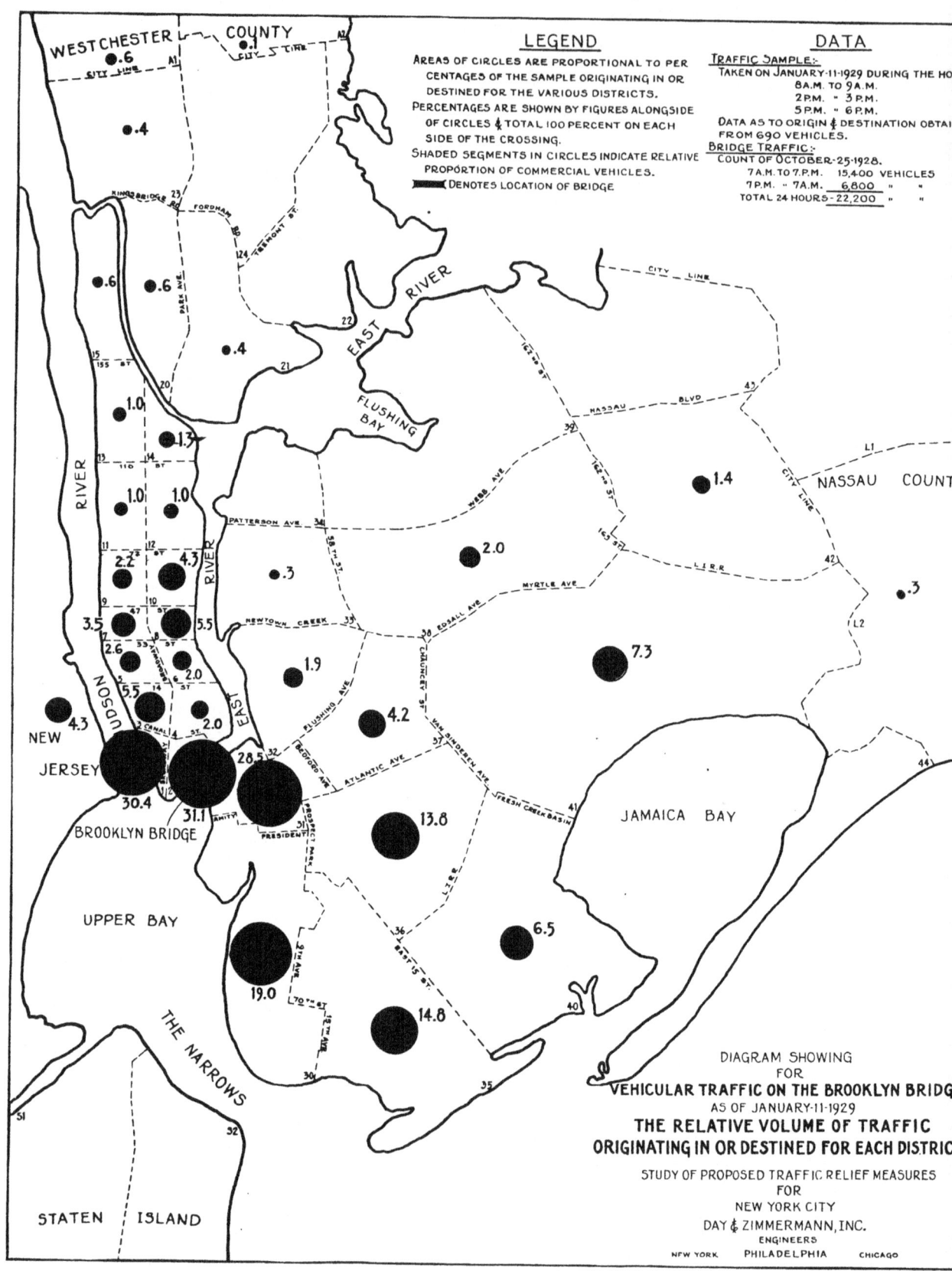

Brooklyn Bridge Traffic.

The diagram on page 184 shows that on the Brooklyn side of the crossing about 83 per cent. of this traffic originates in or is destined for points south of the bridge. The district immediately adjacent to the bridge accounts for about 28 per cent. of all the traffic, and the water front district to the south accounts for 19 per cent. On the west side of the crossing about 61 per cent. of the total traffic moves to or from points south of Canal street.

Routing studies indicate that the traffic moving below Canal street uses miscellaneous streets in that section, and that approximately three-fourths of the remaining traffic uses Lafayette street.

The commercial car traffic is only 6 per cent. of the total vehicular traffic, this type of traffic being limited to mail and newspaper trucks by the regulations governing the use of the Brooklyn Bridge.

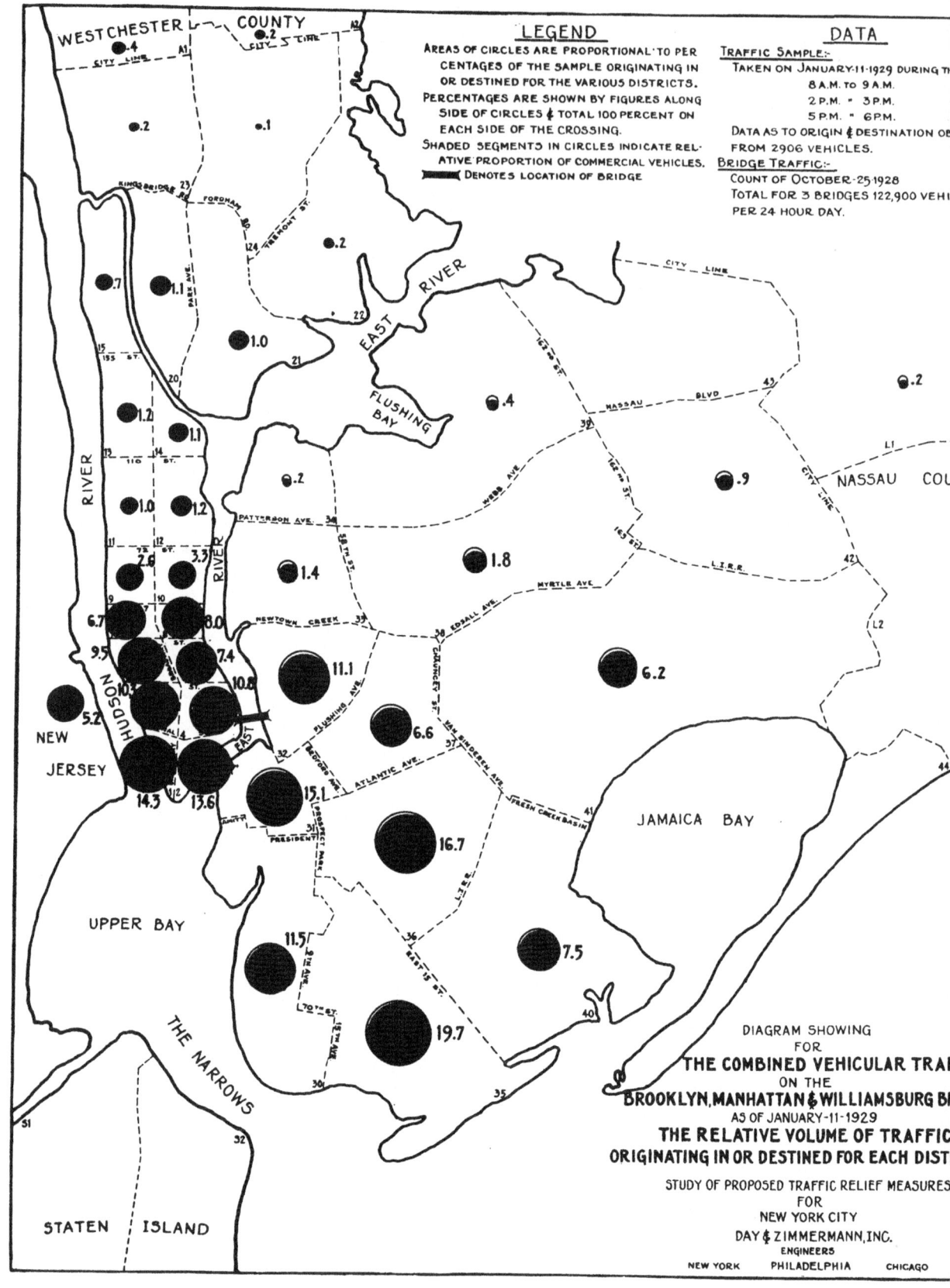

Williamsburg, Manhattan and Brooklyn Bridges, Combined.

Due to the close spacing of these three bridges and to the fact that in a large measure they serve traffic from the same areas, a study has been made of the origin and destination of their combined traffic. The diagram on page 186 shows that on the east side of the crossings about 95 per cent. of all the traffic moves to or from points below Newtown Creek. The bulk of the traffic is concentrated in the districts adjoining the East River and Upper Bay, the Prospect Park district immediately south of the Prospect Park area.

On the Manhattan side of the crossings, the diagram indicates that about 86 per cent. of the total traffic originates in or is destined for points below 47th street in Manhattan or in New Jersey. The west side districts below 47th street account for approximately 46 per cent. of all the traffic. It will also be noted that about 6 per cent. of the combined traffic moves to or from points north of 110th street in Manhattan or in The Bronx.

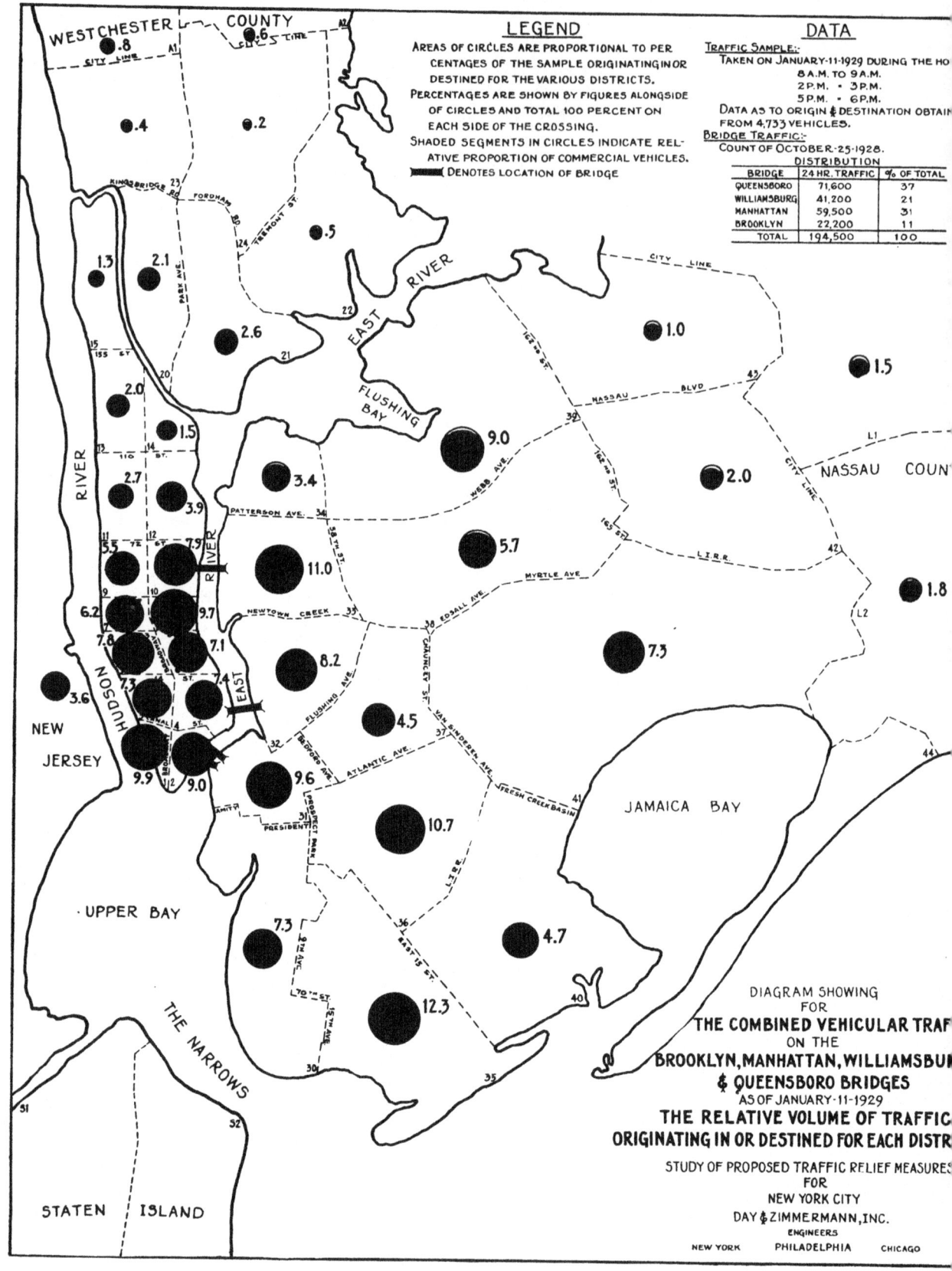

Queensboro, Williamsburg, Manhattan and Brooklyn Bridges, Combined.

The diagram on page 188 shows that on the east side of the crossings approximately two-thirds of the combined traffic on all the bridges originates in or is destined for points below Newtown Creek. The studies of the individual bridges show that the bulk of this portion of the traffic makes use of the three lower bridges. However, a small portion moves over the Queensboro Bridge and likewise a small portion of the traffic from above Newtown Creek uses the three lower bridges.

On the Manhattan side of the crossings, the diagram indicates that the bulk of the combined traffic moves to or from points below 72d street with a very even distribution throughout this area. Approximately 12 per cent. of the total moves to points above 110th street in Manhattan or in The Bronx. The west side districts in Manhattan account for about one-half of the total traffic.

The commercial car traffic is about 24 per cent. of the total combined vehicular traffic. There is a concentration of this class of vehicles on the east side of the crossings near the East River and Upper Bay. There is no marked concentration on the west side of the crossings, although there are slightly greater proportions of commercial traffic in the districts below Canal street, in west side districts below 47th street and in New Jersey.

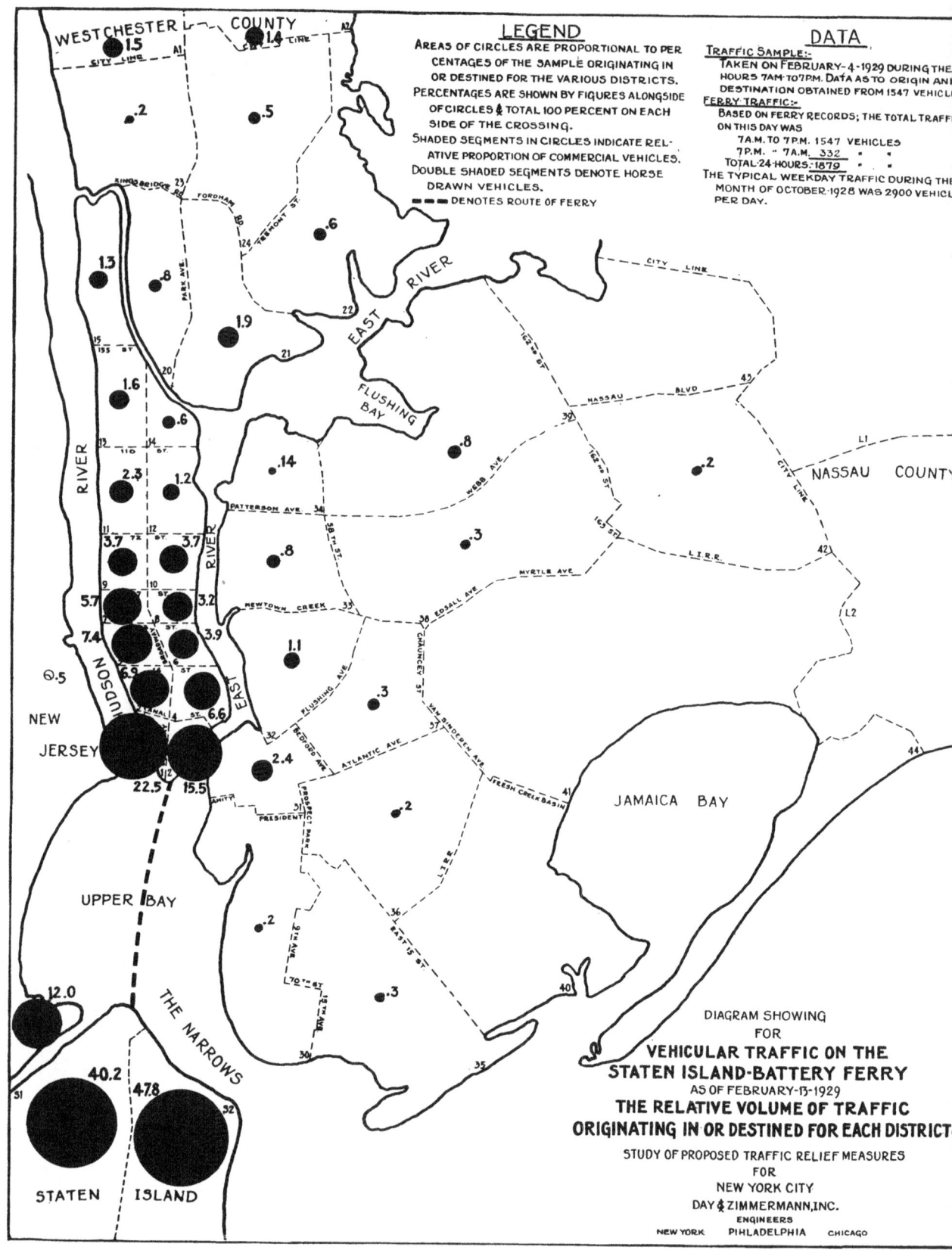

FERRY TRAFFIC.

While the total volume of ferry traffic is small in comparison with that over the bridges, it appears desirable to develop the characteristics of certain more or less special situations of growing importance, particularly with regard to the Staten Island and Clason's Point Ferries.

The traffic volumes involved, shown in detail in a preceding section, are summarized in the following table:

Municipal Ferries.	1928 Vehicular Traffic.	October Weekday Traffic.
Staten Island-Battery	1,072,000	2,900
Staten Island-Brooklyn	325,100	890
Clason's Point-College Point	832,000	2,300
East River ferries	866,700	3,300
Total	3,095,800	9,390

The data as to the origin and destination of weekday vehicular traffic on the various ferries was obtained by means of direct inquiry. The counts were made between 7 a. m. and 7 p. m. between February 4 and 15, 1929, and included practically every vehicle movement during the 12-hour period selected for each ferry. The results of these counts, made on a winter weekday, of necessity cannot reflect the characteristics of summer and Sunday traffic which, based on the general knowledge of ferry officials, not only has a greater volume, but includes a larger proportion of vehicles traveling between more distant points.

Staten Island-Battery Ferry.

The diagram on page 190 shows the distribution of traffic on both sides of the crossing as indicated by the study of 1,545 movements on February 4, 1929. Commercial cars and trucks comprised 52 per cent. of the total sample and horse-drawn vehicles 2 per cent., which proportions are about double those found in the East River bridges.

The distribution of traffic on the Staten Island side shows that 88 per cent. originated in or was destined for points on Staten Island and 12 per cent. for points in New Jersey. The New Jersey traffic was distributed approximately as follows: 8 per cent. over the Outerbridge Crossing, 3 per cent. over the Goethals Bridge and 1 per cent. over the Bergen Point Ferry at Bayonne.

The distribution on the Manhattan side indicates that over 50 per cent. of the traffic stopped short of 14th street and about 14 per cent. moved between the Battery and points north of 72d street, including 7 per cent. which crossed the Harlem River. About 7 per cent. of the total flowed over the East River bridges and ferries to and from widely scattered points throughout Brooklyn and Queens. A very small portion, one-half of one per cent., used either the Holland Tunnel or the Hudson River ferries between Manhattan and New Jersey.

Staten Island-Brooklyn Ferry.

The Municipal Ferry from Staten Island to 39th street, Brooklyn, is paralleled by a privately owned line which is estimated to carry about the same volume of traffic, with substantially the same characteristics. The distribution of traffic on either side of the crossing shown by the diagram on page 192 is based on a study of 608 vehicle movements over the ferry on February 13, 1929. Commercial and horse-drawn vehicles were found in approximately the same percentages of total traffic as stated above for the Staten Island-Battery Ferry.

On the Staten Island side about 80 per cent. of the total traffic was local to points on the Island and 20 per cent. slightly more than in the case of the Battery line, moved to and from New Jersey. The latter traffic was distributed approximately as follows: 13 per cent. over the Outerbridge Crossing, 6 per cent. over the Goethals Bridge and 1 per cent. over the Bergen Point Ferry at Bayonne. The distribution on the Brooklyn side showed an absence of traffic moving through Brooklyn to Manhattan and The Bronx. About two-thirds of the traffic originated in or was destined for the districts immediately adjacent to the Brooklyn Terminal.

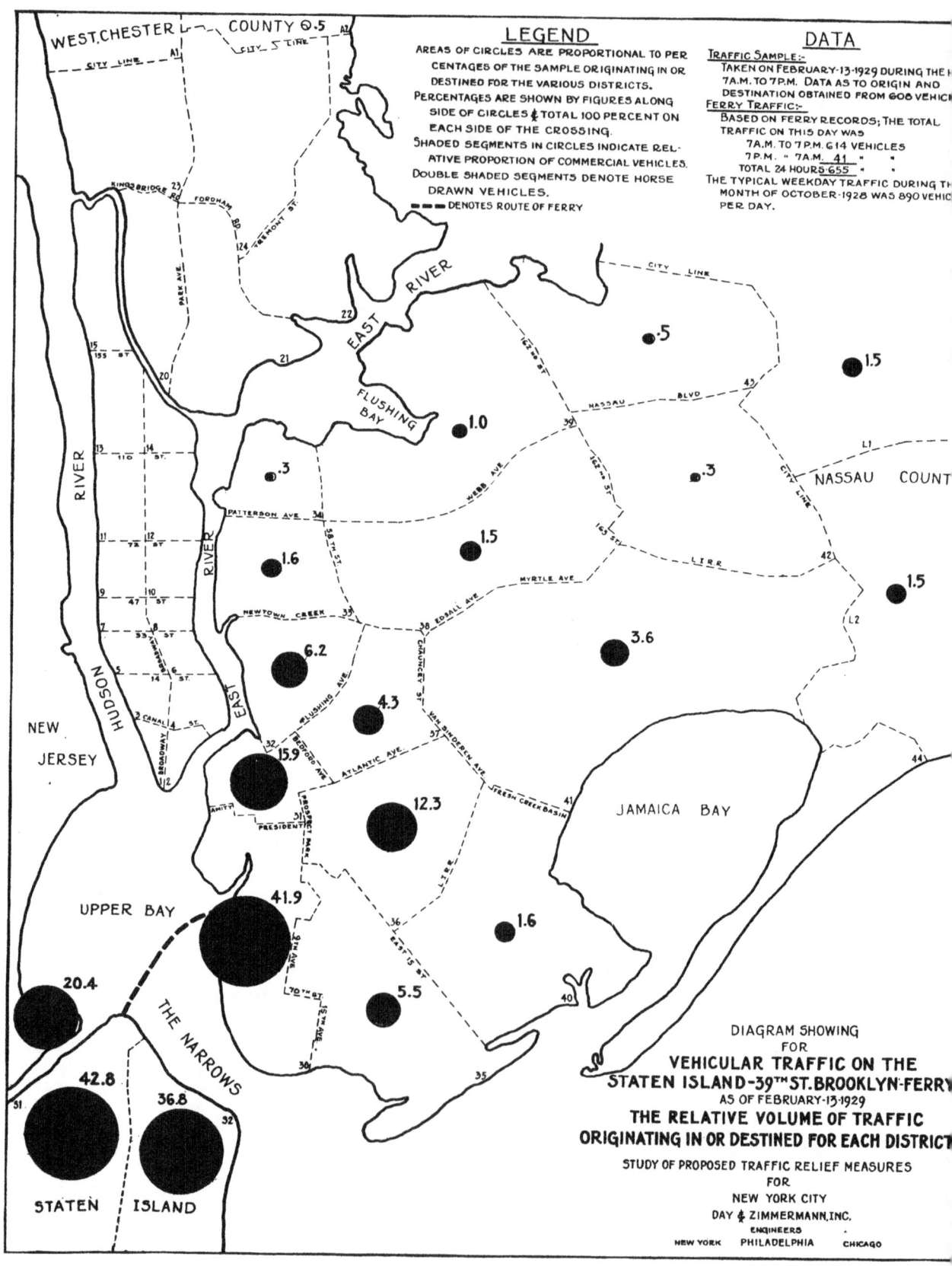

Clason's Point-College Point Ferry.

The line between Clason's Point, Bronx, and College Point, Queens, is important as the only direct facility for vehicles connecting these two Boroughs. A study of 1,000 vehicular movements made on February 6, 1929, indicates that only a small portion, about 9 per cent, was strictly local traffic between Districts 21 and 39, in which the terminals are located. On the Queens side of the crossing about one-third of the total traffic originated in or was destined for District 39, the terminal district; about one-third for points on Long Island beyond the City line, and about one-third widely scattered over Brooklyn and Queens. On The Bronx side over one-third of the total traffic originated in or was destined for the southeastern portion of The Bronx, Districts 21 and 22. About 40 per cent. traveled through The Bronx to and from points north of the City line and the remainder to scattered points in the Bronx, Manhattan and New Jersey.

East River Municipal Ferries.

The Municipal ferries on the East River include the Astoria, Greenpoint, Grand Street, Atlantic Avenue, Hamilton Avenue and 39th Street, Brooklyn Lines, all plying between Manhattan and Brooklyn or Queens. The counts made indicate that most of the vehicular traffic on these lines originates in or is destined for the terminal areas. The percentage of the total sample on each line which moved between the terminal areas only is shown in the following table.

Ferry.	Local Traffic, Per Cent. of Total.
Astoria	30%
Greenpoint	30%
Grand Street	41%
Atlantic Avenue	75%
Hamilton Avenue	81%
39th Street, Brooklyn	73%

There is a similarity in the proportions of strictly local traffic for the three ferries in the upper and in the lower groups, respectively.

Astoria Ferry.

About 50 per cent. of the total traffic over this ferry, based on a study of 601 movements, originated in or was destined for the terminal districts on each side of the crossing. The remainder of the traffic on both sides was largely confined to adjacent districts, diminishing in volume as the distances from the terminal areas increase. The weekday traffic over this ferry amounts to 1,600 vehicles or about one-half of the total traffic using the six East River ferries.

Greenpoint and Grand Street Ferries.

The characteristics of vehicular traffic over these two ferries is similar, about three-quarters of their total traffic originating in or being destined for the respective terminal districts and the distribution of the remainder being limited to nearby points. Their combined weekday traffic volume in October amounted to 750 vehicles, of which the Greenpoint Ferry carried 500 and the Grand Street Ferry 250. The total number of movements studied amounted to 456.

Atlantic, Hamilton and 39th Street Ferries.

A study of the origin and destination of vehicles using the Atlantic Avenue, Hamilton Avenue and 39th Street (Brooklyn) Ferries indicates that no wide distribution occurs on the Brooklyn side, the traffic being concentrated in the sections adjacent to the waterfront along the Upper Bay. On the Manhattan side over three-quarters of the traffic originated in or was destined for the area south of Canal street. The foregoing statements show the local character of vehicular traffic on these ferries, which, we are informed, is largely comprised of commercial vehicles traveling between the wharves and warehouses in lower Manhattan and South Brooklyn.

TRAFFIC ON MANHATTAN AVENUES AT 51ST STREET.

In order to develop information concerning the origin and destination of traffic moving on the avenues of Manhattan, the routes followed by such traffic and the distances moved in the north and south direction, counts were made on all avenues at 51st street during the hours of 8 to 10 a. m., 12 to 2 p. m. and 4 to 6 p. m. on January 13-15, 1929, inclusive. This location, lying to the south of the Queensboro Bridge and within the region in which avenue traffic reaches its greatest densities and in which relief is most needed, appeared to offer an opportunity of obtaining the essential

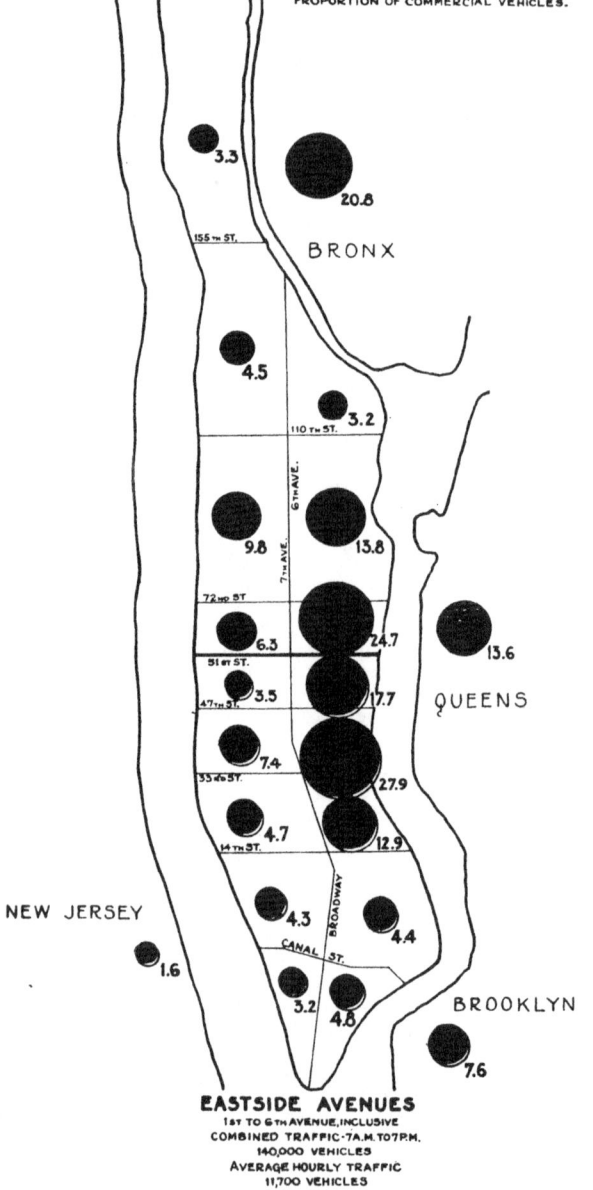

necessary data without duplication of effort by other counts made at locations farther north or farther south.

The Traffic Sample.

Traffic officers stationed on all avenues in the vicinity of 51st street gave out return postal cards similar to those used on the East River bridges, but in spite of efforts to bring about greater co-operation on the part of the public, the proportion of cards returned was less than on the bridges, being only about nine per cent. of those given out. The traffic sample thus obtained totaled 4,553 vehicle movements, equivalent to about four per cent. of the traffic flowing during the hours in which it was collected.

Volume of Traffic.

In order to simplify the presentation and enable the characteristics of this traffic to be more readily determined, the data obtained on individual avenues was combined by grouping them, designating the avenues from 1st to 6th avenues, inclusive, as "East Side" avenues and those from 7th to 11th avenues, inclusive, as "West Side" avenues.

Based on the 1928 counts of traffic moving between the hours from 7 a. m. to 7 p. m., the average hourly flows in the vicinity of 51st street are substantially as follows:

On east side avenues, 1st to 6th, inclusive..........................	11,700 vehicles
On west side avenues, 7th to 11th, inclusive.........................	5,900 vehicles
On all avenues..	17,600 vehicles

The combined flow on all avenues totalling some 211,000 vehicles between 7 a. m. and 7 p. m. may be compared with a combined flow over the four East River bridges of 132,000 vehicles during the same hours of an October weekday in 1928.

Distribution on Basis of Districts.

The diagrams shown on page 194 are similar in general form and meaning to those used for bridge and ferry traffic, the "crossing" in this case being the line of 51st street, designated by a heavy line on the diagram. The most striking indication is the general similarity in the relative distribution of the traffic for the east side and west side avenues, respectively, although it should be kept in mind that the volume of traffic, total vehicles per hour, on the east side avenues is practically twice that on the west side avenues.

The diagrams also show the large portion of the traffic making an L-shaped journey by moving from the west side of Manhattan to an east side avenue, or vice versa, before reaching 51st street. This tendency is substantially equal above and below 51st street, and somewhat greater for the traffic using east side avenues. About 24 per cent. of the east side traffic and 20 per cent. of the west side traffic moved "across town" on its way to or from the point where it crossed 51st street.

The diagrams develop clearly the very considerable portions of the traffic moving to or from points far to the north and to the south of the midtown sections, as well as to or from points in Brooklyn and Queens. There is a considerable volume of traffic moving over the three lower bridges to or from midtown points below 51st street, which is not included in these figures and which has been referred to in connection with the origin and destination studies of East River bridge traffic. There is no marked difference between the east side and west side avenues in respect to the proportion of commercial car traffic coming from or going to the various districts.

Distribution on Basis of Distance Traveled.

The diagram on page 196 based upon the same traffic sample, shows for the northbound and southbound vehicular traffic crossing 51st street the distribution of the traffic flow on the basis of the distance traveled in a north and south direction, no regard being had to whatever crosstown movements may have been involved. The chief purpose of the diagram is to develop the amount and distribution of "long haul" traffic.

The diagram is drawn to scale for distances in a north and south direction, but not for distances east and west. It is about 2 miles from 33d street to 72d street, approximately 5 miles from the Harlem River at 6th avenue to 51st street, and about 7 miles to 14th street.

Referring to the diagram for west side avenues for purposes of illustration, it will be seen that the traffic crossing 51st street has been divided into three bands on the basis of origins or destinations between 51st and 33d streets, 33d and 14th streets, and below 14th street, respectively. Each of these bands in turn shows in its upper sections the extent to which the various districts north of 51st street contributed to the total flow at 51st street. It should be kept in mind that the diagram does not show the total flow in the avenues at any point other than at 51st street. At other points, as for example at 110th street, the widths of the bands are proportional to the traffic at that point which moves to or from points beyond 51st street.

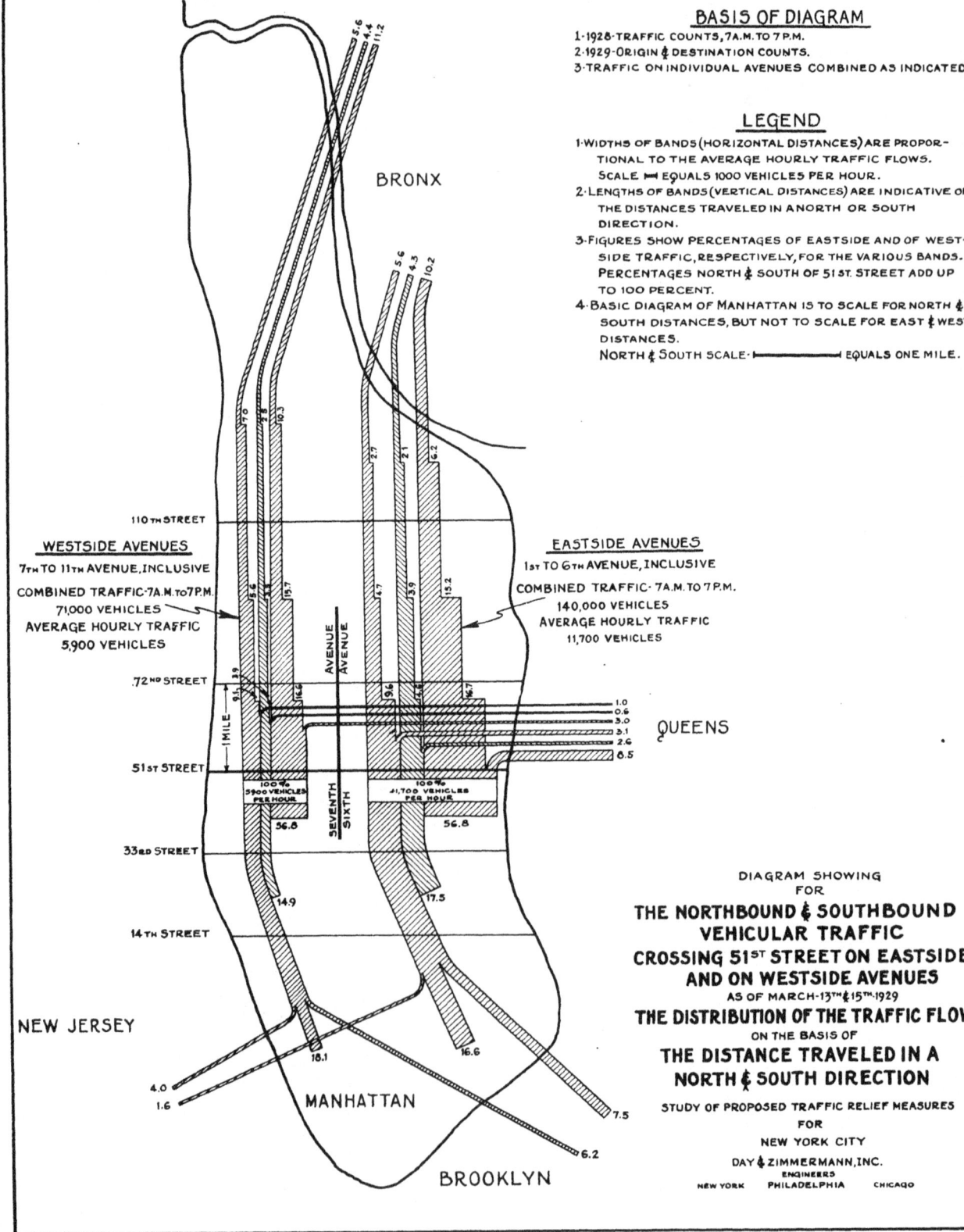

For further illustration, 14.9 per cent. of the traffic crossing 51st street on west side avenues moved to or from points in Manhattan between 33d and 14th streets. of which almost one-third comes from or goes to points in The Bronx. Similarly, 5.6 per cent. of the west side avenue traffic moved between points in The Bronx and points in Manhattan below 14th street or in Brooklyn or New Jersey.

The proportions and distribution of long haul traffic may be determined more concretely from the following tabulation, which shows the percentage of the total avenue traffic crossing 51st street moving between any two of the districts indicated along the side and the top of the table respectively.

Percentage of Avenue Traffic Crossing 51st Street Moving Between the Districts Indicated.

Districts.	51st to 33d Street.	33d to 14th Street.	Below 14th Street.	Total.
Queens	6.6	2.0	2.4	11.0
51st-72d street	16.6	4.3	9.4	30.3
72d-110th street	15.4	3.8	5.0	24.2
North of 110th street	7.6	2.3	4.1	14.0
Bronx	10.5	4.4	5.6	20.5
Total	56.7	16.8	26.5	100.0

Of the 17,600 vehicles per hour crossing 51st street, about 21 per cent., or some 3,700, were commercial vehicles. An analysis of their movements showed characteristics quite similar to those shown for the total traffic and is summarized in the following tabulation of its distribution.

Percentage of Commercial Car Traffic Crossing 51st Street on All Avenues Moving Between the Districts Indicated.

Districts.	51st to 33d Street.	33d to 14th Street.	Below 14th Street.	Total.
Queens	7.5%	2.1%	4.5%	14.1%
51st to 72d street	16.5%	6.7%	11.0%	34.2%
72d to 110th street	9.1%	3.1%	4.3%	16.5%
North of 110th street	6.1%	2.9%	5.3%	14.3%
Bronx	7.9%	4.1%	8.9%	20.9%
Totals	47.1%	18.9%	34.0%	100.0%

Extent of Long Haul Traffic.

The large proportion of the avenue traffic crossing 51st street which moved distances in a north and south direction in excess of approximately 2 miles is indicated by the following statements:

  43 per cent. of the total moved to or from points south of 33d street.
  26 per cent. of the total moved to or from points south of 14th street.
  59 per cent. of the total moved to or from points north of 72d street.
  34 per cent. of the total moved to or from points north of 110th street.

About 4,400 vehicles per hour or practically one-quarter of the total flow, moved between points lying north of 72d street and south of 33d street, passing on its way through about 2 miles of congested mid-town section.

About one-fifth of the total flow, or 3,700 vehicles per hour, moved to or from points in The Bronx to at least 51st street, and of these 1,700 or almost one-half passed through mid-Manhattan on their way to or from points south of 33d street, a journey of at least 6 miles on Manhattan avenues.

About 2,500 vehicles per hour moved between points in Manhattan north of 110th street and points south of 51st street, and of these over 1,100 went to or came from points south of 33d street, involving a journey of at least 4 miles on the avenues.

A more concrete measure of the proportion of long haul traffic on the avenues is afforded by the following statements based on the distribution of traffic previously shown and on the average distances between the respective districts. The distances used are for movements in a north and south direction only, and disregard any distances moved across town or in other Boroughs.

About 39 per cent. of the total avenue traffic crossing 51st street or practically 7,000 vehicles per hour traveled between districts involving north and south movements ranging from 5 to 8 miles, and averaging 6¼ miles.

About 31 per cent. of the total traffic involved movements ranging from 2.5 to 3.5 miles and averaging practically 3 miles.

The remaining 30 per cent. involved movements in a north and south direction ranging from 2 miles downwards and averaging a little over 1 mile. It represents the portion of the total avenue traffic crossing 51st street, which may be considered local to the midtown section of Manhattan.

Traffic South of 51st Street.

The movements of traffic crossing the three lower East River bridges or moving through the Holland Tunnel and originating in or destined for districts above 51st street, have been reflected in the foregoing studies, but there is in addition an appreciable volume of traffic using the facilities enumerated that moves to or from points south of 51st street in Manhattan and hence is not so reflected.

Dealing only with the portion of this last mentioned traffic moving north of Canal street, there are about 800 vehicles per hour now moving on east side avenues between the lower bridges or Holland Tunnel and points between 33d and 47th streets, traveling an average distance of 2.5 miles on north and south avenues. About 900 vehicles per hour move on east side avenues between these facilities and points between 14th and 33d streets, making an average journey of 1.5 miles in a north and south direction. Approximately 400 vehicles per hour move on west side avenues between these bridges or tunnels and points between 33d and 47th streets, and substantially the same volume moves between these facilities and points between 14th and 33d streets.

Traffic counts show that the average hourly volume of traffic on all avenues crossing 14th street consists of about 11,000 vehicles. Of this traffic the movements of some 7,000 vehicles per hour have been accounted for in the foregoing statements. The remaining 4,000 vehicles per hour are local traffic moving between points south of 14th street in Manhattan and points between 14th and 51st streets in Manhattan.

EASTBOUND AND WESTBOUND TRAFFIC IN MID-MANHATTAN.

For the purpose of developing information concerning the origin and destination of crosstown traffic in mid-Manhattan, and particularly the distances travelled on the crosstown streets, counts were made at 5th avenue on all streets from 30th to 59th streets, inclusive, during the hours of 8 to 10 a. m., 12 to 2 p. m. and 4 to 6 p. m., on March 7 and 8, 1929.

The Traffic Sample.

Traffic officers, stationed on 5th avenue at the various intersections, not only distributed return postal cards similar to the ones previously used on the East River bridges, but also obtained data by direct inquiry. The traffic sample obtained by the return of postal cards, together with the questionnaires, totaled 7,556 vehicle movements, equivalent to about 12.5 per cent. of the traffic flowing during the hours in which it was collected. The questionnaires alone comprised a sample of 6,167 vehicle movements, or approximately eight per cent. of the traffic flowing during the same periods. The sample used for the studies of the distances travelled on crosstown streets was made up of both the postal card returns and the questionnaires, whereas for the origin and destination studies the questionnaires only were used.

The Volume of Traffic.

For the purposes of presentation and analysis, the traffic on the individual streets was combined in three groups as shown below.

Based on 1928 counts of traffic moving between the hours from 7 a. m. to 7 p. m., the average hourly flows at 5th avenue on the crosstown streets involved are substantially as follows:

On 30th to 39th street, inclusive..................................... 4,000 vehicles
On 40th to 47th street, inclusive..................................... 3,600 vehicles
On 48th to 59th street, inclusive..................................... 5,700 vehicles

On 30th to 59th street, inclusive..................................... 13,300 vehicles

The combined flow on all streets from 30th to 59th street, inclusive, of about 160,000 vehicles between 7 a. m. and 7 p. m. may be compared with a combined flow on all avenues in the vicinity of 51st street of some 211,000 vehicles during the same hours.

Distribution on Basis of Districts.

The general features of the diagrams on page 200 are similar to the ones previously presented, the principal variation being a subdivision of the districts. Reference to the diagrams will show the streets comprising each group, and attention is called to the volume of traffic represented on each group of streets.

The most striking indication of these diagrams is the large proportion of traffic in all three groups which originates in or is destined for districts directly east or west of the "crossing." There are also very considerable portions of the traffic in each group moving to or from districts north or south of the ones directly opposite the "crossing," supporting our general observations as to the presence of a large amount of Z and L movements in this section of Manhattan.

In group "B" the traffic to or from district 8c, the Grand Central area, represents about 48 per cent. of the total. Of this traffic 40 per cent. moves to or from districts directly to the west of it, 27 per cent. above 47th street, and 33 per cent. below 40th street.

Referring to diagram "C", district 8a accounts for approximately 29 per cent. of the total, of which portion 61 per cent. moves to or from districts directly to the west of it, 21 per cent. above 39th street and 18 per cent. below 30th street.

As is the case with avenue traffic, there is no marked difference between the three groups in respect to the proportion of commercial car traffic, and the distribution of this traffic on the streets, as shown in the diagrams on page 7507, is in general accord with this indication.

Distribution on Basis of Distance Traveled.

The diagram on page 201 shows for the eastbound and westbound vehicular traffic crossing 5th avenue between 30th and 59th streets, inclusive, the distribution of the traffic flow on the basis of the distance traveled on the said crosstown streets. The traffic on the individual streets has been combined into three groups in the same manner as for the origin and destination studies. The volume of traffic flowing is indicated by the width of the bands, the distances traveled across town by the length of the bands, and the class of vehicle by the weight of the cross hatching. The principal purpose of the diagram is to develop the amount and distribution of "long haul" crosstown traffic.

Referring to the diagram showing the combined flow on 48th to 59th streets, inclusive, for purposes of illustration, it indicates that of the total traffic 12.5 per cent. consists of passenger vehicles moving to points west of 9th avenue, of which number about one-half move to points east of 3d avenue, and that 8.9 per cent. of the total flow consists of commercial cars moving to points west of 9th avenue, of which about two-thirds move to points east of 3d avenue. A further analysis, the results of which are not shown on the diagram, indicate that of the total traffic crossing 5th avenue in this group, about 14 per cent. moves over the East River. Of this portion approximately 29 per cent. is made up of commercial traffic.

Similar analysis of the traffic in the other two combinations of crosstown streets also shows that the longer haul traffic includes a relatively larger proportion of commercial cars than of passenger cars.

Extent of Long Haul Traffic.

Applying the percentages of "long haul" traffic shown by our analysis of the sample to the total daytime traffic for each of the combinations of streets enumerated, the following results are obtained:

On the crosstown streets from 48th to 59th streets, inclusive, about 9,000 vehicles move between points west of 9th avenue and east of 3d avenue of which number approximately 4,000 are commercial vehicles.

On 40th to 47th streets, inclusive, approximately 2,000 vehicles move between points west of 9th avenue and east of 3d avenue, about 1,000 of which are commercial vehicles.

On 30th to 39th streets, inclusive, about 3,000 vehicles move between points west of 9th avenue and east of 3d avenue, about one-half of which are commercial vehicles.

Combining the results to include all streets from 30th to 59th street, inclusive, about 9 per cent. of the traffic crossing 5th avenue moves from beyond 9th avenue to beyond 3d avenue. Similar deductions may be obtained with respect to the volume of traffic flowing between other limits by a more detailed study of the diagram.

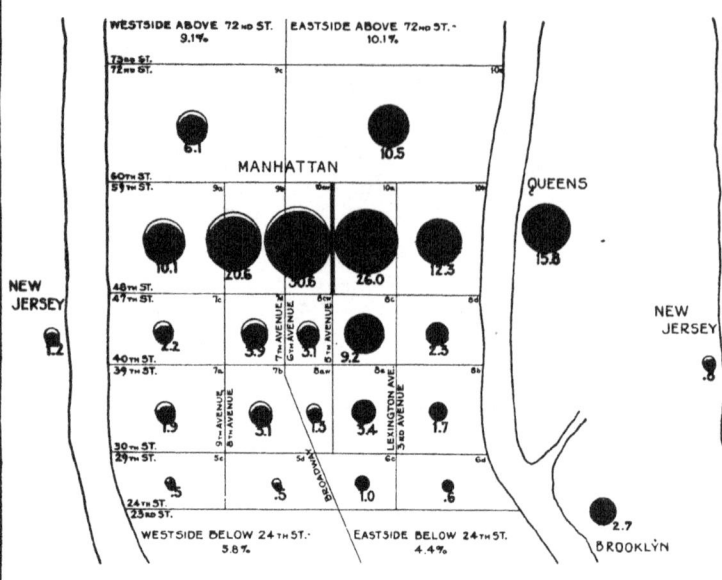

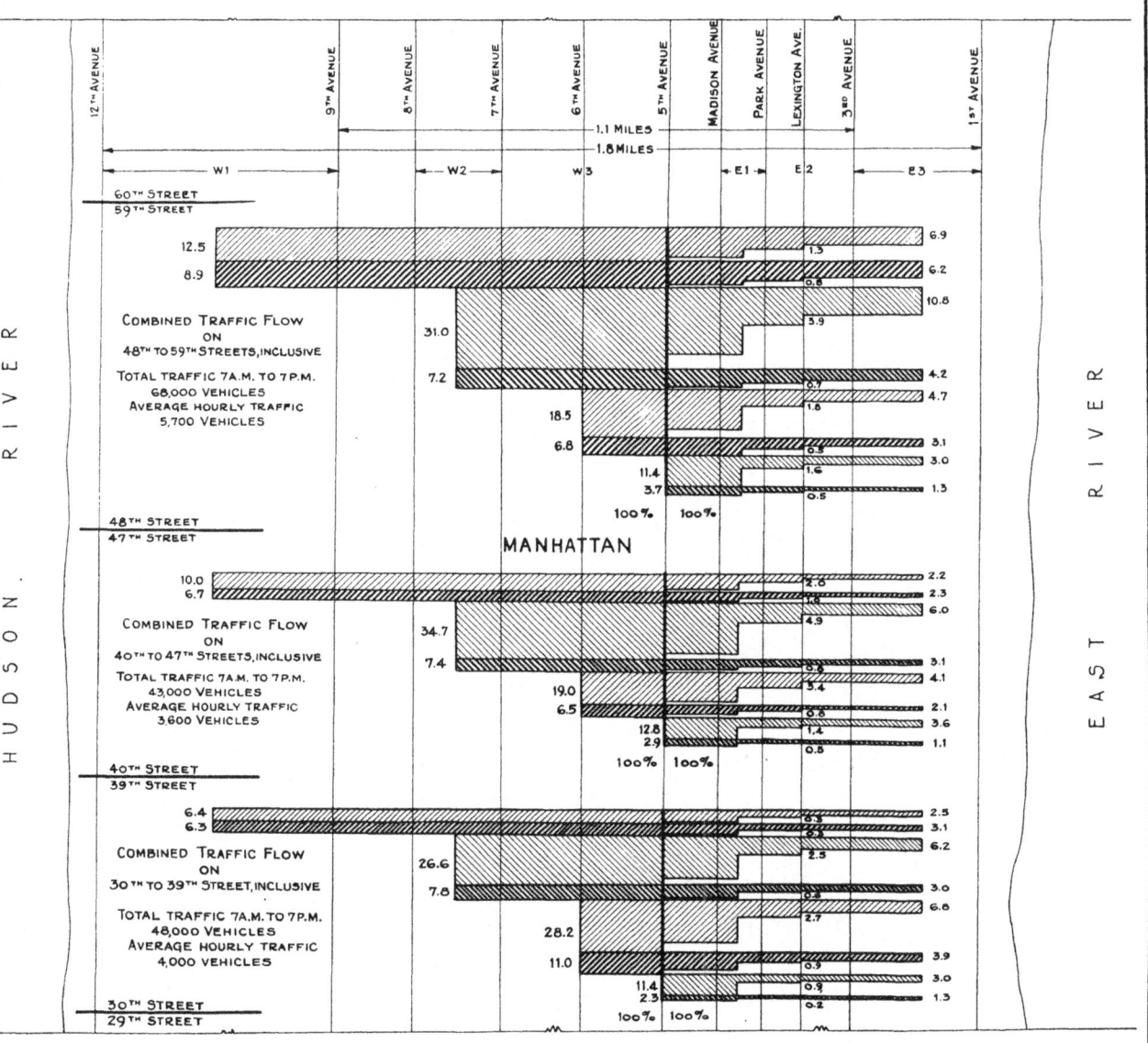

M. B. Brown Printing & Binding Co.,
37-41 Chambers St., N. Y.

ENGIN. - TRANS. LIBRARY
312 UNDERGRADUATE LIBRARY
764-7494
OVERDUE FINE - 25¢ PER DAY

DATE DUE

Printed in Dunstable, United Kingdom